Puppet Best Practices
Design Patterns for Maintainable Code

Chris Barbour and Jo Rhett

Beijing · Boston · Farnham · Sebastopol · Tokyo

Puppet Best Practices

by Chris Barbour and Jo Rhett

Published by O'Reilly Media, Inc., 1005 Gravenstein Highway North, Sebastopol, CA 95472.

O'Reilly books may be purchased for educational, business, or sales promotional use. Online editions are also available for most titles (*http://oreilly.com/safari*). For more information, contact our corporate/institutional sales department: 800-998-9938 or *corporate@oreilly.com*.

Acquisitions Editor: Nikki McDonald	**Interior Designer:** David Futato
Development Editor: Virginia Wilson	**Cover Designer:** Karen Montgomery
Production Editor: Justin Billing	**Illustrator:** Rebecca Demarest
Copyeditor: Octal Publishing, Inc.	**Additional production services:** Jasmine Kwityn
Proofreader: Christina Edwards	**Tech Reviewers:** Linda Bissum, Chris Devers, Ben Ford, Alex Lazar, James Loope, and Jess Males
Indexer: WordCo Indexing Services, Inc.	

September 2018:   First Edition

Revision History for the First Edition

2018-08-23:   First Release

See *http://oreilly.com/catalog/errata.csp?isbn=9781491923009* for release details.

978-1-491-92300-9

[LSI]

Table of Contents

Preface

This book will do more than help solve problems that you are experiencing today; it is intended to help you prepare for the future. We discuss how to build and deploy highly maintainable Puppet code, with a focus on avoiding problems that you'd only need to fix later (*technical debt*).

This book does not attempt to explain the basics of using Puppet; instead, we look at how to use Puppet most effectively. This includes the following:

- A review of the design decisions behind Puppet features
- An exploration of patterns for organizing code and data
- A look at the powerful features of Puppet that you might not be using today
- Discussions of common pitfalls and traps when deploying Puppet infrastructure

What Is a Best Practice?

A *best practice* is the best-known way to use something for positive value while minimizing unnecessary risk. This isn't defined by the manufacturer, rather by practical experience of users in the field.

Do Best Practices Apply to Us?

This question was posed by a manager not certain that Puppet best practices were something in which his team should invest:

"We don't make Puppet. We use Puppet to provide our business' services. We have our own best practices in our field. Do Puppet's best practices apply to us?"

Best practices don't tell you how to operate your business or provide your product. That function is provided by the regulatory, legal, and competitive environment in which the business operates.

Best practices inform you how to safely use the tool in your hand. Best practices on power tools aren't just for carpenters: they're for everyone who uses a power saw. In fact, they are essential guidance for people who aren't using it every day and need to avoid costly mistakes.

A best practice does not tell you why to use a tool, it informs you how to use the tool safely and effectively.

There isn't always an objectively correct best practice for every conceivable tool or use case. Worse yet, there can be conflicting best practices that apply to a given usage. This book provides criteria to judge what makes a solution effective, and how to apply that understanding for the best possible results.

 Best practices don't come in a manual—they come from years of *burned hands and deep scars from using the tools in anger*...uh, sorry! We mean practical, hands-on experience using the tools. Of course we did!

Who Should Read This Book

This book explores concepts, designs, and practices useful for Puppet novices and experts alike. It specifically aims to provide the following benefits for Puppet users:

- Identify alternate design approaches and their benefits for experienced DevOps or SRE engineers developing *infrastructure as code* today.
- Emphasize best-practice code patterns for system administrators and developers. Enumerate useful structures for organization of code and data.
- Review solution evaluation criteria and iterative improvement suggestions for architects and infrastructure engineers.
- Demonstrate declarative coding practices for Puppet novices of any type. Provide warnings about pitalls to avoid during the learning process.

We do intend for this book to be valuable for all professionals working with Puppet. if you're interested in improving your understanding of configuration management (CM), continuous integration (CI), continuous delivery (CD), automation tools, and infrastructure as code, you should find the concepts and designs in this book useful and practical. Even if you are only peripherally related to the usage of Puppet in your organization, you will find the following here:

- The design principles and major components of a working Puppet ecosystem
- Best-practice implementations of Puppet architecture that you should consider

- Guidelines to implement or upgrade Puppet effectively in your organization
- Strategies to get the most value out of Puppet with the least effort

Whether you are an expert responsible for designing large-scale Puppet infrastructure, or a novice learning to deploy a single application, we intend for this book to be valuable to you. The content should be immediately useful if you work with Puppet today, but it also can provide a conceptual foundation if you're just learning about Puppet, taking Puppet training courses, or migrating from other configuration management tools.

 This book is not intended to train you in how to use Puppet; rather, it complements existing Puppet books, documentation, and training courses. *Learning Puppet 4* (O'Reilly, 2016) provides an in-depth training guide to using and deploying Puppet, making it a useful introduction to the concepts discussed in this book.

The concepts and strategies presented are applicable to both *green field* (new build) and *brown field* (update in place) deployments of Puppet. We present concepts key to a stable foundation design that provides flexibility to grow and change. We explore strategies to eliminate pain points in existing environments, and make improvements that accelerate change velocity while reducing risk and minimizing impact.

Why We Wrote This Book

Our objective for this book is to share our professional experience to help IT, operations, security, and developer professionals solve problems and improve the overall quality of code and infrastructure deployed in the real world.

This book draws heavily from our experiences as Puppet consultants. Any site deploying Puppet can do more with less, and thus many grow both quickly and organically. The consequences of design decisions that were made early in development often had repercussions that were not obvious when originally made. As code became established and moved to production, it became more and more difficult to correct those problems without risking the stability of the site that code manages.

Many folks who have deployed Puppet on their own are bright and talented individuals, quick to learn and make use of the many features of Puppet. As they take on more demanding needs with Puppet, they often find very innovative, even superlative, ways of using Puppet features to solve problems. Unfortunately, some of those innovative designs produce code that is difficult to understand and nearly impossible to refactor or reuse in a general manner.

This problem isn't specific to Puppet. Any powerful tool can be used in ways the designers never intended. As the configuration management codebase grows to handle all applications and services, it can quickly dwarf any other single codebase maintained by your organization.

This book highlights design patterns, both good and bad, that you can use when deploying Puppet environments, and discusses the impact of each decision. The conceptual designs and implementation patterns contained in this book will help you to create solutions that can be extended, maintained, and supported—not only by yourself, but by diverse global teams and the people who might inherit your work down the road.

A Word on Puppet Today

First, we'd like to take a moment to acknowledge all of you who have been waiting for this book. Compiling the best of existing practices on a product and community that are constantly evolving and refining is more difficult than you might expect. Some of these practices were updated just hours before the book went to press.

Puppet Best Practices have evolved continuously since Puppet's early releases. In every way, Puppet is much easier to work with and support than it was five years ago. For example, puppet lookup and the new multilayered approach to Hiera data that allows data hierarchies in environments and modules have made it much simpler to create and reuse community modules.

On the other hand, change requires adaptation and refactoring. The new parser used by Puppet 4 and higher have introduced new syntax and deprecated some older features. Puppet design patterns have evolved, and the demarcation points between various systems aren't always clear. Even just picking which versions to support—never mind which practices to highlight—involved many hours of debate between two authors who wanted to help the most people possible.

We feel that this is the very best book we can give you today. Best practices will continue to evolve. Common complaints will be resolved. New issues will be discovered. This process will iterate indefinitely. We look forward to seeing you present a new pattern that we hadn't imagined when this book was written, either in your blog, at a Puppet camp, or a conference. We are absolutely confident that you will.

We intend to keep updating this book as Puppet and its usage evolves, keeping it current and relevant. As you read this, the next update to this book is already in progress —with an entire new chapter about Puppet Tasks—as the community development starts to find common ground.

Navigating This Book

This book is organized as follows:

- Chapters 1 through 3 discuss design concepts, philosophy, and practices that drive the recommendations made throughout this book.
- Chapters 4 through 8 provide concrete recommendations for major components of Puppet, such as Modules, Hiera, *roles and profiles*, and external node classifiers.
- Chapter 9 covers development and release management practices for Puppet developers, including `r10k`, test environments, linting, and editors.
- Chapter 10 covers extending Puppet—the development of new resource types, providers, facts, and features for Puppet.

This book is organized so that you can read it front to back; however, most of the chapters in this book are fairly self-contained and will provide references to other topics where appropriate. After you've read through it entirely, it is our sincere hope that you will return to individual sections when needed to address a difficult problem, to refresh your knowledge, or to pick up strategies that you might have overlooked on the first read.

 We encourage you to read linearly through Chapter 3, because key concepts are introduced that we refer to throughout the book. After that, feel free to skip around to topics that interest you.

If you find anything in this book confusing or incomplete, we encourage you to reach out for clarification. Our goal is to produce the best work we possibly can. Your feedback is invaluable to this effort, and very much appreciated.

Online Resources

Following are some resources that you might find useful:

- Official documentation (*https://puppet.com/docs*)
- Where to find help (*https://ask.puppet.com*)
- Puppet community chat (*https://slack.puppet.com*)
- Mailing lists, local user groups, and so forth (*https://puppet.com/community*)

Conventions Used in This Book

The following typographical conventions are used in this book:

Italic
> Indicates new terms, URLs, email addresses, filenames, and file extensions.

`Constant width`
> Used for program listings, as well as within paragraphs to refer to program elements such as variable or function names, databases, data types, environment variables, statements, and keywords.

`Constant width bold`
> Shows commands or other text that should be typed literally by the user.

`Constant width italic`
> Shows text that should be replaced with user-supplied values or by values determined by context.

 This icon signifies a tip, suggestion, or general note.

 This element signifies a general note.

 This icon indicates a warning or caution.

Using Code Examples

This book is here to help you get your job done. In general, if example code is offered with this book, you may use it in your programs and documentation. You do not need to contact us for permission unless you're reproducing a significant portion of the code. For example, writing a program that uses several chunks of code from this book does not require permission. Selling or distributing a CD-ROM of examples from O'Reilly books does require permission. Answering a question by citing this book and quoting example code does not require permission. Incorporating a significant amount of example code from this book into your product's documentation does require permission.

We appreciate, but do not require, attribution. An attribution usually includes the title, author, publisher, and ISBN. For example: "*Puppet Best Practices* by Chris Barbour and Jo Rhett (O'Reilly). Copyright 2018 Chris Barbour and Joe Rhett, 978-1-491-92300-9."

If you feel your use of code examples falls outside fair use or the permission given above, feel free to contact us at *permissions@oreilly.com*.

O'Reilly Safari

Safari (formerly Safari Books Online) is a membership-based training and reference platform for enterprise, government, educators, and individuals.

Members have access to thousands of books, training videos, Learning Paths, interactive tutorials, and curated playlists from over 250 publishers, including O'Reilly Media, Harvard Business Review, Prentice Hall Professional, Addison-Wesley Professional, Microsoft Press, Sams, Que, Peachpit Press, Adobe, Focal Press, Cisco Press, John Wiley & Sons, Syngress, Morgan Kaufmann, IBM Redbooks, Packt, Adobe Press, FT Press, Apress, Manning, New Riders, McGraw-Hill, Jones & Bartlett, and Course Technology, among others.

For more information, please visit *http://oreilly.com/safari*.

How to Contact Us

Please address comments and questions concerning this book to the publisher:

O'Reilly Media, Inc.
1005 Gravenstein Highway North
Sebastopol, CA 95472
800-998-9938 (in the United States or Canada)
707-829-0515 (international or local)
707-829-0104 (fax)

We have a web page for this book, where we list errata, examples, and any additional information. You can access this page at *http://bit.ly/puppet-best-practices*.

To comment or ask technical questions about this book, send email to *bookquestions@oreilly.com*.

For more information about our books, courses, conferences, and news, see our website at *http://www.oreilly.com*.

Find us on Facebook: *http://facebook.com/oreilly*

Follow us on Twitter: *http://twitter.com/oreillymedia*

Watch us on YouTube: *http://www.youtube.com/oreillymedia*

Acknowledgments

Chris Barbour: This book would not have been possible without the patience and support of my wife and son.

Jo Rhett: The teams at every shop I've worked at and the Puppet community, especially including Vox Populi, have contributed tremendously to my own understanding as represented in this book. The patience and support of my fiance has made it possible for me to make this available to you.

Thanks most especially to Brian Anderson and Virginia Wilson, who have expended numerous hours aiming procrastinating writers in the right direction so that this book would be available and hopefully valuable to you. And to our reviewers and technical editors, who gave us feedback, helped us focus the content, and made this more complete than we'd ever thought possible.

## CHAPTER 1

The Puppet Design Philosophy

Before we begin to explore best practices with Puppet, it's valuable to understand the reasoning behind these recommendations.

Puppet can be somewhat alien to technologists who have a background in shell scripting. Whereas most scripts are *procedural*, Puppet aims to be *declarative*. This allows it to take a node from an unknown state and converge it to a known, desired state.

Puppet's declarative design principles drive the practices in the coming chapters. Although the declarative language has many advantages for configuration management, it does impose restrictions on the approaches used to solve problems. Understanding the philosophy behind the design will help contextualize the recommendations covered in this book.

Declarative Code

As we discussed a moment ago, the Puppet domain-specific language (DSL) is a declarative language, as opposed to the *imperative* or procedural languages with which system administrators tend to be most comfortable and familiar.

Imperative language declares the actions to accomplish a task. Declarative language declares the desired result. You'll see examples of these differences as we proceed.

In theory, a declarative language is ideal for baseline configuration tasks. Because declarative language defines the result, and not the path to get there, the Puppet language is (mostly) verbless. Using the Puppet DSL, we describe only the desired state of our nodes. Puppet handles all responsibility for making sure the system conforms to this desired state. Understanding and internalizing this paradigm is critical when working with Puppet.

Unfortunately, most of us are used to a procedural approach to system administration. The vast majority of the bad Puppet code I've seen has been the result of trying to write procedural code in Puppet rather than adapting existing procedures to a declarative approach. Attempting to force Puppet to use a procedural or imperative process quickly becomes an exercise in frustration and produces fragile code.

If your infrastructure is based around modern open source software, Puppet's built-in types and providers offer declarative methods to handle most operational tasks. This means that writing declarative Puppet code will be relatively straightforward. In other circumstances, we might be tasked to deploy software that demands a procedural installation process. A large part of this book attempts to address how to handle many of the uncommon or irregular requirements in a declarative way.

Implementing a procedural process in Puppet might be unavoidable due to interactions with external components. If your infrastructure includes Windows nodes and enterprise software, writing declarative Puppet code can be significantly more challenging. Simply putting procedural code in Puppet is rarely elegant, often creates unexpected bugs, and is always difficult to maintain. We explore practical examples and best practices for handling procedural requirements when we look at the exec resource type in Chapter 5.

A major challenge that system administrators face when working with Puppet is our own mindset. Our daily job responsibilities have often been solved with an imperative workflow. How often have you manipulated files using regular expression substitution? How often do we massage data using a series of temp files and piped commands? Even though Puppet offers many ways to accomplish the same tasks, most of our procedural approaches do not map well into Puppet's declarative language. We must learn a different mindset to translate imperative design into a declarative model. We explore examples of these situations and discuss declarative approaches to solving it.

What Is Declarative Code, Anyway?

As mentioned earlier, declarative code should not have verbs.

*We don't **create** or **remove** users.*
    We declare that users should be present or absent.

*We don't **install** or **remove** software.*
    We declare that software should be present or absent.

Whereas create and install are verbs, present and absent are adjectives. The difference seems trivial at first but proves to be very important in practice. Let's examine a real-world example. Imagine that you're being given directions to the Palace of Fine Arts in San Francisco:

1. Head North on 19th Avenue.
2. Get on US-101S.
3. Take Marina Boulevard to Palace Drive.
4. Park at the Palace of Fine Arts Theater.

These instructions make a few major assumptions:

- You aren't already at the Palace of Fine Arts.
- You are driving a car.
- You are currently in San Francisco.
- You are currently on 19th Avenue or know how to get there.
- You are heading north on 19th Avenue.
- There are no road closures or other traffic disruptions that would force you to a different route.

Compare this to the declarative instructions:

1. Be at 3301 Lyon Street, San Francisco, CA 94123 at 7:00 PM

The declarative approach has major advantages in this case, namely:

- It requires no variants based on your current location or mode of transportation.
- This instruction is valid whether your plans involve public transit or a parachute.
- This instruction is valid regardless of your starting point.
- This instruction empowers the driver to route around road closures and traffic.

In short, the declarative approach is simpler and easier to write. It allows you to choose the best way to reach the destination based on your current situation.

Resource Types and Providers

Declarative languages don't implement the declared state with magic. Puppet's model uses a *resource type* to model an object, and a *resource provider* to implement the state the model describes. To map this to the previous example, when an address and time is declared as the implementation, the provider is you. You are capable of navigating to the destination, calling a taxi, or flinging yourself out the window as necessary to reach that state.

 Resource providers are backends that implement support for a specific implementation of a given resource type.

The major limitation imposed by Puppet's declarative model is obvious. If a resource provider doesn't exist for the resource type, Puppet won't be able to ensure the modeled state. Declaring that you want a red two-story house with four bedrooms won't accomplish anything if a construction engineer (the provider) isn't available to implement it.

There is some good news on this front, however, because Puppet includes types and providers for common operating system (OS) resources such as users, groups, services, and packages. Further, the Puppet community and product vendors contribute additional models for add-on software. If you are considering using the **exec** resource type, look around and make sure someone hasn't already created a declarative type and provider to handle it.

Procedural Example

Let's examine some common procedural code intended for user management. We later discuss how to replace this code with a robust, self-healing equivalent in Puppet.

Imperitive/procedural code

Example 1-1 presents an imperative process implemented using a Bash script. It creates a user and installs an Secure Shell (SSH) public key for authentication on a Red-Hat–family Linux host.

Example 1-1. Imperative user creation in Bash

```
# groupadd examplegroup
# useradd -g examplegroup alice
# mkdir ~alice/.ssh/
# chown alice:examplegroup ~alice/.ssh
# chmod 770 ~alice/.ssh
# echo "ssh-rsa AAAAB3NzaC1yc2EAAAABIwAAAIEAm3TA...EnMSuFrD/E5TunvRHIczaI9Hy0IMXc= \
alice@localhost" > ~alice/.ssh/authorized_keys
```

What if we decide that this user should also be a member of the wheel group? Let's try it:

```
# useradd -g examplegroup alice
# usermod -G wheel alice
```

And if we want to remove that user and that user's group? Let's give that a try:

```
# userdel alice
# groupdel examplegroup
```

Notice a few things about this example:

- The correct process to use depends on the current state of the user.
- Each process is different.
- Each process will produce errors if invoked more than one time.

Imagine for a second that we have several types of nodes:

- On some nodes, the Alice user is absent.
- On some nodes, Alice is present but not a member of the wheel group.
- On some nodes, Alice is present and a member of the wheel group.
- On some nodes, Alice is present but does not have an SSH key installed.
- On some nodes Alice is present but does not have the correct SSH key installed.
- ...and so on.

Imagine that we need to write a script to ensure that Alice exists, is a member of the wheel group on every system, and has the correct SSH authentication key. Example 1-2 illustrates what such a script would look like.

Example 1-2. Robust user management with BASH

```
#!/bin/bash

if ! getent group examplegroup; then
  groupadd examplegroup
fi

if ! getent passwd alice; then
  useradd -g examplegroup -G wheel alice
fi

if ! id -nG alice | grep -q 'examplegroup wheel'; then
  usermod -g examplegroup -G wheel alice
fi

if ! test -d ~alice/.ssh; then
  mkdir -p ~alice/.ssh
fi
```

```
chown alice:examplegroup ~alice/.ssh

chmod 770 ~alice/.ssh

if ! grep -q alice@localhost ~alice/.ssh/authorized_keys; then
    echo "ssh-rsa AAAAB3NzaC1yc2EAAAABIwAAAIEAm3TAgMF...AkxEnMsu\
    FrD/E5TunvRHIczaI9Hy0IMXc= alice@localhost" >> ~alice/.ssh/authorized_keys
fi
```

That's quite a bit of code and it's very specific to the current needs. This example covers only the use case of creating and managing two properties about the user. If our needs changed, we would need to write a much larger script to manage the user. Even fairly simple changes, such as revoking this user's wheel access, could require significant changes.

This approach has another major disadvantage: it works only on RedHat–based platforms that implement the same commands and arguments. Entirely different scripts would need to be written for other Linux platforms, Solaris, FreeBSD, MacOS, and Windows.

Declarative replacement

Let's look at our user management example using Puppet's declarative DSL. Example 1-3 presents the code.

Example 1-3. Declarative user creation with Puppet

```
group { 'examplegroup':
  ensure => 'present',
}

user { 'alice':
  ensure     => 'present',
  gid        => 'examplegroup',
  managehome => true,
}

ssh_authorized_key { 'alice@localhost':
  ensure => 'present',
  user   => 'alice',
  type   => 'ssh-rsa',
  key    => 'AAAAB3NzaC1yc2EAAAABIwAAAIEAm3TAgMF/2RY+r7...vRHIczaI9Hy0IMXc='
}
```

Adding alice to the wheel group requires changing only one attribute of the user, as shown here (bolded in the example):

```
user { 'alice':
  ensure     => 'present',
  gid        => 'examplegroup',
```

```
  groups      => 'wheel',
  managehome => true,
}
```

Likewise, removing the example group and alice requires changing only one attribute of each:

```
group { 'examplegroup':
  ensure  => 'absent',
  require => User['alice'],
}

user { 'alice':
  ensure     => 'absent',
  gid        => 'examplegroup',
  groups     => 'wheel',
  managehome => true,
}
```

This was a simplified example. Compliance needs usually require disabling accounts rather than removing them to avoid user identifier (UID) reuse and preserve audit history.

In this example, we are able to remove the user by changing the ensure state from present to absent on the user's resources.

Gain by replacing procedural code

Our procedural example showed a long script that could handle only a few attributes of a single user on a Red Hat Linux system. Each step of the example script had to analyze the current state to determine what action to take.

The much simpler resource declaration removes the need to compare each individual attribute as a new decision point. And it would work just fine on Ubuntu, a BSD Unix, or Windows. Perhaps most important, every line of the declarative example is focused on the data rather than how to do it. To add another user who is a member of two groups, we would need to add only the group to the groups attribute.

Rather than managing the user Alice as three unique resources, abstract this into a *defined type* that implements the related resources based on input parameters.

Nondeclarative Code with Puppet

Most people use the operating system's package provider (Yum, Apt, MSI, etc.) for consistency and reporting. But they use it most of all for convenience. When they are required to install a package outside of that system, they often revert to an imperative process that does the steps they would have followed. Example 1-4 shows it is possible to write nondeclarative code with Puppet. *But that doesn't mean that this won't hurt.*

Example 1-4. Nondeclarative application installation

```
$app_source  = 'http://www.example.com/application-1.2.3.tar.gz'
$app_tarball = '/tmp/application.tar.gz'

exec { 'download application':
  command => "/usr/bin/wget -q ${app_source} -O ${app_tarball}",
  creates => '/usr/local/application/',
  notify  => exec['extract application'],
}

exec { 'extract application':
  command     => "/bin/tar -zxf ${app_tarball} -C /usr/local",
  refreshonly => true,
  creates     => '/usr/local/application/',
}
```

Example 1-4 shows a common example of nondeclarative Puppet code, often used to handle software unavailable in a native packaging format. This example has a few major problems:

- exec resources have a set timeout. This example might work well over a fast corporate network connection, but fail completely from a home DSL line. The solution would be to set the timeout attribute of the exec resources to a reasonably high value.

- This example does not validate the checksum of the downloaded file, which could produce some odd results upon extraction. We might use an additional exec resource to test and correct for this case automatically.

- A partial or corrupted download can wedge this process. You can work around this problem by overwriting the archive each time it is downloaded.

- This example makes several assumptions about the contents of *application.tar.gz*. If any of those assumptions are wrong, these commands will repeat every time Puppet is invoked.

- This example is not portable and would require a platform-specific implementation for each supported OS.

- This example would not be useful for upgrading the application.

Another common pattern is the use of conditional logic and custom facts to test for the presence of software. Example 1-5 looks quick and easy, but it is fragile and leaves Puppet completely unaware of the state of the system.

Example 1-5. Nondeclarative application install

```
# ensure custom app version 1.2.3
if $facts['custom_app_version'] != '1.2.3' {
  exec { 'download application':
    command => "/usr/bin/wget -q ${app_source} -O ${app_tarball}",
  }

  exec { 'extract application':
    command => "/bin/tar -zxf /tmp/${app_tarball} -C /usr/local",
    require => Exec['download application'],
  }
}
```

This particular example has the same problems as the previous example and introduces a new problem: it breaks Puppet's reporting and auditing model. The conditional logic happens during the catalog build process and thus removes the application resources from the catalog following initial installation. Puppet can no longer validate nor report on the state of those resources.

This approach is also sensitive to version issues in so much as future versions might have differing needs. This will lead to an imperative testing if/then/else tree, as shown in the Bash script in Example 1-1.

 An if or unless block adds or removes resources from the catalog entirely. Conditional evaluation is performed during the catalog build, and thus invisible to the Puppet agent implementing the changes.

This implementation will fail in unexpected ways; for example, not installing the software when expected to or continually reinstalling it when using the cached catalog. Using cached catalogs is a recommended and often-used practice to minimize disruption in production environments.

It is much better to let the resource provider determine compliance rather than trying to make compliance decisions by adding or removing things from the catalog. This allows the providers to report the current state and determine any necessary action. Consider this *enabling the driver to adjust for traffic conditions*. Example 1-6 presents a declarative example using the puppet/archive (*https://forge.puppetlabs.com/puppet/archive*) module that doesn't require a custom fact to gather the application version.

Example 1-6. Declarative, provider-implemented application installation

```
$app_source  = "http://www.example.com/application-${app_version}.tar.gz"
$app_tarball = '/tmp/application.tar.gz'
$app_version_canary = "/usr/local/application/README.v${app_version}"
# canary contains a file that exists only in that version

archive { 'custom_application':
  path         => $app_tarball,
  source       => $app_source,
  extract      => true,
  extract_path => '/usr/local/',
  creates      => $app_version_canary,
  cleanup      => true,
}
```

As you can see, the simple declarative version uses of all the same data, without attempting to imperatively describe how to reach the end goal. This resource's state will be tracked and reported by Puppet, making it visible for orchestration and reporting tools in the Puppet ecosystem.

Idempotency

In computer science, an *idempotent* function returns the same value each time it's called, whether that happens once or 100 times. For example, X = 1 is an idempotent operation. X = X + 1 is a nonidempotent, impactful operation.

The Puppet language was designed to be idempotent. A large part of this idempotency is owed to its declarative resource type model; however, Puppet also enforces a number of rules on variable handling, iterators, and conditional logic to maintain idempotency.

Idempotence has major benefits for a configuration management language:

- The configuration is inherently self-healing
- State does not need to be maintained between invocations
- Configurations can be safely reapplied

For example, if for some reason Puppet fails part way through a configuration run, reinvoking Puppet will complete the run and repair any configurations that were left in an inconsistent state by the previous run.

Convergence Versus Idempotence

Configuration management languages are often discussed in terms of their convergence model. Some are designed to be *eventually convergent*, whereas others are immediately convergent or *idempotent*.

Convergence implies the existence of a diverged state. *Divergence* is the act of moving the system away from the desired *converged* state. This typically happens when someone manually alters a resource that is under configuration management control.

With an eventually convergent model, the configuration management tool is invoked over and over: each time the tool is invoked, the system approaches a converged state in which all changes defined in the configuration language have been applied, and no more changes take place. During the process of convergence, the system is said to be in a partially converged or inconsistent state.

Whether Puppet functions as an immediately convergent model depends entirely on the code it is enforcing. For a Puppet codebase to be idempotent, it must reach a convergent state in a single application, and remain in the same state for any subsequent applications.

In most cases, breaking Puppet's idempotence model would be considered a bug. There are some cases for which eventual convergence is unavoidable, such as the numerous postinstallation reboots required by Windows software upgrades. However, it is encumbent on us to not introduce these problems if they can be avoided.

Side Effects

In computer science, a side effect is a change of system or program state that is outside the defined scope of the original operation. Declarative and idempotent languages usually attempt to manage, reduce, and eliminate side effects. With that said, it is entirely possible for an idempotent operation to have side effects.

Puppet attempts to limit side effects but does not eliminate them by any means; doing so would be nearly impossible given Puppet's role as a system management tool.

Some side effects are designed into the system. For example, every resource will generate a notification upon changing a resource state that can be consumed by other resources. The notification is used to restart services in order to ensure that the running state of the system reflects the configured state. The `filebucket` operation that stores a backup of a file modified by Puppet is an intentional and beneficial side effect.

Some side effects are unavoidable. Every access to a file on disk will cause that file's atime to be incremented unless the entire filesystem is mounted with the noatime attribute. This is of course true whether or not Puppet is being invoked in noop mode.

Resource-Level Idempotence

Many common tasks are not idempotent by nature, and will either throw an error or produce undesirable results if invoked multiple times.

The following code is not idempotent because it will set a state the first time, and throw an error each time it's subsequently invoked, as shown here:

```
$ sudo useradd alice
$ sudo useradd alice
useradd: user 'alice' already exists
```

This code is not idempotent because it will add undesirable duplicate host entries each time it's invoked:

```
echo '127.0.0.1 example.localdomin' >> /etc/hosts
```

The following code is idempotent, but will probably have undesirable results:

```
echo '127.0.0.1 example.localdomin' > /etc/hosts
```

To make our example idempotent without clobbering /etc/hosts, we can add a simple check before modifying the file:

```
grep -q '^127.0.0.1 example.localdomin$' /etc/hosts \
    || echo '127.0.0.1 example.localdomin' >> /etc/hosts
```

The same example is simple to write in a declarative and idempotent way using the host resource:

```
host { 'example.localdomain':
  ip => '127.0.0.1',
}
```

In this example, the resource is modeled in a declarative way and is idempotent by its very nature. Under the hood, Puppet handles the complexity of determining whether the line already exists and how it should be inserted into the underlying file. Using the host resource, Puppet also determines what file should be modified and where that file is located. The preceding declarative example will work on Windows and MacOS, for example.

The idempotent examples are safe to run as many times as you like. This is a huge benefit in large environments; when trying to apply a change to thousands of hosts, it's relatively common for failures to occur on a small subset of the hosts being managed. Perhaps the host is down during deployment? Perhaps you experienced some sort of transmission loss or timeout when deploying a change? If you are using an idempotent language or process to manage your systems, you can run the process repeatedly on the entire infrastructure with impact only on the exceptional cases that didn't converge the first time.

When working with Puppet resources, you typically don't need to worry about idempotence; most resource providers are idempotent by design. A couple of notable exceptions to this statement are the exec and augeas resources. We explore those in depth in Chapter 5.

Puppet does however attempt to track whether a resource has changed state. This is part of Puppet's reporting mechanism and used to determine whether a signal should be sent to resources with a notify relationship. Because Puppet tracks whether a resource has made a change, it's entirely possible to write code that is functionally idempotent without meeting the criteria of idempotent from Puppet's resource model.

The code example that follows is functionally idempotent: this command will always result in the same state. However, because the exec resource knows only whether or not a command succeeded—not the resulting configuration created—it will report a state change with every Puppet run. This will make monitoring convergence reports for unexpected changes more difficult.

```
exec { 'grep -q /bin/bash /etc/shells || echo /bin/bash >> /etc/shells':
  path    => '/bin',
  provider => 'shell',
}
```

Puppet's idempotence model relies on a special aspect of its resource model. For every resource, Puppet first determines that resource's current state. If the current state does not match the defined state of that resource, Puppet invokes the appropriate methods on the resource's provider to bring the resource into conformity with the desired state. This usually happens in a transparent manner; however, there are a few exceptions that we discuss in their respective chapters. Understanding these cases is critical in order to avoid breaking Puppet's simulation and reporting models.

The following example uses state verification to prevent the resource from being converged unnecessarily:

```
exec { 'echo /bin/bash >> /etc/shells':
  path   => '/bin',
  unless => 'grep -q /bin/bash /etc/shells',
}
```

In this example, the unless attribute provides a condition Puppet can use to determine whether a change actually needs to take place.

Using the state verification attributes `unless` and `onlyif` properly will help reduce the risk of `exec` resources. We will explore this in Chapter 5.

An even better implementation would be to forego `exec` in favor of a resource type that would manage the state for us. For example, we could implement this using the *file_line* resource from the puppetlabs/stdlib module (*https://forge.puppet.com/puppetlabs/stdlib/*):

```
file_line { 'bash_in_shells':
  path => '/etc/shells',
  line => '/bin/bash',
}
```

Do you see how much simpler and easier to read it is when you no longer need to describe how to accomplish the change?

A final surprising example of unintended side effects is the `notify` resource, used to produce debugging information and log entries:

```
notify { 'example':
  message  => 'Danger, Will Robinson!'
}
```

The notify resource generates an alert every time it is invoked and will always report as a change in system state. As such, you should use `notify` resources only to bring attention to exception cases, not for general-purpose information. If you'd like to display informational messages without causing a change report, you would need to use alternatives like the ipcrm/echo module on the Puppet Forge.

Run-Level Idempotence

Puppet is designed to be idempotent both at the resource level and at the run level. Much like resource idempotence means that a resource applied twice produces the same result, run-level idempotence means that invoking Puppet multiple times on a host will be safe. Puppet's default agent run model performs a state evaluation every 30 minutes, and is widely used in live production environments.

You can run Puppet in nonenforcing `--noop` (no-operation) mode so as to only report on variance from the model in change-sensitive production environments.

Run-level idempotence is a place where Puppet's idea of change is just as important as whether the resources are functionally idempotent. Remember that before performing any configuration change, Puppet must first determine whether the resource currently conforms to policy. Puppet will make a change only if resources state doesn't match the declaration. If Puppet does not report having made any changes, the practical implication is that the resources were already in the desired state.

 Determining where your Puppet runs are not idempotent is fairly simple: If Puppet reports a change on an immediately successive invocation, that change identifies Puppet code that fails to be idempotent.

Because changes to a Puppet resource can have side effects that affect other resources, Puppet's idempotence model can be broken if we don't carefully declare resource dependencies, as illustrated here:

```
package { 'httpd':
  ensure => 'installed',
}

file { '/etc/httpd/conf/httpd.conf':
  ensure => 'file',
  content => template('apache/httpd.conf.erb'),
}

Package['httpd'] -> File['/etc/httpd/conf/httpd.conf']
```

The file resource will not create paths recursively. In the preceding example, the *httpd* package must be installed before the *httpd.conf* file resource is enforced, which depends on the existence of the */etc/httpd/conf/* directory, which is only present after the *httpd* package has been installed. If these dependencies are not managed, the file resource becomes nonidempotent; upon first invocation of Puppet it might throw an error, and enforce the state of *httpd.conf* only upon subsequent invocations of Puppet.

Such issues will render Puppet *eventually convergent*. Because Puppet typically runs on a 30-minute interval, eventually convergent infrastructures can take a very long time to reach a converged state.

Nondeterministic Code

As a general rule, the Puppet DSL is deterministic, meaning that a given set of inputs (manifests, facts, exported resources, etc.) will always produce the same output with no variance.

For example, the language does not implement a random() function; instead, a fqdn_rand() function is provided that returns predictable and repeatable random values derived from a static seed (the node's fully qualified domain name). This function is neither cryptographically secure nor random. It produces the same randomish number every time it is called for the same node. This is commonly used to distribute the start times of load-intensive tasks.

Nondeterministic code can pop up in strange places with Puppet. A common cause of nondeterministic code pops-ups is when our code is dependent on a transient or changeable value.

The following code uses the Puppet server's name in the file:

```
file { '/tmp/example.txt':
  ensure  => 'file',
  content => "# File managed by Puppet, server ${::servername}\n",
}
```

This code will not be idempotent when used with a cluster of Puppet Servers. The value of $::servername changes depending on which server compiles the catalog for a particular run. This means that change reports won't differentiate between nodes with unexpected changes and those that received a different Puppet server from the compile cluster but had no changes to their resources.

For each invocation of Puppet with nondeterministic code, some resources will change. The node catalog will converge, but it will always report your systems as having been brought into conformity with its policy rather than being conformant. This makes it virtually impossible to determine whether changes would be made to a node. Unexpected changes are far easier to pick out when there are only a handful of change reports instead of hundreds or thousands of false positives.

Nondeterministic code that utilizes subscribe or notify can create unintended side effects. If a resource is converged that notifies or is subscribed to by a service, the service will restart. This can cause unintended service disruption.

Stateless

A stateless interface does not preserve state between requests; each request is completely independent from previous requests.

 Puppet uses a RESTful API over HTTPS for client–server communications.

Puppet's agent/server API is stateless. The catalog build process does not consult data from a previous request to produce a new catalog for the node. Unless state information is provided by custom node facts, node classifiers, or Hiera lookups, node catalogs are built in a completely stateless, deterministic manner.

Benefits of Stateless Design

 This section discusses implementations in which the Puppet Server (master) process builds the catalog for the node. The catalog build process is identical in every way for *serverless* Puppet implementations, except that `puppet apply` builds the catalog locally.

Puppet uses the facts supplied by the node to build a catalog for it. The catalog building process doesn't know or care whether this is the first time it has generated a catalog for this node, whether the last run was successful, or if any change occurred on the node during the last run. The node's catalog is built from scratch every time the node requests a catalog. The catalog builder (master) creates the model. The Puppet agent on the node has the responsibility of comparing the current state of the node to the catalog and applying change as necessary to match the model.

Keeping Puppet stateless can be tremendously useful. In a stateless system, there is no need to synchronize data or resolve conflicts between masters. There is no locking to worry about. There is no need to design a partition-tolerant system in case you lose a datacenter or uplink, and there's no need to worry about clustering strategies. You can easily distribute load across a pool of masters by using a load balancer or DNS SRV record.

It is possible to track state on the agent, and submit state information to the master using Puppet facts. The catalog build is customized with the values provided by facts. There are cases for which security requirements or particularly idiosyncratic software will necessitate creating custom facts to manage bespoke dependencies with Puppet's DSL.

If you keep your code declarative, it's easy to work with Puppet's stateless agent/server configuration model. If a manifest declares that a `user` resource should exist, the catalog builder is not concerned with the current state of that resource. The catalog declares the desired state, and the Puppet agent enforces that state.

Puppet's stateless model has several major advantages over a stateful model:

- Lack of state allows Puppet servers to scale horizontally.
- Catalogs can be compared.
- Catalogs can be cached locally to reduce server load.

It is worth noting that there are a few stateful features of Puppet. It's important to weigh the value of these features against the cost of making your Puppet infrastructure stateful, and to design your infrastructure to provide an acceptable level of availability and fault tolerance. We discuss how to approach each of these technologies in upcoming chapters, but we provide a quick overview here.

Sources of State Information

In the beginning of this section, we mentioned that a few features can provide state information for use in the Puppet catalog build. Let's look at some of these features in a bit more depth.

Filebuckets

Filebuckets provide history of changes to files by Puppet, an under-appreciated feature of the `file` resource. If a filebucket is configured, the file provider will create a backup copy of a file before changes are made. You can store the backup locally, or you can submit it to a server-based bucket.

Bucketing your files is useful for keeping backups, auditing, reporting, and disaster recovery. It can be immensely useful for restoring a file broken by a Puppet change, or to compare when testing changes to Puppet resources. Both command-line utilities and web consoles can display and compare the contents of files stored in the bucket.

Exported resources

Exported resources provide a simple service discovery mechanism for Puppet. When a Puppet master builds a catalog, resources can be marked as exported by the compiler. After the resources are marked as exported, they are recorded in Puppet's database, PuppetDB. Other nodes can then collect the exported resources and apply those resources locally. Exported resources persist until they are overwritten or purged by a later Puppet run on the same node. Be aware that exported resources introduce a source of state into your infrastructure.

In this example, a pool of web servers export their pool membership information to a HAproxy load balancer using the puppetlabs/haproxy (*https://forge.puppetlabs.com/ puppetlabs/haproxy*) module and exported resources.

Each node would create an exported resource with its own information, as demonstrated here:

```
# Export a balance member resource with our details
@@haproxy::balancermember { $::fqdn:
  listening_service => 'web',
  server_names      => $::hostname,
  ipaddresses       => $::ipaddress,
  ports             => '80',
  options           => 'check',
}
```

The load balancer collects all of these balance members to create the service pool:

```
# Define the frontend listener
haproxy::listen { 'web':
  ipaddress => $::ipaddress,
  ports     => '80',
}

# collect all exported backends for the service
Haproxy::Balancermember <<| listening_service == 'web' |>>
```

 The preceding example shows a fairly safe use of exported resources. If PuppetDB became unavailable the pool would continue to work. New nodes would be added when PuppetDB was available again.

Exported resources rely on PuppetDB, which stores the data in a PostgreSQL database. Although there are several methods available to make PuppetDB fault tolerant, including the Puppet Enterprise high availability configuration (*http://bit.ly/2Lem9Gq*), the use of exported resources does introduce into the infrastructure a dependency and possible point of failure.

Hiera

Hiera is by design a pluggable system. By default, it provides YAM, JSON, and HOCON backends, all of which are stateless. However, it is possible to design a custom backend for Hiera that sources a database or inventory service, such as PuppetDB. If you use this approach, it can introduce a source of state information for your Puppet infrastructure. We explore Hiera in depth in Chapter 6.

Inventory and reporting

Puppet Server stores a considerable amount of information pertaining to the state of each node. This information includes the facts supplied by the node, the catalog last sent to the node, and the convergence reports produced by each Puppet application on the node. Even though this information is stateful, it is not typically consumed when building the node's catalog. We take a close look at inventory and reporting services in "Inventory and Infrastructure Management ENCs" on page 205.

There are Puppet extensions that provide inventory information for use during the catalog build; however, these are not core to Puppet.

Custom facts

Custom facts can provide current node state information for use in Puppet manifests. Facts provided by the node avoid creating scaling and availability problems inherent in server-side state storage and management.

Example 1-5 showed how the use of custom facts for conditional inclusion can create nondeclarative, fragile code.

Summary

In this chapter, we reviewed how Puppet's declarative design provides simplicity, flexibility, and power. We also reviewed how declarative design requires new approaches, and restricts the usage of simple imperative approaches.

Here are some takeaways from this chapter:

- Puppet is declarative, idempotent, and stateless by default.
- In some cases violation of these design ideals is unavoidable.
- You should write declarative, idempotent, and stateless code whenever possible.

Each chapter in this book provides concrete recommendations for the effective usage of Puppet's language, resource types, and providers. Building code that uses Puppet's declarative model will be the major driving force behind each topic in future chapters.

## CHAPTER 2

High-Level Code and Data Design

In this chapter we review the primary structures of a Puppet codebase, and discuss how the structure of code and data will affect the cost of module maintenance, code reuse, debugging, and scaling.

 A codebase is the *complete body of source code for a software program or application*. For our purposes, it is the total body of code used to build Puppet catalogs.

This chapter covers best-practice use of core features of Puppet, including the following:

- Node facts
- Hiera data
- Puppet modules

We introduce broad categories for code and data used with Puppet, creating a common vocabulary for use in later chapters. This shared basis makes it easier for us to discuss appropriate ways of handling the concerns of each topic.

As with Chapter 1, this chapter focuses primarily on "why" rather than "how."

Code and Data Organization

The organization of your Puppet codebase is critical for all of the following reasons:

- Organization-based structures for data allow multiple teams to share responsibility for Puppet data.
- Separation of code and data promote code reuse as you bring up new applications with similar needs.
- Puppet modules provide independently testable implementations that are simpler to debug and improve.
- Independent and dynamic environments improve testing opportunities, and minimize the disruption caused by local environmental changes.
- Versioning and release management allow highly customized controls for stability and speed of change in each environment.

All of these work together to reduce the impact of changes to business logic and operational requirements driven by ever-changing business requirements.

Code and Data Categories

When discussing Puppet implementations, it helps to identify the types of code and data seen in the infrastructure. Naming these categories enables discussions about the organization of your code and how it maps to the various features and design patterns of Puppet. We have found the following categories useful for that discussion:

- Application logic
- Business logic
- Site-specific data
- Service-specific data
- Node-specific data

Why is it important to categorize information in this manner? These categories loosely map to a number of Puppet features and design patterns. The following outlines a common data source pattern used by many organizations:

- The logic to configure and deploy a single application fits within a Puppet module (code).
- You can find business logic that informs app configuration in the following:
  — Static information stored in Hiera
  — Role and profile definitions declared in Puppet code
- Site-specific data is often static, and usually stored in Hiera
- Service-specific data is usually:
  — Static information stored in Hiera.

— Stateful information can be pulled from PuppetDB or another service discovery system
- Node-specific data is usually:
  — Facts submitted by the node
  — Static information stored in Hiera
  — Infrastructure data provided by a node classifier

As you can see from this structure, each type of data has different sources and can have diverse needs for accuracy and freshness. Although these categories have different sources and needs, a good structure for the code and data will allow a single Puppet module to provide the complete logic to manage a single application, service, or subsystem, regardless of the diversity of data sources we just outlined.

Types of Code Logic

Taking time to evaluate which type of logic is being implemented might seem strange, but this provides essential knowledge useful to untangle the intertwined layers of an implementation. Take the time now, or you'll spend the time plus significant interest later.

Application logic

Application logic is the logic to manage a single application or component and optionally its dependencies. A MySQL database, the Postfix mail processor, and the Chocolatey windows package packager (*https://chocolatey.org/*) are applications that a Puppet module can configure by using application logic.

Application logic can contain logic and data to handle platform-specific implementation details. For example, an Apache module should contain platform-specific logic to ensure the following:

- The correct package is installed (e.g., `httpd` on Red Hat and `apache2` on Debian)
- The configuration file is installed to the platform-appropriate location.
- The configuration contains platform-specific configurations.
- The correct service name is used when managing the Apache service.

The Apache module contains a lot of data about Apache: package names, configuration details, file locations, default port numbers, docroot, and file ownership information.

In some cases, the application might include some default data that can be overridden with site- or service-specific data. For example, the NTP module includes a set of publicly available Network Time Protocol (NTP) servers for use if specific servers are not configured.

Site-specific data

 We use the term *site* to refer to a distinct grouping that has some shared configuration. In most situations, this maps cleanly to a physical or logical location such as an office or datacenter. In cloud environments, it would depend on how shared resources are managed. This could be unique on the VPC (Amazon Web Services) or Virtual Network (Microsoft Azure) level, or could be shared at the Account or Subscription layer.

Site-specific data is the data that is unique to your site, and isn't fundamental to any of your applications. Following are some examples of site-specific data:

- The package repositories used by nodes for installation and updates
- The authoritative time sources used by nodes for time synchronization
- The passwords used by applications to authenticate to database servers

Node data

Node-specific data is a super-localized instance of site-specific data. Node-specific data identifies properties specific to a single node, such as the following:

- Location
- Node name
- IP addresses
- Tier or group

Although this data can be maintained in static form with your site-specific data (such as Hiera), it's more commonly sourced from external data sources used to manage node inventory. In these days of cloud computing, nodes are constantly brought up, shut down, modified, and reassigned. Nodes are often maintained by a different team (or company!) than the one that manages the services.

 In Puppet terms, a *node* is a unique instance configured by a Puppet agent. It's not uncommon for a virtualization engine to be a node managed by Puppet and for each virtualized node provided by that engine to also run Puppet.

In the early days of Puppet, nodes were managed by using node statements within a site-wide Puppet manifest. Node classification was a mix of code and data that attempted to group configurations using *node inheritance*. This mixture of code and data led to inconsistent, often surprising results.

These days, node definition is entirely data, often retrieved by lookup from an external node management service (e.g., Foreman or the cloud provider's API).

Service data

Service data provides configuration details for a specific service as part of a specific technology stack. This kind of data is prevalent with horizontally scaled, multitier applications.

For example, the classic three-tier technology stack consisting of frontend web servers, mid-tier application servers, and backend databases would typically have two pools of service data that would need to be maintained to configure every host in the stack:

- Service data for the Tomcat servers would be consumed by the frontend web servers to load balance requests to the application servers.
- Service data for the database instances would be consumed by the application servers to balance read requests across a pool or identify the write master.

Service data can be defined as static site-specific data; however, this manual approach does not facilitate automatic scaling or failover. Service discovery from PuppetDB or other APIs enables dynamic Puppet configuration that adjusts to instance availability and automatic node provisioning by autoscaling groups.

We discuss service discovery data access in "Service Discovery Backends" on page 170.

Business logic

Business logic provides configuration data at a higher level than applications or instances. Logic at this level isn't concerned with package names or the platform-specific implementation details of services. For example, it would define a web server instance without specifying whether to use Apache or NGINX. The implementation details of each component are abstracted away as application code.

Business data commonly contains organization-wide requirements, such as compliance requirements for password expirations or log retention.

Examples of Logic Types

The following presents an example breakdown of the data types in action:

- The application logic for Apache contains resources to install the Apache *httpd* package, manage the *httpd.conf* configuration file, and ensure that the *httpd* service is running.

- The service logic for a web service hosted by Apache might define an Apache virtual host to provide service for the application.

- The site-specific logic might identify shared resources for the application, such as backend databases.

- The load balancer might utilize node data to configure nodes in the service pool.

- The business logic might describe instance names, user policies, and operational constraints.

Because a server can host multiple applications, services, and their dependencies, there can be a bit of overlap in possible places for data to be relevant. Don't stress too much about nailing each one down, but do spend some time thinking about the appropriate category for each type here. You'll gain tremendous insight into how data is used in your organization.

Mapping Data Types to Puppet Use Cases

Let's take a look at how these concerns map to the features and common design patterns of Puppet.

Application Logic and Puppet Modules

For high-level design purposes, when we discuss module design, we are almost always looking at modules from the perspective of service or application management using the Puppet DSL. The Puppet documentation describes modules as "self-contained bundles of code and data." Modules serve many purposes in Puppet, and it's difficult to provide a more specific description while remaining concise and accurate. With this scope in mind, well-designed Puppet modules configure applications or services utilizing business and site-specific data.

Modules are most effective when they serve a single purpose, limit dependencies, and concern themselves only with state related to their named purpose. A well-designed module will usually manage a single service and accept enough input parameters to be used in multiple ways. Modules need not contain nor declare their dependencies: doing so invariably embeds business logic in the module. The prerequisites and dependencies of the service can be managed by other modules, and multiple modules can be used together to create technology stacks.

Single Purpose and Focus

Let's consider the example of a Java application that requires a Java Runtime Environment (JRE) to be available.

It might seem logical to install a JRE as part of our application. However, there are several JRE offerings available, each with its own releases and feature sets. If we bundle a specific JRE (like OpenJDK) into our module, a conflict would arise when another application profile installs a different JRE.

Rather than force both applications to be coded with the same dependency, a more flexible approach would be to document the Java dependency and allow each implementation to select a specific JRE. This approach allows different teams to resolve interdependencies using their own business, service, or site-specific logic.

Example component module

The NTP module is fairly simple as far as Puppet modules are concerned. It contains few resources, and a lot of data. However, all of this data is specific to the NTP module. You can easily use this module by applying it with default parameters or override the default parameters with your own site-specific data.

Although this module is concerned with the NTP service, the list of authoritative NTP sources tends to remain static. Service configuration data can be provided as site-specific data stored in Hiera.

From a business logic perspective, this module would be part of your baseline system profile, and would most likely be applied to every node in your infrastructure.

Identifying business logic in Puppet modules

There's no absolute guide for identifying the business logic antipattern, but it's not terribly difficult to spot. As a general rule, the code implements business logic rather than application logic when the following conditions are met:

- The module conflicts with another module that does not overlap in functional intent.
- The module includes a dependency outside the explicit scope or concern of this module.
- The module implements a subsystem that could be a standalone application or service.

- The module implements a feature that has been implemented by a module focused on that feature.

When a module's code meets one or more of the aforementioned criteria, consider whether you could split the module into smaller, more focused modules that each implement one feature.

Identifying site-specific data in Puppet modules

Modules tend to contain a lot of data: package and filenames, network ports, and application-specific default values. The ideal module contains no data specific to your organization, service, or site, but does contain the minimum necessary data to bring this application or service up in a generic way with appropriate values for supported platforms.

An example of application-specific data is the name of a package that should be deployed and the format of the configuration file. This is specific to the application and necessary to configure the application.

An example of site-specific data is a URL to download a file from an internal server. This is clearly specific to a given site's implementation.

There are several important reasons to keep site-specific data out of your module, even if your module is completely proprietary and would never be released to the public:

Embedding data in the module creates module interdependencies
> When a module contains data about your site, it's tempting to de-duplicate the data by referencing it from other modules. Using the module as a data source creates explicit interdependencies and violates the principles of interface-driven design. Refactoring this module will be impossible without breaking other modules.

Data changes—constantly
> This is by far the greatest issue created by embedding site-specific data in modules. If the site-specific data is spread across multiple modules, simple changes to your site's configuration can demand a massive effort to refactor all interdependent modules.

Data stored inside a module isn't easily accessible
> The site-specific data in a module will be placed for the convenience of the module author. This will rarely be formatted in a consistent way and might be spread across a large set of files. Making use of the data can require manipulation within another module to get the necessary values, causing the two modules to be tightly interwoven and thus fragile.

Modules are rarely stored in the same source repository as data

Data stored in modules might not have the appropriate permissions for the resource manager to keep it up to date. Worse yet, the data's existence within the module might not be documented, forcing a person to manually track down data that is used in multiple locations.

All of these problems can be avoided by keeping site-specific and business data out of Puppet component modules. By adhering to this pattern, you encourage more flexible module design, module reuse within diverse profiles, and centralize site-specific data within Hiera.

Business Logic Should Not Be Written into Component Modules

A major feature of Puppet is module reuse. Component modules provide a way to model applications and services in a portable and reusable way. Technology stacks can be created by combining component modules together in interesting ways using the *roles and profiles* pattern.

For example, an instance of WordPress would need a technology stack containing the following components:

- A database server (MySQL)
- A web server (such as Apache)
- PHP
- WordPress

Even though a monolithic Puppet module could configure WordPress and all of its dependencies, such a module would be quite complex and inflexible. It would likely have conflicts with other modules used on the same node.

Less is more

A module that concerns itself only with the deployment of WordPress and relies on other modules to provide the dependencies would be much more flexible. For example, the WordPress module could depend on the following:

- The Puppet Supported puppetlabs/apache (*https://forge.puppetlabs.com/puppet labs/apache*) module
- The Puppet Approved mayflower/php (*https://forge.puppetlabs.com/mayflower/php*) module
- The Puppet Supported puppetlabs/mysql (*https://forge.puppetlabs.com/puppet labs/mysql*) module

Using this approach allows us to rely on the high-quality *Puppet-supported* modules for Apache and MySQL, along with a Puppet-approved module for PHP. Using the community-supported modules takes advantage of their shared experience, improvements, and bug fixes.

Small components are flexible building blocks

The modular approach facilitates code reuse. By writing a module that focuses on WordPress, the consumer of your module (different team, different site, different service within your own group) could easily swap in a different web server or database server.

Distinct components avoid conflicts

If two modules assigned to a node both depend on Apache, which of those modules should be the one to configure it? If one of the modules expects the other module to configure Apache, both modules are required. Refactoring one module risks breaking the other.

Using shared, flexible modules allows you to avoid this design problem. A node could apply multiple modules that depend on Apache without conflict.

Small components are easily testable

A self-contained module makes it simpler to test each system in isolation and helps reduce the amount of code that would need to be reviewed to identify and isolate bugs.

Business Logic with Roles and Profiles

If you should keep modules small and focused on specific applications, how should you configure a complete technology stack? You can do this cleanly and safely by abstracting the application stack into *roles and profiles*.

Roles describe business logic and site-specific configurations

A role contains responsibility for implementing a site-specific configuration. To this end, a role is often no more than a list of profiles to be applied to a node.

Profiles implement technology stacks

The profile simply declares the modules needed to build a given technology stack, their ordering dependencies, and any profile-specific parameters that should be passed to the component modules. Because a profile is site- or service-specific, profiles provide all site-specific details to the component modules about the stack requirements.

For example, we could have a WordPress profile include the WordPress, Apache, PHP, and MySQL component modules. It would configure Apache appropriately for the WordPress service, configure WordPress' dependencies in PHP, and ensure that WordPress has a database available for its use in MySQL. Thus, the profile defines the technology stack.

We take a closer look at the *roles and profiles* design pattern in Chapter 7.

Roles and profiles versus node classifiers

Roles and profiles provide a necessary abstraction layer between your modules and your node classifier. Before roles and profiles became common, it was necessary to use external node classifiers (ENCs) to manage Puppet node assignments, which presented a wide variety of data management problems. Now the ENC is best suited to identify the role to be assigned to the node and pass along provisioning and node-specific details it is well suited to manage.

We explore roles and profiles and how they have replaced other node classification mechanisms in Chapter 7.

Business, Service, Site, Node, and Application Data

Hiera is the data store for node, application, service, site, and business-specific data. Hiera contains three layers for data, each of which can implement a unique hierarchy specific to that layer's needs. With the addition of pluggable modules to provide external data lookup, Hiera has become the omnipresent, ubiquitous data source for Puppet.

Having all data lookup available through a consistent data access mechanism makes it easy to query data using a standard tool, puppet lookup, without knowledge or care about the origin of the data. This can be extremely valuable for debugging modules when data comes from diverse sources or multiple teams.

Global layer: business data

The global layer is best used for business data that should never vary on a site-specific basis. As it comes first in the data lookup, any value it contains will override values in a lower layer.

Depending on your business needs, you might want to put security controls and mandatory compliance data at this layer. If the site-specific configurations are diverse, it might not be useful to have any data in the global layer.

Environment layer: site, service, and node-specific data

A node's catalog is built for a specific *environment*. The data hierarchy in the environment should provide a layered lookup to retrieve node, service, and site-specific data.

Following are some examples of site-specific data appropriate for the environment layer:

- User account information or authentication services
- Local data storage replicas
- DNS resolvers and NTP synchronization sources

Site-specific data is local to a specific implementation and tends to change more often than application code or business logic. New sites come up, infrastructure changes, nodes are added or removed. Placing the data describing your service or site in the Puppet environment makes it easy to localize data that is relative to the context in which it is used.

Module layer: application defaults

As a general rule, application defaults do not belong in the global or environment layers of Hiera. Default values for basic usage of the module should be provided within the module data.

One of the most eagerly awaited features provided by Hiera v5 was *data in modules*. Instead of writing code to introspect the environment (as done in the older *params.pp* pattern) the Hiera data hierarchy within a module provides a consistent data lookup mechanism for returning application defaults. This allows application defaults to be based on node facts, like `os.family` or `os.version.major`.

 A module may not contain data outside its own namespace. This prevents a module from declaring values for the environment or a different module.

Hiera Data Sources

Hiera provides a data lookup hierarchy with pluggable backend data providers. We examine usage of Hiera in depth in Chapter 6; however, we mention it here to discuss how Hiera can provide access to the different types of data.

Static data in Hiera

Hiera has built-in data backends to read text files in three different formats:

- YAML
- JSON
- HOCON

In a small site that changes infrequently or with stable services, service data can be staticly declared in Hiera data files. Any change to the data can be made by pushing changes to those files. Even when service discovery data is available, it's not uncommon for core services such as DNS servers or package repositories to be maintained in static data.

Service discovery from Hiera

Modern computing environments are rarely static. Autoscaling pools are increasingly common, service clusters are increasingly large, and dynamic cloud provisioning has become the new normal. In these cases, manually editing data files every time a node comes up becomes burdensome and unrealisticly slow. It also creates high levels of churn in your data, which can increase and magnify human error.

Service discovery is the act of discovering information about services from live (as opposed to preconfigured) data. Dynamic service discovery allows internode relationships to be retrieved on demand. For example, a load-balancer module can create service pools using a list of nodes that provide the application.

If you have a large, autoscaled environment, it might be necessary to acquire service discovery data from another source. We cover the use of Hiera backends that access exported resources from PuppetDB for service discovery in "Service Discovery Backends" on page 170.

Accessing third-party external data sources in Hiera

You can configure any level of the Hiera hierarchy to source data from an external third-party database, application, framework—really anything that can be queried. This makes reuse of existing data sources easy to manage.

Node Classification

Node data is a form of site-specific data usually handled separately from general site data. Site-specific data tends to be relatively static, whereas nodes are added to your data store every time a node is brought up or down. The node data contains unique information about each node, such as the IP address of the node, the physical location of the node, and the Puppet environment assigned to that node.

ENCs

An ENC utilizes node information provided by a data source to determine what roles (and thus profiles) should be assigned to a specific node. Such data sources are typically provisioning systems that maintain their own host databases and manage more properties of a node than Puppet requires.

Besides tracking node details, the ENC can provide a list of Puppet classes for the node. This is best used to assign the node's role.

There are many options available for external node classification:

- Puppet Enterprise includes a node management interface and classifier.
- Mature infrastructure management solutions such as Foreman and Cobbler provide node classification for Puppet.
- Node data can be retrieved from the Lightweight Directory Access Protocol (LDAP), a database, or a NoSQL implementation like MongoDB.
- Node data can be queried from cloud or infrastructure vendor APIs.

Because ENCs are simple to write, you can use any data source that can provide information about the nodes.

 Using an external data store as a classifier does not preclude you from using PuppetDB for reporting and analysis purposes.

Hiera as a node classifier

An alternative to using an external classifier is to assign roles and profiles to the node based on information the node knows about itself. The node supplies `facts`, which can be used in the Hiera hierarchy to include the role appropriate for node. This is usually done with custom facts used specifically to assist with node classification.

Appropriate uses of node data

The best use of node classification is to gather enough data to assign the appropriate role to a node and, optionally, to provide node-specific configuration details. Attempts to source site and service data from node provisioning systems invariably lead to painful duplication and inconsistency in the data.

Provisioning systems rarely match the flexibility of Hiera for assigning roles, defining application profiles, and general node configuration. For example, the node classifier in Cobbler cannot set class parameters and has limited support for defining groups of classes. The Puppet Enterprise node classifier and Foreman both use all features of the Classifier API, but the API was never intended to provide dependencies, class ordering, or relationships. These are business logic that should be expressed in the roles and profiles.

Summary

This chapter introduced categories for code and data used in a Puppet deployment and discussed how categories are related to components of Puppet. The *roles and profiles* design pattern was introduced for effective usage of code and data to deploy a complete application stack.

Here are this chapter's takeaways:

- Before writing code, take a moment to categorize the scope of the data using the list presented at the beginning of this chapter.
- Keep modules small, focused, and modular so that you can reuse them.
- Isolate application logic to the Puppet module.
- Manage business logic and application dependencies using the *roles and profiles* pattern.
- Use an ENC to retrieve node data from your provisioning system.
- Use Hiera at the environment layer to localize site- and service-specific data.
- Consider using service discovery to dynamically manage internode relationships and service data.

## CHAPTER 3

Coding Practices

In this chapter, we look at best practices related to using the Puppet language. This chapter focuses predominantly on Puppet's conditional logic, operators, function calls, and data structures. We concentrate on resource types and classes at a high level so that we can delve deeper on those subjects in Chapter 4 when we discuss module design, and Chapter 5 when we explore best practices relating to a number of common resource types, and Chapter 7 when we look at code organization and intermodule relationships.

The Style Guide

We advise you to review the Puppet language style guide (*https://docs.puppetlabs.com/guides/style_guide.html*), which covers recommended usage and what validation and testing tools to expect. We do not repeat the style guide in this chapter; instead, we expand upon the information Puppet provides in the guide, emphasizing a few key and often overlooked aspects of the guide.

The Puppet style guide focuses on keeping code clear and easy to understand, as well as maintaining a clean revision history. A major benefit of the official style guide is that development and testing tools automatically identify and correct violations of the guide.

The Puppet style guide is now updated for each version of Puppet. Always refer to the version you are coding for, like so:

- Puppet 5.5 style guide (*https://puppet.com/docs/puppet/5.5/style_guide.html*) or Puppet 4.10 style guide (*https://puppet.com/docs/puppet/latest/style_guide.html*)
- *https://puppet.com/docs/puppet/4.10/style_guide.html*

Be aware that the style guide often contains recommendations made to ensure backward compatibility with older Puppet releases. This is useful for shared modules used by a wide audience. If you're planning to release code that might be used with older versions of Puppet, the style guide will keep you safe. Otherwise, it's usually best to code to current best practices, and leave those deprecations behind.

 The style guide once recommended use of the *params.pp* pattern for compatibility with 3.x releases. Use it if you still have Puppet 3 deployed, but otherwise leave the past behind. Puppet 4, 5, and 6 all support the significantly more powerful *data in modules* pattern.

Having a set style guide is invaluable for peer review. Consistent style helps reviewers focus on the changes in your code, without struggling to read past differences in style. Simple rules such as indentation can make errors stand out. Correct use of white space, variable assignment, and interpolation make the code easier to follow. If you choose to not follow the Puppet style guide, we recommend documenting and publishing an internal style guide for your site. Your internal guide could be based on the Puppet standard, with your own internal adjustments documented.

When working in a team that uses its own style guide for other projects, it can be a good idea to adapt that style for use in Puppet for team or project consistency. One consistent *imperfect* style is much better than multiple coding styles, though this doesn't mean adopting bad practices in the name of consistency.

Install `puppet-lint` (*http://puppet-lint.com/*) and use it in a `pre-commit` hook to encourage conformity to the style guide. We discuss `puppet-lint` more extensively in "Testing" on page 250.

Coding Principles

Principles for development improve the quality of your code. Books such as *Practical Object-Oriented Design in Ruby* (*http://bit.ly/practical-object-oriented-design*) by Sandi Metz and *Clean Code* (*http://bit.ly/clean-code-orm*) by Robert C. Martin go into great depth on coding practices and do so in a way that is applicable beyond the scope of the language examples used in the book.

Many object-oriented development principles apply to Puppet, though some principles are procedural in nature and can thus be counterproductive due to the nature of Puppet's declarative language and idempotent design. This section introduces declarative and object-focused coding principles that are referenced throughout the book.

KISS: Keep It Simple

Good Puppet code is not clever. Good code is straightforward, obvious, and easy to read. There is no twist, no mystery. Although there are many neat tricks that can reduce the number of characters used, you and others will spend a lot more time *reading* your code than you did *writing* it. Readable code is less fragile, easier to debug, and easier to extend. Code reduction is most beneficial when it eliminates potential bugs and improves readability.

Clever code tends to make sense when written, but often becomes confusing when read months later. Clever code often hides subtle bugs, and can be difficult to extend or refactor. In the worst cases, it solves unexpected problems in nonobvious ways, and bites anyone who attempts to refactor it.

If a trick improves the readability and clarity of your code, by all means use it. If the neat trick has obtuse inner workings or makes the person next to you scratch their head, consider using a more readable approach that's easier to understand.

> Code that's obvious to you today might not be so to the person who must read or update it. Even you likely won't recall your own intent after enough months or years have passed.

Even documented design patterns and techniques can be confusing to those new to Puppet or that particular technique. The benefit of documented tricks is that they tend to be well understood and well explained. Example 3-1 demonstrates needless complexity.

Example 3-1. Violating the KISS principle using create_resources()

```
$files = {
  '/tmp/foo' => {
    'content' => 'foo',
  },
  '/tmp/bar' => {
    'content' => 'bar',
  }
  '/tmp/baz' => {
    'ensure' => 'link',
    'target' => '/tmp/foo',
  }
}

$defaults = {
  ensure => 'file',
  mode   => '0644',
}
```

```
create_resources('file', $files, $defaults)
```

Using `create_resources` to iterate over a hash is a well-known pattern and is a best practice when iterating over a large number of items sourced from an external data source. But the implementation in Example 3-1 is both more lines of code—and less readable—than simple `file` resource declarations. See "DRY: Don't Repeat Yourself" on page 44 later in this chapter for more examples.

The Single Responsibility Principle

Resources, defined types, and function calls in Puppet should have one responsibility, and no more than one responsibility. Examples of statements that violate the *single responsibility principle*:

- This module installs Java and Tomcat.
- This conditional sets the ensure state and determines the correct version.
- This resource downloads and extracts a tarball.
- This class configures NGINX and installs a baseline environment.
- This module encrypts data and synchronizes the system clock.

A module built with this description attempts to solve multiple problems in a single place, thus embedding limitations and contraints on reuse. The single responsibility principle suggests that code built around singular responsibilities will be better designed and reusable. We can achieve a key difference simply by defining responsibilities without using the word "and," as shown here:

- This class manages Apache's packages.
- This select statement retrieves platform-specific defaults.
- This function call validates URLs.
- This resource downloads a file.
- This module installs Tomcat.
- This role builds our three-tier application stack on a single node.

A Puppet module that follows the single responsibility principle is easy to reuse, maintain, and extend. It doesn't include its own copy of Java; it allows you to use a class designed specifically for that need. The class' structure is broken down into child classes, each of which are named appropriately for their single purpose. This allows the reader to easily grasp the flow of the module and its relationships.

When you apply the single responsibility principle, modular, extensible, and reusable code is created. It helps ensure that side effects are minimized, and simplifies debugging. It's easy to create unit and acceptance tests for Puppet modules built around the principle. The behavior of each bit of functionality will be uniform, easy to document, and easy to test.

Reusable Building Blocks

Modular code is less likely to be rewritten as your site grows and changes. For example, if a monolithic *base* module contains policy enforcement, user accounts, drivers, and packages, it will be difficult to accomodate nodes that need a nonstandard base configuration.

We've often seen parameters added to monolithic modules to allow special exceptions; however, this only digs the hole deeper. Each time base is changed, it may affect nodes for which no change was intended.

Stop digging! Treat each component module as a separate build block, and allow each profile to use and combine the blocks as necessary. This gives each profile complete flexibility, without forcing yet another exception into a shared base.

Separation of Concerns

The separation of concerns (SoC) principle makes it possible to create loosely integrated, modular code. It is is strongly related to interface-driven design and the single responsibility principle.

Many of the concepts discussed in Chapter 2 service the SoC:

- Modules implement a single application or component.
- Data sourced from Hiera describes the implementation.
- Roles and profiles incorporate business and service logic for complete stack implementations.

SoC requires thought to where a particular bit of code or data belongs. It means asking questions such as the following:

- Is this business logic or application data?
- Should this be specified in data or static in this profile?
- Is this configuration part of the application logic or profile-specific logic? Example: Should a VMWare-specific time setting be in the NTP or the VMWare module?

In the last scenario, the NTP configuration change is applicable only to VMware nodes. Therefore, the correct choice is to create a profile that includes both modules and implements this one change common to, but outside of, both of them.

SoC can be difficult to maintain. Referencing an existing variable from another module seems like a quick and easy way to access data. It avoids duplicating data and avoids the need to reconsider structure. Unfortunately, this is always a trap. Violating another module's interface makes your code tightly interwoven with that module, making any change a risk for both modules. It is thus difficult to debug and maintain, constrains improvements, and hampers refactoring.

 Failing to keep modules discrete creates situations where it's impossible to test a module without deploying the entire code-base.

Modular Puppet code minimizes dependencies, allowing quick instantiations of the module to validate the module's functionality. With modular code, you can test and debug one component at a time. With an interwoven codebase, understanding and troubleshooting any single component of the system involves troubleshooting the entire application stack.

 Properly implementing SoC manifests the design goal of low coupling and high cohension (*http://bit.ly/2nXwNbu*): the module resources are tightly focused on its core concerns while loosely bound to other modules.

Interface-Driven Design

Puppet modules should interact with one another using well-defined interfaces. In most cases, this means that you interact with classes via class parameters and class relationships rather than using fully qualified variables and direct resource relationships.

Because Puppet is a declarative language and does not offer *getter* or *setter* methods, interface-driven design tends to enforce a structure to the way data flows through your site.

- Data originates from sources such as Hiera, ENCs, and your *site.pp* manifest.
- The data is consumed by roles and profiles.

- component modules. This all happens by having the `component` modules receive parameters from the roles and profiles.

With this approach, the business logic instructs the general-purpose application modules how to build the site-specific requirements.

Using class parameters as your primary interface providers troubleshooting benefits. Information about the classes and class parameters applied to a node are sent to that node as part of its catalog. Referring to the built catalog, you can isolate and debug a single module without worrying about *how* its parameters are being generated. You can also use the parameters to better understand how data flows through your manifests.

Example 3-2 presents code that makes two bad choices that violate the principles of interface-driven design.

Example 3-2. vhost template violating the principle of interface-driven design

```
class myapp {
  include apache
  $vhost_dir = $apache::vhost_dir

  file { "${vhost_dir}/myapp.conf":
    ensure  => 'file',
    content => epp('myapp/vhost.conf.erb', {
                hostname => 'myapp.example.com',
                port     => '443',
                docroot  => '/srv/my_app/root',
              })
  }
}
```

This module does two things wrong:

- It violates the module interface to retrieve the configuration directory.
- It writes a file into the module's managed configuration directory.

Example 3-3 provides the same delivery as Example 3-2 except that it uses the module's public interface. This ensures that the usage will work, regardless of whether the Apache module uses a different variable for the configuration directory in the future, or purges unmanaged content from its directory.

Example 3-3. Interface-driven virtual host creation virtual host creation

```
class myapp {
  include apache
```

```
  apache::vhost { 'myapp.example.com':
    ensure  => 'present',
    port    => '443',
    docroot => '/srv/my_app/root',
  }
}
```

In Example 3-2, the code reaches into the Apache module and grabs the contents of an internal variable. If this is not a documented interface of the class, there is no guarantee that the variable or its contents will be available or consistent between releases.

Rather than querying the Apache module to determine the directory and then inserting custom content there, in Example 3-3 we utilize a defined type provided by the Apache module that creates the vhost for us. This approach uses a stable interface provided by the Apache module while retaining our ability to control the virtual host definition our application requires. Because apache::vhost is provided by the Apache module, it has safe access to Apache internals without violating the principles of interface-driven design.

Although versions up through Puppet 6 don't prevent you from directly accesssing variables from other modules, Puppet has indicated that it is considered deprecated behavior and might be removed in future versions of Puppet. The best reason to avoid direct access of variables internal to another module is that it will improve the quality of your code, facilitate debugging and analysis, and avoid headaches when the module is refactored.

DRY: Don't Repeat Yourself

The DRY principle suggests that if you write the same code or data more than once, it could be abstracted into a class, defined type, or function call.

Puppet provides the ability to extend the language with Ruby facts, functions, custom Hiera backends, data providers for environments, and modules. Puppet 4 and higher support facts and functions written entirely in the Puppet DSL to reduce repetition in your code.

The best application of the DRY principle can be subjective and might differ from one use case to another. If reducing repetition in your code makes it unreadable, it reduces the code quality rather than enhance it. We advise preferring readability over DRY for any case in which the principles conflict.

Consider Example 3-4:

Example 3-4. Repetitive resource declarations

```
file { '/etc/puppet/puppet.conf':
  ensure => 'file',
```

```
  content => template('puppet/puppet.conf.erb'),
  group  => 'root',
  mode   => '0444',
  owner  => 'root',
}

file { '/etc/puppet/auth.conf':
  ensure => 'file',
  content => template('puppet/auth.conf.erb'),
  group  => 'root',
  mode   => '0444',
  owner  => 'root',
}

file { '/etc/puppet/routes.yaml':
  ensure => 'file',
  content => template('puppet/routes.yaml.erb'),
  group  => 'root',
  mode   => '0444',
  owner  => 'root',
}
```

You could make this example DRY by using default attribute values, as shown in
Example 3-5.

Example 3-5. Resource declarations with attribute defaults

```
file {
  default:
    ensure => 'file',
    owner  => 'root',
    mode   => '0444',
    group  => 'root',
  ;

  '/etc/puppetlabs/puppet/puppet.conf':
    content => template('puppet/puppet.conf.erb'),
    group   => 'wheel',
  ;

  '/etc/puppetlabs/puppet/auth.conf':
    content => template('puppet/auth.conf.erb'),
    mode    => '0400',
  ;

  '/etc/puppetlabs/puppet/routes.yaml':
    content => template('puppet/routes.yaml.erb'),
  ;
}
```

As shown in this example, readability is improved by setting resource default values. The code is condensed, and exceptions stand out clearly to the reader.

 Default attribute values in a resource expression are more readable and less prone to breakage than default resource definitions (e.g., File), which can affect resources off the page. Default resource definitions can have wide-randing but inconsisent impact and produce surprising behavior when minor changes to the catalog affect class load order.

You could further simplify this example by using a defined type, as demonstrated in Example 3-6.

Example 3-6. Resource declarations with a defined type

```
$files = [
  '/etc/puppet/puppet.conf',
  '/etc/puppet/auth.conf',
  '/etc/puppet/routes.yaml',
]

mymodule::myfile { $files: }
```

Although this approach uses fewer characters, the implementation is hidden from the viewer. The resulting behavior relies on the implementation of the *Mymodule::Myfile* defined type, which could change outside of the scope of this example. This highlights the inherent problem with this approach: it hides implementation details and forces cross-reference when extending or debugging this code.

You can accomplish the same thing using an each() loop.\, as shown in Example 3-7.

Example 3-7. Resource declarations with an each() loop

```
include 'stdlib'

$files = [
  '/etc/puppet/puppet.conf',
  '/etc/puppet/auth.conf',
  '/etc/puppet/routes.yaml',
]

$files.each |$file| {
  file { $file:
    ensure  => 'file',
    content => template("puppet/${file}.erb"),
    group   => 'root',
    mode    => '0444',
```

```
    owner  => 'root',
  }
}
```

This approach is preferable to a defined type by keeping the resource declaration logic and iterator in the same file, and often on the same page of code. The code is better contextualized for the reader, and there is no latent dependency on external code.

In practice, Example 3-5 is the most readable approach, despite being less DRY than Example 3-6 or Example 3-7. This is a case for which simplicity wins out over other considerations.

There are a few cases in which very DRY code can be produced using array resource declaration and depending on automatic relationships:

```
$directories = [
  '/tmp',
  '/tmp/example1',
  '/tmp/example2',
  '/tmp/example1/foo',
  '/tmp/example1/bar',
]

file { $directories:
  ensure => 'directory',
  mode   => '0755',
}
```

In this example, each of the directories is created by passing an array of directory paths to the file resource. This simple example depends on autorequire logic in the File resource to automatically create relationships between the higher- and lower-level directories. Without this automatic relationship, you'd need to break these out to create the relationships one by one, as shown here:

```
file { '/tmp':
  ensure => 'directory',
  mode   => '0755',
}

file { '/tmp/example1':
  ensure  => 'directory',
  mode    => '0755',
  require => File['/tmp'], # redundant, is automatic dependency
}

file { '/tmp/example1/foo':
  ensure  => 'directory',
  mode    => '0755',
  require => File['/tmp/example1'], # redundant also
}
```

The bolded lines in the preceding example are unnecessary given that the `File` resource automatically creates relationships with directories in parent paths.

Don't Reinvent the Wheel

Attempts to reinvent existing tools using the Puppet DSL are the most common cause of fragile, code-heavy Puppet manifests. For example, it can take a lot of conditional logic and exec resources to download, cache, and extract a *.tar* file from a web server. You can perform the same process idempotently with a single `archive` resource.

Puppet is not a software packaging tool; there are more than three dozen package providers purpose-built for this need. The `package` resource makes use of these providers to manage packages. There can be odd situations for which using Puppet to build packages might seem unavoidable, but the quality of code will suffer, and the complexity of the implementation will increase dramatically.

YAGNI: You Ain't Gonna Need It (or You're Not Google)

Avoid taking a small requirement and setting out to build a solution (that you think) Google would be proud of. We have seen far too many simple requests turned into a multiweek deliverable when the need didn't require it. This often results in overly abstracted, difficult-to-decipher implementations that provided the same features that existing functionality like a simple key/value store could provide (unless you count lost hours of effort).

Is the requirement for highly performant code or is it for a well-maintained solution delivered quickly? Most companies without Google's scale would rather throw money at commonly available compute resources than at difficult-to-find, comparatively expensive infrastructure engineers.

We advise being data driven in your selection of efforts. Document the needs that are known at the start. Observe that certain future needs might not be met with a selected existing functionality. But don't go coding *The Best New Key Query Store Evah* until data shows those conditions are necessary. This avoids unnecessary work, known widely as *You Ain't Gonna Need It*, and colloquially as *You're Not Google*.

Code Practices

This section covers best practices relating to code patterns that improve readability with the Puppet language. These are all subjective, but it's usually quite easy to see the difference when you're comparing two different implementations.

Balance of Resources Versus Logic

Puppet code contains instructions on how to build a catalog of resources. Those resources describe the state that the resource providers on the node will ensure.

Conditional logic by definition is not idempotent. It's a procedural construct that guarantees that given the same input, it will return the same output. Although Puppet variables, selectors, and conditionals are a core part of the Puppet language, their ultimate purpose is to declare resources to be added to the node's catalog. Logic implemented in the Puppet language without resources can never be idempotent; only the resources it declares can function idempotently. Puppet works best when decisions about how to implement the declared state are left to the resource providers.

When you find a module heavy with conditional logic, case statements, and variable handling code, take a moment to reassess your approach. Is there a way to refactor this code to be more declarative? To illustrate this further, let's take a look at Example 3-8.

Example 3-8. Resources versus logic

```
# BAD DESIGN: conditionally create resources specific to the data
if( $users['jill']['shell'] == '/bin/bash' ) {
  user { 'jill':
    ensure => 'present',
    shell  => '/bin/bash',
  }
}

# GOOD DESIGN: let the data inform the user provider what to implement
user { 'jill':
  ensure => 'present',
  shell  => $users['jill']['shell'],
}
```

Catalog building works best when the bulk of your manifests comprise resource declarations rather than logic. Declare the desired state, and leave it up to the resource provider to choose when and how to act.

Balance of Code Versus Data

Puppet is often described as *infrastructure as code* because it creates infrastructure with code based on the data provided.

Puppet code is reusable when the code does not contain data values, but instead implements application or business logic based on the data provided. A Puppet module should ideally contain little to no data within the module, instead acting upon data provided by Hiera.

To understand this point better, let's look at Example 3-9, which contains a considerable amount of data.

Example 3-9. Data values in code

```
case $facts['os']['family'] {
  'RedHat': {
    package { 'apache24':
      provider        => 'yum',
      vendor_options => '--enablerepo=epel',
    }
  }
  'Debian': {
    package { 'apache2':
      provider => 'apt',
    }
  }
}
```

This example hardcodes the name of the package, the name of the repository, and the provider into the module. All of these are subject to change. In Red Hat Enterprise Linux (RHEL) version 8 and above, the provider will be DNF, the default Apache version will be 2.6...you get the idea. But most important of all, *none of these data values describe what is being done.* Rather, they provide specifics about how to do it, as shown in Example 3-10.

Example 3-10. Code utilizing supplied data

```
$pkginfo = lookup("myapp::packages::${facts['os']['family']}")

package { $pkginfo['name']:
  ensure         => $pkginfo['should_update'],
  provider       => $pkginfo['provider'],
  vendor_options => $pkginfo['vendor_options'],
}
```

Example 3-10 is much easier to read, and uses values supplied by Hiera for the packages and providers appropriate for each OS.

Conditional Logic

As shown in Example 3-9, you should avoid placing resources inside of conditional logic whenever possible. Doing so makes the generated catalog subject to change and removes important information from the node's catalog and reports. Let's look at this in Example 3-11.

Example 3-11. Resources embedded in conditional logic

```
case $facts['os']['family'] {
  'RedHat': {
    package { 'httpd':
      ensure => 'installed',
    }
  }
  'Debian': {
    package { 'apache2':
      ensure => 'installed',
    }
  }
}
```

When comparing the catalogs of two otherwise identical nodes, `Package['httpd']` and `Package['apache2']` would appear to be different but implement the same functionality for two different platforms. You can achieve the same net result with a consistent resource name and acquiring OS–specific values from data, as demonstrated in Example 3-12.

Example 3-12. Use data to simplify resource management

```
package { 'apache':
  ensure   => 'installed',
  name     => $pkginfo['name'],
  provider => $pkginfo['provider'],
}
```

When reading the code, comparing the catalog or reports of catalog application, these resources will clearly be identical. No lines of code are wasted on OS-specific details better listed in the data.

Example 3-12 is significantly more DRY than Example 3-11 and better communicates its intent.

This concept extends to resources that might be optional within a catalog. Let's look at Example 3-13, which conditionally adds a resource an *autosign.conf* file:

Example 3-13. Conditionally adding a resource to a catalog

```
if $autosign == true {
  file { '/etc/puppet/autosign.conf':
    ensure  => 'present',
    content => template('puppetserver/autosign.conf.erb'),
  }
}
```

This code has two problems:

- It won't remove the file if the value changes from `true` to `false`.

- It causes the `File['autosign.conf']` resource to wink in and out of existence in the catalog.

A significantly more stable implementation is provided in Example 3-14.

Example 3-14. Conditionally managing resource state

```
$autosign_ensure = bool2str($autosign, 'present', 'absent')
file { '/etc/puppet/autosign.conf':
  ensure  => $autosign_ensure,
  content => template('puppetmaster/autosign.conf.erb'),
}
```

Example 3-14 declares what the result should be in either case, rather than the conditional action shown in Example 3-13. In doing so, it ensures the proper state by changing the file declaration to be `absent` and having the file be removed.

There are some cases for which it makes absolute sense to wrap a resource in conditional logic, such as the following:

```
if $pkginfo['uses_sites_available'] {
  file { "/etc/apache2/sites-enabled/${title}.conf":
    ensure => 'link',
    target => "../sites-available/${title}.conf",
  }
}
```

This resource would be nonsensical on a Red Hat–based system because Red Hat does not manage Virtual Hosts using the *sites-available/* and *sites-enabled/* directories. In this case, conditionally adding the resource to the catalog is the correct approach because that directory structure won't exist if the sites-available configuration style is not in use.

Iteration

Iteration is the act of applying the same process to multiple elements in a set. Puppet 3 had limited support for iteration. Puppet 4 and newer introduced iteration functions that are a great deal more readable and flexible than previous solutions.

Iteration with resources

Until Puppet 4, only two features allowed iteration over multiple resources. We cover these because they remain available in newer versions of Puppet.

Resources can be declared with an array of titles

If you declare a resource with more than one title, it will process each one as a distinct resource declaration. This works well only when the attributes are consistent in each resource, although it is most often used to call a declared type that acts on each value.

`create_resources()` *creates a named resource for every entry in the hash*

Call the `create_resources()` function with the name of a resource and a hash of resource attributes. It will create a resource declaration of the named resource for each entry in the hash.

For cases in which you want to declare a bunch of resources with a hash, `create_resources()` interates over an easy-to-maintain data structure, as illustrated in the following example:

```
$services = {
  'puppet'       => { 'ensure' => 'running', },
  'puppetserver' => { 'ensure' => 'running', },
  'httpd'        => { 'ensure' => 'stopped', },
}

create_resources('service', $services)
```

In situations that require something more complex than mapping data to resource attributes, you can call a defined type via `create_resources()` to process or evaluate input. Example 3-15 demonstrates an implementation to automatically adjust the `enabled` attribute of a resource based on the `ensure` parameter.

Example 3-15. Iteration using a defined type

```
$services = {
  'puppet'       => { 'ensure' => 'running', },
  'puppetserver' => { 'ensure' => 'running', },
  'httpd'        => { 'ensure' => 'stopped', },
}

create_resources('ensure_service', $services)

define ensure_service (
  $ensure => undef,
) {
  $enabled = $ensure ? {
    'running' => true,
    default   => false,
  }

  service { $title:
    ensure  => $ensure,
    enabled => $enabled,
```

```
    }
  }
```

Iteration with functions

Functions that iterate across arrays and hashes of data provide a level of flexibility not available prior to Puppet 4.

Puppet 4 introduced a number of block iterators. The functions `filter`, `map`, `reduce`, `scanf`, and `slice` are most useful for data transformation. Each of these functions takes one set of data and processes it to create another form. For example, `filter` can be used to produce an array or hash containing only values that meet certain criteria.

The example that follows filters a hash of users to extract a smaller hash containing only users who are members of the `admin` group.

```
$admins = $users.filter |$username, $values| {
  $values['groups'] =~ /admin/
}
```

For each user in `$users`, a test of the `groups` value is performed. A positive match causes the entire user entry to be added to the `$admins` hash.

In contrast, the `each()` function passes each value to a block of code for processing without returning any value to the calling scope. The following is a very basic reimplementation of `create_resources()`:

```
$services.each |$name, $values| {
  service { $name:
    ensure  => $values['ensure'],
    enabled => $values['enabled']
  }
}
```

Generating Lists

There are a number of cases for which you might want to dynamically generate a list of items. This can happen for benchmarking purposes, or to supply a range of times for *cron* jobs.

The `range()` function from *puppetlabs/stdlib* accepts a beginning value, an end value, and an optional interval value, and then returns an array of values. This makes it useful for specifying intervals, such as with *cron*:

```
cron { 'every_5_minutes':
  command => something to be done every 5 minutes
  minute  => range(0, 55, 5)
}
```

Although the `range()` function can provide some limited iteration of numbers within a string, it's more reliable to generate an array of integers and use `prefix()` and `suffix()` to create names. `prefix()` and `suffix()` each accept an array and a string and return an array with the prefix or suffix applied to each element, as shown in this example:

Example 3-16. Iterating over a flat hash using each

```
$range    = range('0','2')
$prefixed = prefix($range, '/tmp/test')
$complete = suffix($prefixed, '.txt')
```

You can see the output of this code by testing with `puppet apply`. This example uses the less readable but concise function chaining:

```
$ puppet apply -e "notice( range('0','2').prefix('/tmp/test').suffix('.txt') )"
Notice: Scope(Class[main]): [/tmp/test0.txt, /tmp/test1.txt, /tmp/test2.txt]
```

Variables

This section covers a number of best practices relating to the use of variables in the Puppet language.

Variable Naming

Correct naming of variables is very important for both usability and compatibility.

All supported versions of Puppet (4+) have restrictions on variable naming, the most major of which is that you can no longer start variable names with capital letters.

You must follow these guidelines:

- Begin variable names with an underscore or lowercase letter.
- Subsequent characters may be uppercase or lowercase letters, numbers, or underscores.

Most identifiers in Puppet loosely follow Ruby symbol naming restrictions; the identifier cannot begin with a number and cannot contain dashes. Class names are even more strict because they normalize to lowercase (flattening capitals), which will impair readability. We advise erring on the side of using more restrictive conventions and favoring descriptive variable names over terse variable names.

Referencing Variables

We recommend the following guidelines when referencing a variable:

- Avoid variable inheritance.
- Local variables should be unqualified.
- Global variables should be fully qualified.
- Reference facts using the $facts[] array.
- Avoid referencing undefined variables.

Variable should be fully qualified

Local variables should be unqualified, global variables should be fully qualified, and you should avoid fully qualified out-of-scope variable references whenever possible.

Fully qualifying variable names accomplishes two goals:

- Clarify your intent
- Disambiguate local and global variables

When a variable is fully qualified, it becomes clear that your module is attempting to consume a top-level variable and eliminates the possibility that you simply forgot to define that variable or are attempting to inherit a variable from a higher scope. This disambiguation will be important when you revisit your code in the future, either to extend the code or debug a problem.

 Many validation tools assume that unqualified variables are local and will throw a warning if the variable is not defined in scope. puppet-lint allows you to disable this behavior; however, we recommend against doing so because it's an essential tool for identifying subtle bugs.

Although you can fully qualify references to local variables, using unqualified names makes it clear at a glance that the variable is local and has been defined in the current scope. This hint again is used by the validators.

Avoid creating interclass variable references using fully qualified variable names. Such references are a useful stop-gap measure when upgrading code that relies on variable inheritance; however, it usually violates the SoC principle. A major issue with interclass variable access is that there's no way to determine from the referenced class that such a reference exists. As a result, any code change in one class could break the reference. Instead, consider parameterizing your classes, using class parameters to pass data from one module to another, as demonstrated in Example 3-17. A side benefit of this approach is that it tends to reduce and eliminate circular dependencies.

Example 3-17. Passing data using fully qualified variables

```
class parent {
  $foo = 'alpha'
}

class parent::child {
  $foo = $parent::foo
  alert($foo) #Prints 'alpha'
}
```

In this situation, someone refactoring parent wouldn't necessarily be aware that variable $foo is being used elsewhere. In Example 3-18, the data usage is explicit, allowing either or both modules to be refactored without affecting the other.

Example 3-18. Passing variables using class parameters

```
class parent {
  $new_name = 'alpha'

  class { 'child':
    foo => $new_name,
  }
}

class parent::child (String $foo) {
  notice($foo) # logs 'alpha'
}
```

Example 3-18 is more verbose than Example 3-17, but is designed in such a way that variable usage is clearly documented in code. This increase in verbosity improves the quality of the code and reduces the likelihood of breakage as the code evolves.

Avoid referencing out-of-scope variables. Instead, pass variables into classes using class parameters, as shown in the code that follows. This might seem like an arbitrary guideline at first, but it helps to control a flow of data through your code and avoids surprises when refactoring code.

```
class profiles::variable_scope {
  $foo = 'alpha'

  class { 'first':
    foo => $foo,
  }

  class { 'unrelated':
    foo => $foo,
  }
}
```

```
class first (String $foo) {
  notice($foo) # logs 'alpha'
}

class unrelated (String $foo) {
  notice($foo) # logs 'alpha'
}
```

Fully qualified variables make it easy for minor code changes to break things in different codebases, whereas use of parameters for passing values enforces the loosely coupled, SoC approach to data handling.

It used to be necessary to reference fully qualified variables to work around limitations in Puppet. The deprecated *params.pp* pattern discussed in "The params.pp Pattern" on page 91 is an example of such a workaround. But all supported versions of Puppet provide the features necessary to keep the boundary intact.

Other Variable Use Cases

Variables can be tremendously powerful for documenting your code. Well-named variables can create meaning and context for complex data interactions. Further, they can tremendously simplify understanding when complex quoting and escaping are used.

Avoid anonymous regular expressions

A non-Puppet example: the purpose of the following regular expression might not be immediately clear:

```
grep -o '`\b\d{1,3}\.\d{1,3}\.\d{1,3}\.\d{1,3}\b`' logfile
```

The reader is forced to decode the regular expression to understand the usage. Although this is not difficult in this case, it slows down or prevents comprehension depending on the reader's knowledge of regular expressions, or regexes.

Prefer named regular expressions

The purpose of the regular expression can be made apparent by assigning it to a well-named variable before using it:

```
IPV4_ADDR_REGEX='\b\d{1,3}\.\d{1,3}\.\d{1,3}\.\d{1,3}\b'

grep -o $IPV4_ADDR_REGEX logfile
```

This usage makes the same code readable to someone who doesn't understand regular expression syntax and also speeds reading for someone who can parse it but doesn't need to.

Variables containing regex patterns can be invaluable when you have complex quoting requirements, such as working with directory paths containing spaces on Windows hosts. Consider the following example:

```
$sevenzip    = '"C:\Program Files\7-Zip\7z.exe"'
$archive     = '"C:\temp space\archive.zip"'
$output_path = '"C:\temp space\deploy"'

exec { 'extract_archive.zip':
  command => "${sevenzip} x ${archive} -o${output_path} -y"
  creates => $output_path,
}
```

This example is dramatically simplified by declaring our paths as single-quoted strings and interpolating them together in a double-quoted string. Single-quoted strings allow you to embed quotes in the paths containing spaces and avoid the need to double escape the directory-delimiting backslashes.

Trusted Variables

Puppet 3.4 introduced the $trusted[] data hash and Puppet 3.5 introduced the $facts[] data hash. These hashes are enabled by default in all supported versions of Puppet.

The values in the $trusted hash are provided by or validated by the Puppet server/master process. It doesn't matter what version of Puppet agent is running on the node because these values are set by the master only for use when building the catalog. This means that you can rely on the $trusted[] hash to be available. Using it helps disambiguate server-validated facts, and can prevent some injection attacks against exported resource collectors.

If you are supporting a mixture of Puppet 3 and modern Puppet agents, it is crucial to get the Puppet 3 nodes up to the final version of Puppet 3 (3.8.7) so that you'll have consistent access to the $facts hash.

Better yet, get them up to at least Puppet 4.10—the oldest supported version of Puppet at the time this book was released.

Remember that a compromised node can arbitrarily define facts. Data in the trusted[] hash is guaranteed to be supplied or validated by the Puppet server.

If you are using global variables for anything security sensitive, declare them unconditionally in a global manifest or your ENC to avoid the risk of abuse via client-side facts.

Order of Assignment for Top-Level Variables

Global variables can be defined from a number of different sources, including your ENC, your site-wide manifests, by the Puppet interpreter, by the Puppet Master, and via facts supplied by the client.

In some cases, the variables defined by different sources are reserved; for example, interpreter-defined variables such as $name, $title, and $module_name. In other cases, more authoritative data sources will override less authoritative data sources.

Top-level or un-namespaced variables are declared by the following sources:

- Facts provided by the node
- Parameters supplied by the ENC
- Global variables in top-level manifests

Assignment with Selectors

You can use a selector to improve handling of data provided. The following example maps multiple data formats to acceptable values:

```
$file_ensure = $ensure ? {
  'false' => 'absent',    # String value true
  false   => 'absent',    # Boolean value true
  default => 'file',  # anything else
}

file { 'somefile':
  ensure => $file_ensure,
  ...
}
```

This example correctly evaluates either the String 'false' or the Boolean value false to remove the file. This can be a very effective technique when upgrading older modules to use data types, where you cannot immediately update all uses of the module to pass in the correct type.

Attribute Values Chosen by Conditional Evaluation

Although you can use selectors in resource attribute values, doing so produces obtuse code. As you can see in the following example, you are forced to keep reconsidering what is being done at multiple levels:

```
service { example:
  ensure => $ensure ? {
    'absent' => 'stopped',
    default  => 'running',
  },
```

```
  enabled => $ensure ? {
    'absent' => false,
    default  => true,
  },
}
```

This same example is significantly improved by using selectors to declare variables used for the attributes in the resource, as shown in the preceding code.

```
$service_enable = $ensure ? {
  absent  => false,
  default => true,
}

$service_ensure = $ensure ?
  absent  => 'stopped',
  default => 'running',
}

service { example:
  ensure => $service_ensure,
  enable => $service_enable,
}
```

Another easy-to-read implementation groups the value assignments using a `case` statement:

```
case $ensure {
  'present': {
    $service_ensure = 'running'
    $service_enable = true
  }
  'absent': {
    $service_ensure = 'stopped'
    $service_enable = false
  }
}

service { example:
  ensure => $service_ensure,
  enable => $service_enable,
}
```

Variable Inheritance

Variable inheritance has been effectively removed from Puppet. Each version of Puppet since 3.0 has limited variable inheritance even further. Since Puppet 4, nearly all variable inheritence was removed in favor of fully qualified variable names.

Puppet still permits a variable inheritance only when a class inherits from another class, in which case the parent class variables are inherited into the child class. You can use this to override specific values within a specific implementation.

```
class auto {
  $type = 'vehicle'
  $wheels = 4

  notice($type)   # logs 'vehicle'
  notice($wheels) # logs 4
}

class motorcycle inherits auto {
  $wheels = 2

  notice($type)   # logs 'vehicle'
  notice($wheels) # logs 2
}
```

You should avoid class inheritance except in this specific use case for overriding a value in the child class. We explore this in greater depth in Chapter 4.

Strict Variables

With the strict_variables configuration setting enabled, referencing an undefined variable throws an error. Enabling this setting can help you catch all kinds of bugs and typos. Example 3-19 assumes that the unknown variable should resolve to an undefined value and so ouputs nothing. Depending on how that value is used in the code, this can lead to unintended consequences.

Example 3-19. Undefined variables silently fai...succeed!

```
$ puppet apply -e 'notice($unknown_var)'
Notice: Scope(Class[main]):
Notice: Applied catalog in 0.03 seconds
```

In the early days of Puppet, this behavior was commonly used to test for the existence of a fact or variable. While that was convenient, it also made typos prevalent and almost impossible to catch. These days you should use defined($variable) to check for a variable's existence.

When strict mode is enabled in Example 3-20, it immediately throws an error that includes the exact location of the invalid variable:

Example 3-20. Enabling strict variables catches typos

```
$ puppet apply --strict_variables -e 'notice($unknown_var)'
Error: Evaluation Error: Unknown variable: 'unknown_var'.  at line 1:8
```

We encourage you to test modules with this setting enabled. If you happen to encounter a public module that fails with strict_variables enabled, submit a fix to the module author.

Function Calls

Puppet's rich assortment of built-in and stdlib function calls are one of the more frequently overlooked features of Puppet. We recommend that you read through both the list of built-in functions and the list of *puppetlabs/stdlib* function calls once or twice to familiarize yourself with what's already available. Very often there is a function call that can help you debug or solve a problem you're currently experiencing while developing a module.

 puppetlabs/stdlib has four major releases, not all of which are compatible with end-of-life releases of Puppet. If you are using an unsupported version of Puppet, you might find situations in which the `puppet module` tool will not install modules due to version dependency conflicts.

When writing a public module that depends on stdlib functions, determine the minimum version of stdlib your module depends on. If all of the features you require are available in stdlib v4.12, declare that as the minimum version in your module to make life much easier for folks trying to use your module with obsolete versions of Puppet. (*Caveat emptor.*)

Always Use Parentheses

In previous versions of Puppet, and in the Ruby language upon which Puppet is based, it was popular to leave off parentheses when calling functions. In a top-level manifest, the code `warning $message` would generally evaluate the same as `warning($message)`. Unfortunately this is not always true when used within enclosed blocks, such as lambdas, where there is an implicit context. This requires you to be constantly vigilant about usage, especially when code is copied from one context to another.

Always implement functions with parentheses around the parameter input.

Functions for Logging and Debugging

If you have access to the logs of the Puppet server or agent that creates the catalog, `alert()`, `crit()`, `debug()`, `emerg()`, `err()`, `info()`, and `warning()` are useful for adding debug logs to your code. These function calls are less impactful than the `notify` resource type, because they do not insert extra resources into the catalog and do not increment the change counter on the node report.

Due to their report of a convergence event, you should use `notify` resources when you do want to see a change reported in the convergence report (and the Puppet console).

If in doubt, use a function call rather than a `notify` resource.

`fail()` terminates catalog compilation and returns a message. It is commonly used by module authors to stop a Puppet run when critical dependencies are not available. `fail()` is also valuable when decommissioning obsolete code. You can insert a `fail()` statement to make it clear that a module or code path has been intentionally removed, and supply a message explaining what the user should do to rectify the problem.

String Manipulation Functions

The list of string manipulation functions in *puppetlabs/stdlib* is fairly extensive. For a complete list, read the stdlib documentation. Here are a few noteworthy function calls:

`split()`
> Converts a string into an array, splitting at a specific character. This is very useful for handling delimited inputs, or for performing directory and filename manipulation.

`join()`
> From the *puppetlabs/stdlib*, you can use this to convert an array back into a string.

`strip()`, `lstrip()`, *and* `rstrip()`
> These are useful for trimming white space from input. With Puppet, most input is machine generated, and stripping the data is rarely necessary, except perhaps to remove problematic newline characters.

`downcase()`
> This accepts a string as input and returns it converted to lowercase. `upcase()` and `swapcase()` are also available.

Path Manipulation

You can use `dirname()` and `basename()` to parse the filename or directory name out of a fully qualified file path. This is often very useful for file manipulation.

You can also use `split()`, `join()`, and array indexing to perform more complex path manipulation if necessary. This approach can be useful when working with older releases of *puppetlabs/stdlib*, which do not provide the `dirname()` function call.

Input Validation Functions

puppetlabs/stdlib and Puppet data types provide a rich assortment of input validation features. In many cases, the calls simply accept an input parameter and produce a useful failure message if the input fails validation. In other cases, you can use function calls with conditional logic to declare the `fail()` function.

Here's a recommendation regarding input validation: unlike your typical web application, you probably don't need to validate every data input as a possible attack vector, especially if the data is sourced from the node facts. Data supplied by the node is returned directly to the node and is unlikely to have a tangible impact on any other node in your infrastructure. The goal of input validation in a module should focus on ensuring the values are sane or usable for the methods intended. Sanitizing the data values also enforces a passive resistance to most forms of tampering.

If you are operating in a multitenant environment and cannot trust the authors of your code, you need to ensure security above the code layer. In this situation, we strongly recommend using a code review process to audit code and data before it is deployed. For a deeper dive into release management concerns in multiteam environments, see Chapter 9.

Do, however, consider validating inputs that might be executed locally to the Puppet master via function calls, or might be exported to other nodes in the infrastructure.

Input validation can create problems when it rejects otherwise valid inputs. Use validation to improve user experience by producing more useful information than the user would otherwise have by allowing malformed data to create failures elsewhere.

We discuss input validation in more depth in Chapter 4.

Data validation functions

These function calls accept an input and automatically cause the Puppet run to fail with a useful error if the input does not match the type expected, as demonstrated in the following code:

```
assert_type(Stdlib::Absolutepath, $provided_path) |$expected, $actual| {
  fail("The path provided was ${actual}, should be ${expected}")
}
```

Each value can be checked against the expected data type in this manner. Because the `assert_type()` core function can validate any data type, it provides an extensible replacement for a long list of `validate_type()` functions in stdlib: `validate_abso lute_path()`, `validate_bool()`, `validate_array()`, and so forth have all been made obsolete by this general-purpose function.

Having a general-purpose test in Puppet's core functionality ensures that any data type provided by any module can be tested. Here are some examples of replacements for the obsolete validate functions:

Old function	Data-type test
`validate_numeric($input)`	assert_type(Numeric, $input)
`validate_float($input)`	assert_type(Float, $input)
`validate_ip_address($input)`	assert_type(Stdlib::IP::Address, $input)
`validate_v6_address($input)`	assert_type(Stdlib::IP::Address::v6, $input)
`validate_mac_address($input)`	assert_type(Stdlib::MAC, $input)
`validate_domain_name($input)`	assert_type(Stdlib::Fqdn, $input)

Data type comparison

In the same vein, the `ip_type()` functions provided by stdlib have been obsolete by the built-in conditional. As shown in the code that follows, a value on the lefthand side of the `=~` and `!~` operators will be checked against the type on the righthand side. This can be any Puppet data type.

```
if ($provided_path =~ Stdlib::Absolutepath) {
  do something
}
```

Value existence comparison

There do remain some useful validation functions in stdlib focused on evaluating values within data types.

The `has_interface_with()`, `has_ip_address()`, and `has_ip_network()` functions use the *interfaces* facts to validate that the supplied IP address, network name, or interface is present on the node. Because these tests rely on node-supplied facts, it is possible to spoof them from a compromised node.

Most of the other data-checking functions have been made obsolete by methods specific to their data type. For example, `grep()`, `has_key()`, and `member()` have been replaced by the `in` operator, as shown here:

```
unless $ensure in ['present','absent'] {
  fail("$ensure must be 'present' or 'absent'")
}

if 'hacker' in $users {
  warning("The hacker has access here.")
}
```

Catalog Tests

The following functions return a Boolean value if a resource exists in the catalog:

- `defined()`

- `defined_with_params()`

These functions do a similar test, but declare the missing resource if it already exists:

- `ensure_packages()`
- `ensure_resource()`

At first glance, these functions appear to be a useful way to solve duplicate resource declaration issues, as illustrated here:

```
unless defined(Package['openjdk']) {
  package { 'openjdk':
    ensure => 'installed',
  }
}
```

Unfortunately, this code won't work, because it's parse order-dependent. If OpenJDK is added to the catalog after this block is evaluated, a resource conflict will still be created, as demonstrated here:

```
notice( defined(Package['openjdk']) ) # returns false

package { 'opendjk':
  ensure => 'installed',
}

notice( defined(package['openjdk']) ) # returns true
```

You might think the fix would be to wrap every potentially conflicting resource in a `defined()` test, or to declare every resource using the `ensure_resource()` function calls. Doing so creates other potential issues, such as the following:

```
ensure_resource('package', 'jre', {'ensure' => '1.7.0'})
ensure_resource('package', 'jre', {'ensure' => '1.8.0'})
```

This example raises a duplicate resource declaration error. The same code written using the `defined()` function call would result in nondeterministic and potentially nonidempotent Puppet runs. `defined_with_params()` works around the problem but creates other issues.

Managing conflicts using `defined()` or `ensure_resource()` also subtly violates the SoC principle; it requires that all modules use the same approach to handling package version tests. To update the test or resource declaration in one module, you would need to update all potentially conflicting modules.

These function calls have only two valid use cases:

- A defined type can safely use these tests to ensure that it declares a resource one time, even when invoked more than once.

- Classes within the same module could safely declare the same resource by using ensure_resource().

When dealing with the problem in a larger scope, there are two ways to effectively solve the problem:

- Declare the common requirements as *virtual resources*, which can be safely realized by each dependent class.
- Move the shared resources to their own class, which can be safely included by each dependent class.

You'll need to determine which solution is the most robust and understandable for your needs.

Data Transformation

Data transformation is the act of manipulating data in one or more ways. We've already seen a few examples of data transformation, such as Example 3-16, in which we converted an array of integers into a list of filenames.

Puppet does not transform data in place; data can be transferred when passing it between classes or transformed when defining a new variable.

You should avoid transforming data unless necessary. When you must transform data, do so in the same class that initially defines the data or within the *init* manifest of the module that consumes the data.

Take, for example, the following list of filenames:

```
files:
  - foo.txt
  - bar.txt
  - baz.txt
directory: /tmp
```

In Example 3-21, we use that data in a role and profile to make use of a file implementor.

Example 3-21. Classes utilizing the YAML data

```
class roles::myfiles {
  Array  $files     = lookup('files')
  String $directory = lookup('directory')

  class { 'profiles::myfiles':
    files     => $files,
    directory => $directory,
  }
```

```
}

class profiles::myfiles (
  Array  $files,
  String $directory,
) {

  $apnfiles = prefix($files, $directory)

  class { 'create_files':
    files => $apnfiles,
  }
}

class create_files (
  Array $files,
) {
  file { $files:
    ensure => 'present',
  }
}
```

This somewhat confusing chunk of code retrieves data from Hiera and passes it to the profile. The data is transformed in `profiles::myfiles`, with the transformed data being sent to the `create_files` class. Imagine for a moment that the `file` resource contained in the class `create_files` was producing an unusual result. Our first reaction would be to look at the class `create_files` and then perhaps to look at the data in Hiera that feeds `role::myfiles`. Unfortunately, we would not be seeing the full picture, because the data is transformed in `profiles::myfiles`. In this case, debugging will go slowly because we must follow the path by which data transverses our codebase to identify the step where the transformation takes place.

This example could be improved significantly using one of several approaches:

- Store the data in its final form.
- Transform the data in Hiera using interpolation tokens.
- Transform the data in the class `create_files`.

In this case, the correct solution would be to store the absolute pathname in Hiera. When that is not feasible, the next best solution is usually to pass the data verbatim to the module, transforming the data in the same class that applies it. Even though this approach might violate the DRY principle, it's much simpler to debug.

There are a number of cases for which data must be transformed inside the module. One such use case for which the default of one parameter should be based on the value supplied to another parameter. You can see examples of this in Chapter 4.

Whenever possible, it's best to avoid passing data needlessly through multiple classes. The Hiera data terminus can be very helpful this way. For an in-depth discussion of the pros and cons of various approaches relating to Hiera, see Chapter 6.

Templates

Templates provide a traditional way of separating *presentation logic* from *business logic*. In the case of Puppet, templates allow us to interpolate data from Puppet into files, creating a layer of separation between the source configuration files and the logic used to populate those files.

ERB Templates

The Embedded Ruby (ERB) template parser provided by the `template()` and `inline_template` functions allow the use of Ruby language interpolation within a file. Puppet has supported this since its early days, and it is used in many other systems than Puppet.

There are a few best practices relating to the use of ERB templates:

Never source a template from another module. This violates SoC, and often results in problems down the line when someone changes the template in the other module without realizing your module will be affected. If you need to pass templates between modules, render the template in the source module, and pass the template in its rendered form as parameter data.

You should try to avoid referencing out-of-scope variables within a template. And you should absolutely avoid referencing variables from other modules. The reason for this recommendation is that it's often difficult to determine which variables are being used by a template, especially when reviewing Puppet code, as illustrated here:

```
class alpha {
  file { '/etc/alpha.conf':
    content => template('alpha/alpha.conf.erb'),
  }
}

template alpha.conf.erb:
  # This will silently fail if beta module changes
  important setting = '<%= scope["beta::foo"] %>'
```

This situation hides the out-of-scope variable down in a data file (the template). Besides creating maintenance problems, out-of-scope variable lookup methods have inconsistent behaviors when tested as a Boolean value, and evaluate to `true` in unexpected situations.

Instead, you should copy out-of-scope variables into the manifest's scope and reference the local variable, like so:

```
class alpha {
  # Get necessary value from related module 'beta'
  $important_setting = $beta::foo

  file { '/etc/alpha.conf':
    content => template('alpha/alpha.conf.erb'),
  }
}
```

```
template alpha.conf.erb:
  # this won't silently become nil if the variable reference is no longer good
  important setting = '<%= @important_setting %>'
```

Referencing only local variables guarantees that any variable used by your template is defined in the same class that declares the template. This also helps avoid subtle bugs created when out-of-scope variables change names and are treated as nil values by the template rather than throwing an exception.

EPP Templates

Embedded Puppet Programming Language (EPP) templates have been available in all versions of Puppet from 4.0 onward.

EPP is stylistically similar to ERB templating; however, it uses Puppet language variables, functions, and iterators rather than embedded Ruby. The advantage of using EPP templates over ERB templates is that EPP templates are written in the same language used to write your modules.

EPP provides enhanced security features, permitting you to pass an explicit list of parameters to the template, as shown in Example 3-22. The template cannot query variables that exist outside the template. This provides a huge maintainability improvement.

Example 3-22. Customizing an EPP template with parameters

```
$example_content = epp('example_module/template.epp', {
  'arg_a' => 'Value 1',
  'arg_b' => 'Value 2',
})
```

Always pass variables into your EPP templates using this explicit syntax. Within the template, declare the parameters in a comment block on the first line. Input type checking works exactly the same as in classes:

```
<%- | String[1] $arg_a,
      String[1] $arg_b
```

```
|-%>
arg_a is <%= $arg_a %>
arg_b is <%= $arg_b %>
```

Don't declare EPP input parameters with a resource declaration; instead, either assign the output of the EPP template to a variable and pass that to the resource, or assign the variables to a hash and pass that to the EPP statement (both approaches are demonstrated in Example 3-22).

The general recommendations for ERB templates also apply; do not reference out-of-scope variables, and never render templates stored outside the scope of your module.

EPP Versus ERB

The ability to explicitly pass input parameters to EPP templates (and have their data type checked) is a significant advantage over the ERB templating engine. You should seriously consider adopting EPP templates for this reason alone.

ERB is a very common templating language in Ruby frameworks. As a result, it enjoys a lot of tooling that isn't available with EPP templates. If you are a Ruby shop, this might be an important issue for you.

Otherwise, the choice between the two comes down to whether you want to write your templates in the Puppet Ruby DSL.

Other Language Features

There are many language features that we haven't covered in this quick run-through of Puppet features and conceptual design, but we do delve into them later in the book as follows:

- Resource relationships, exported resources, metaparameters, and virtual resources (discussed in Chapter 5)
- Classes and defined types (discussed in Chapter 4)
- Node statements (discussed in Chapter 8)
- Puppet node convergence run stages (discussed in Chapter 7)

Summary

This chapter discussed both good and bad coding practices, and provided an overview of useful function calls. Applying clean coding practices as discussed in this chapter will help make your code easier to understand and thus easier to maintain. In many cases, simple and clean code will often result in fewer defects, as well.

Takeaways from this chapter include the following:

- Apply common development principles to improve the quality of your code.
- Reduce the amount of code in your Puppet manifests.
- Separate your code from your resource declarations.
- Use clearly named variables to clarify the purpose of your code.
- Separate your code into modules for reusability.
- Avoid creating additional scope needlessly.
- Use Puppet's built-in and stdlib function calls to enhance your code.
- Be extremely careful with scope when using templates.

CHAPTER 4
Puppet Module Design

Puppet modules are self-contained bundles of code and data. A module extends Puppet features with any number of the following optional components:

- Manifests written in the Puppet language
- Files and templates used by the module
- Facts about the node
- Parsing and manipulation functions
- New resource types
- New providers for existing resource types
- Module-specific data files or providers
- Unit and acceptance tests and test fixtures

This chapter focuses on module manifests containing Puppet language code and their resources: files, templates, metadata, and tests. We cover these additional aspects of module design in the following chapters:

- Creation of modules for roles and profiles in Chapter 7
- Distribution and deployment of modules in Chapter 9
- Extending modules with plugins in Chapter 10

The Puppet Development Kit

This section examines the minimum set of tools necessary for installing, testing, and extending Puppet modules.

Installing the Puppet Agent

It might seem obvious, but Puppet novices often forget the value of installing the Puppet agent on their developer machines. Testing locally with Puppet can catch common errors that would otherwise result in a long push, run, fail, repeat-until-success cycle.

Using the Ruby that Comes Bundled with Puppet

If you've been working on Puppet for many years, you probably have configured a wide array of Ruby environment managers for testing your Puppet code. If you are new to all of this, we have good news: *This is no longer necessary.* If you don't maintain other Ruby projects, ignore old instructions that tell you to install Ruby Version Manager (RVM) or rbenv and multiple Ruby interpreters on your workstation. The Puppet Development Kit (PDK) has made that environment setup obsolete.

Installing the Puppet Development Kit

The PDK provides all of the Ruby environment, dependency management, and testing tools necessary for testing Puppet code. You can download the PDK here (*https://puppet.com/download-puppet-development-kit*).

All of the following instructions that you might find on the internet have been rendered obsolete by the PDK:

- You no longer need to manually install Ruby gems for testing. Add them to the module's Gemfile, and the PDK will install them for you.

- You no longer need to run `bundle install` or prefix each test command with `bundle exec`.

- You no longer need to run `puppet parser validate`, `puppet-lint`, or `rubocop`. `pdk validate` does all of that and more.

- You no longer need to find and add Puppet testing libraries to your Gemfile. The PDK installs every one we've used before.

- You no longer need to define standard node facts for rspec; the PDK includes a complete set of node facts for you and provides a single file to add your own customizations.

- You no longer need to build test environments for each version of the Puppet agent and/or Ruby. The PDK bundles and tests all supported versions.

In short, you no longer need to be an expert in Ruby testing toolkits to test modules for a given purpose. For 90% of testing situations, the PDK will do everything you need right out of the box.

Favor Editors or IDEs with Puppet Plugins

You can use any IDE or text editor for Puppet development. Because the recommendations for all of them are basically the same, in the following, we mention only the things that you likely will want to utilize.

- Enable syntax highlighting for Puppet, Ruby, JSON, YAML, and HOCON.
- Install plugins for the editor that provide inline Puppet code validation.
- Configure the editor to strip carriage returns automatically from Puppet, Ruby, JSON, HOCON, and YAML files.
- Ensure that the editor can preserve existing line endings if you need to edit Windows configuration files on Linux, or vice versa.

If you have nodes from heterogenous environments, ensure that your editor can handle linefeed conversation properly.

 At the time this was written, Visual Studio Code (*https://code.visual studio.com/*) was the best free tool for editing Puppet code and data in Windows. It preserves the original line endings used in any file it opens.

Using Vendor-Provided or Community Modules

Before you begin the process of developing a new module, check what's already available on the Puppet Forge (*http://forge.puppet.com*). In many cases, someone might already have developed a module suitable for your needs. It's almost always easier to write a profile that customizes one or more component modules from the Forge than to build your own from scratch. At the very least, it would give you a head start on development.

Modules from the Puppet Forge have a number of benefits:

- You don't need to spend time developing or updating the module.
- Quality control is performed by a large community of users (not just you).
- Bug fixes and new features developed by others appear without effort on your part.
- Public modules often include good documentation and test scenarios.

For all of these reasons, begin by finding a module that does what you need. If you find the need to expand the module, submit your improvements back to the community.

Picking Good Modules

There are thousands of modules available on the Forge, and for the most part, Puppet does a good job of highlighting the best modules. Download statistics, ratings, platform support, test results, and module documentation are published.

There are many well-written modules on the Puppet Forge. There are also half-baked ideas that were never finished. The Forge is not a curated list; anyone can write and publish a module of any quality. The following markers provide indicators of quality design:

- Modules marked *supported* are officially supported by Puppet and used in the Puppet Enterprise product. There are millions of users for these modules.
- Modules marked *approved* are certified by Puppet to meet their standards for high quality. It also indicates that it is the *best-in-class* module for that particular need. Puppet does not approve two modules that do the same thing.
- A high community score. This number is a star-vote by community members who have downloaded it.
- A high code-quality score. This is an automated code-quality analysis, the detailed results of which you can read there.

Module Checklist

If you've found a large number of modules that may meet your needs, the following list provides key points to review when choosing a module for your needs:

Module completeness:
    ❏ Is the module well documented?

    ❏ Does the module include unit tests?

    ❏ Does the module include acceptance tests?

    ❏ Has the module received updates recently?

    ❏ Does the module support the operating systems or applications frameworks you use?

Code quality:
    ❏ Does the module appear to follow the single responsibility principle?

    ❏ Is the module *supported* or *approved* by Puppet?

    ❏ Does the module follow the Puppet Lab's style guide?

    ❏ Does the module conform to module development best practices?

Local needs:
- ❏ Does the module license meet your requirements?

- ❏ Does the module pull in a lot of dependencies? Will those dependencies conflict with modules you are using today?

- ❏ Is the module source hosted in a public location (i.e., GitHub)? Do the authors allow you to submit pull requests back to them?

Testing/integration needs:
- ❏ Is the author responsive to pull requests and issues?

- ❏ Do the unit tests pass in your environment?

- ❏ Will the acceptance tests operate in your environment?

In general, if any one of these items is missing, this is not necessarily a deal-breaker, but if large numbers of your requirements are not met, it might be useful to investigate other modules.

Module Applicability to Your Needs

Sometimes, otherwise good modules simply won't be suitable for your site, or your specific needs. It's important to carefully consider your own use case when selecting a module. Following are some key questions to consider:

Platform support
Does the module support the platforms you have deployed?

If all nodes run CentOS Linux, there's a high probability most published modules will work. If you must support Solaris or Windows nodes, your choices might be somewhat more limited. Although there are great multiplatform modules available, many published modules support only a few platforms. If the module doesn't support your platform, consider how difficult it would be to wrap or extend the module. Otherwise, you can fork the module and submit changes back to the original author.

Features
Does the module support the application features you require?

Some modules manage only specific features of an application or service. Other modules can be incredibly comprehensive in their ability to manage every aspect of the application. It will be fairly easy to establish the difference between these by reading through the manifests.

Scaling
What are your scaling requirements and limitations? The design considerations that went into creating the module might create unnecessary complexity. Or the

implementation used might not be flexible enough to scale to your deployment size. What is the sweet spot between enough features and brutally fast simplicity for needs?

Modules that rely on exported resources will require an investment in PuppetDB infrastructure to provide the resource storage and query interfaces. Is that infrastructure available everywhere you plan to use this?

If the module recursively synchronizes directories using Puppet `file` resources (which are processed in memory and superfast for small files or directories), it might not be suitable for synchronizing terabytes of files. A more specialized resource provider might be necessary for specialized needs.

The `puppetlabs/apache` module is very feature-complete and manages a lot of complexity to provide every Apache feature for any given application. This makes it very powerful and useful in nearly all scenarios. However, the complexity makes the module resource intensive to apply, which might be unsuitable for a large-scale bulk hosting provider that adds and removes a customer every few seconds.

> The important point is to understand your needs. The vast majority of us need flexibility and features more than we need to dredge the last bit of performance gain from something that runs only periodically. Avoid taking on unnecessary effort and reinventing the wheel for a potentially unnecessary optimization.

Embracing and extending modules

If you find a module that meets most but not all of your requirements, you have two choices:

- Write a wrapper module that depends on this module and then adds the missing bits.
- Fork the module and add your extensions directly in the source tree.

You should contribute improvements upstream whenever possible. Code accepted into the mainline branch will be maintained and tested by the original author and community. Improvements accepted into the mainline release have a much lower risk of being broken by future releases.

> The r10k code deployment tool simplifies switching between an upstream module and an independent fork. When local changes are accepted upstream, you can flip back to the original module transparently. For more instructions on module management with r10k deployments, see Chapter 9.

Contributing Modules

If you've written a new and interesting module or if you've improved significantly upon modules already available on the Forge, consider publishing your module. The `puppet module` utility will package your module for upload to the Puppet Forge.

Designing Modules Well

Good module design relates strongly to good code design. We touched on a number of coding principles and practices in Chapter 3, including *separation of concerns* (SoC), the *single responsibility principle*, *KISS* (Keep It Simple), and *Interface-Driven Design*. We put these principles into practice in this chapter.

Make Use of Module Structure

Puppet modules are self-contained bundles of code and data. Being self-contained allows modules to be portable:

- The module occupies a single directory in the module path.
- Its code is loaded upon request (declaration).
- Files and templates specific to the module are stored within their respective directories.
- Facts and functions required by the module are within its *lib/* directory.
- Data provided by the module can be referenced within the module namespace.

Each directory in the module contains specific files. This structure allows those features to be autoloaded. Although it's possible to use files outside of that structure, it defeats expectations, confuses the reader, and could likely fail in unexpected ways when Puppet is upgraded.

Keep the Module Focused

Your modules should have a clearly defined purpose, and the use case should be likewise clearly documented. When building a module, ask, "Is this data or dependency part of the application or does it contain information specific to my business?" Use the answer to this question to determine which of the following types most appropriately matches the need:

Component modules
    Component modules should minimize dependencies and contain only the application-specific data needed for generic situations. Component modules should be free of business logic or data.

Profile modules

> Profile modules supply the business logic and data to instruct the application of component modules. Profile modules can have many dependencies on component modules.

Design Modules for Public Consumption

You should design every module as if you plan on releasing it to the public. This is not to say that you should release all modules to the public—it means that the design patterns for public modules are the design patterns for creating good modules in general. Even if you never intend to release them, it helps you to maintain consistency.

Designing modules for portability ultimately makes them simpler to support and extend. It helps to eliminate technical debt. The design patterns for creating public modules encourage reuse. Reuse means that you won't need to rewrite the module from scratch every time your requirements or environment change.

Planning and Scoping Your Module

Before you begin writing your module, it's important to first determine your module's scope. For many of us, our first instinct is to write a jumbo module that installs and manages all of its dependencies. Unfortunately, this approach tends to create problems down the line; such modules are often inflexible and become difficult to maintain. They can create compatibility problems when they manage a dependency that's needed by another module.

You should always design your modules using SoC (see "Separation of Concerns" on page 41 and "The Single Responsibility Principle" on page 40 as guidelines). As a rule of thumb, if a resource in your module might be declared in any other module it should probably be its own module.

Dependencies outside the scope of your module should be externalized into their own modules. Domain logic should be handled using the *roles and profiles* pattern described in Chapter 7.

> In many cases you can rely on the package manager to handle dependencies.

The Java dependency for Tomcat is a classic example of a dependency that you should externalize as domain logic. By separating the management of Java from the management of Tomcat, the process of upgrading Java is simplified, and potential conflicts with other modules also attempting to deploy Java are eliminated.

Even if you never plan on ever distributing the module, you should design it as if you were. By designing your modules to be portable, you can adapt them to new requirements and new environments with minimal effort.

Basic Module Layout

A puppet module has a fairly standardized structure made up of a number of *optional* components. The `pdk new module` command populates a module skeleton with the following elements:

manifests/
> Puppet manifests written in the Puppet DSL

facts.d/
> Facts written in YAML or any language

files
> Files made available through the `modules` Puppet file server mountpoint

templates/
> ERB and EPP templates

examples/
> Test manifests used for system testing, experimentation, and demonstration

spec/
> RSpec unit tests and Beaker acceptance tests

docs/
> Module documentation generated from the code

lib/
> Native Ruby extensions for Puppet

README.md
> Documentation describing your module and its requirements

REFERENCE.md
> Documentation of the modules classes, types, functions, and so on

Gemfile
> Gem dependencies for testing and extending Puppet

Rakefile
> Rake tasks for validating and testing the module

metadata.json
> Metadata about the module for puppet tools to use

hiera.yaml
> The module data hierarchy for `puppet lookup`

.fixtures.yml
> Dependencies for `puppet apply`, RSpec, and Beaker testing

There is also additional metadata for CI, editing, Git, and other tools.

Every one of these components is (technically) optional. Although each one will be automatically generated using `pdk new module`, empty directories should be removed to simplify the module layout and clarify the design and intent of your module. For example, if the module contains only native Puppet extensions, there's no need to have a *manifests/* directory. Likewise, if your module contains no files or templates, you should remove those directories to focus attention on what the module does provide.

You should always update the autogenerated *README.md* file and the *metadata.json*, even if only to simplify them. These are data for the reader and tools, and bad data creates big problems.

The Module's Main Class

The Puppet manifest in *manifests/init.pp* contains the main class of your module. It is optional but rare for it to not exist. In most modules, *init.pp* is the most likely starting point to see what input the module accepts, to understand the basic layout of the module, to perform input validation, and to handle user input and transformation of input data.

As a general rule, we recommend grouping resources in classes, and performing all class inclusion and relationship handling in the main class. This approach makes the module easier to understand, and centralizes the flow and features of the module.

Although the main class manifest is often the main entry point into your module, this is a convention rather than a rule. It's perfectly okay to have defined types or classes in your module that might be declared or referenced from outside your module.

An example main class

Let's look at the main class for the Apache module in Example 4-1. This example is simplified for instructional use; a real Apache module would likely accept many more input parameters.

Example 4-1. Example main class for a simple Apache module

```
class apache (
  String[1] $ensure      = 'installed',
  String[1] $servername  = $facts['fqdn'],
```

```
    Integer[0,65535] $listen = 80, ❶
    String[1] $user,
    Stdlib::Absolutepath $documentroot,  # defaults to
    String[1] $package_name,             # os-dependent data ❷
    String[1] $service_name,             # sourced from Hiera
) {

    # Validation phase
    unless $package_name =~ /^[[:print:]]+$/ {
      fail("invalid package name")
    }
    unless $service_name =~ /^[[:print:]]+$/ {
      fail("invalid service name")
    }

    # servername must match apache's specifications ❸
    unless $servername =~ /^([a-z]+:\/\/)?[\w\-\.]+(:[\d]+)?$/ {
      fail("servername invalid
          http://httpd.apache.org/docs/2.4/mod/core.html#servername")
    }
    # valid POSIX user name
    unless $user =~ /^[_.A-Za-z0-9][-\@_.A-Za-z0-9]*\$?$/ {
      fail("username must be POSIX compliant")
    }

    # Declaration phase
    class { 'apache::install':  ❹
      package => $package_name,
      ensure  => $ensure,
    }

    class { 'apache::config':
      servername   => $servername,
      documentroot => $documentroot,
      listen       => $listen,
      user         => $user,
    }

    class { 'apache::service':
      service => $service_name,
    }

    # Relationship definitions
    contain apache::install ❺
    contain apache::config
    contain apache::service

    Class['apache::install'] -> Class['apache::config']  ~> Class['apache::service'] ❻
}
```

❶ Type checking input avoids the need for validation tests in the code block.

❷ This assumes that the module has a *hiera.yaml* file specifying the module's data hierarchy.

❸ Some input validation such as printable characters are self-documenting. This regular expression is not, so it's a good idea to add a comment regarding its purpose.

❹ This demonstrates resource-style class declaration for child classes. Other approaches are discussed in "Modularizing Classes" on page 95.

❺ Containment is critical so that modules are not required to create relationships with child classes. For more on this, see "Class Containment" on page 96.

❻ Class relationships are dramatically simpler than a web of resource relationships. We use chaining arrows because they are easier to read at a glance.

This simplified example demonstrates a complete layout usable for larger, more complex modules:

1. The class begins by accepting a set of input parameters. Defaults that are universal for all platforms are declared here, and platform-specific defaults are pulled from module data. Each value is explicitly checked for type and minimum size.

2. The validation phase checks for valid values by using regexes. In older versions of Puppet there would have been dozens of `validate_` function calls for type checking, but this is greatly reduced with inline input checking.

3. Data transformation would happen after input validation. None was needed in this example, but if a value was determined by or from other values, it could be handled here.

4. The validated input is passed to child classes in the declaration phase.

5. The declared classes are contained using the `contain()` function, and ordered using chaining arrrows in the relationship phase.

Module Parameters

Modules receive external input via class parameters.[1] Class parameters are a well-defined interface that permit you to supply values when declaring the class. This data can be passed directly to your module's resources or it can alter the behavior of your

---

[1] This statement seems obvious now, but in the past it was common to use global variables to pass data into modules.

module using conditional logic. The following snippet shows an example of a class with a single parameter:

```
class ntp (
  $servers = 'pool.ntp.org',
) {
  # Resources go here
}
```

If your module has special case input needs, such as to look up data using hiera_hash(), the best approach is to still define an input parameter and to set the default value of that parameter so that the lookup you wish to use is performed automatically if no value is explicitly supplied, as demonstrated here:

```
class ntp (
  $servers = lookup('ntp::servers', Array, 'unique', ['pool.ntp.org']), ❶
) {
  # Resources go here
}
```

 Note that we still supply an optional default value in our Hiera lookup to be used in case Hiera is not available.

The approach demonstrated in the previous code example has several major advantages over alternatives:

- It automatically looks up values in Hiera.
- It allows you to declare the class without an explicit value.
- It facilitates debugging by embedding the result of the lookup in your catalog.

Parameter defaults

It's a good idea to supply default values for all parameters, even if those defaults aren't necessarily going to be useful in a real-world environment. In many cases, a default of undef is a perfectly valid and simple value.

There are two main reasons for this recommendation:

- It simplifies experimentation with your module.
- It avoids creating Hiera dependencies during unit testing.

There are many situations for which you might want to test or experiment with one or many modules. This is common when deciding whether a module from the Puppet Forge is suitable for a site.

In these cases, it's ideal to be able to test the module by installing it into a temporary module path and then testing the module with the `apply` command, as shown in the following:

```
$ mkdir -p example
$ puppet module install --modulepath=example puppetlabs/ntp
Notice: Preparing to install into /home/vagrant/example ...
Notice: Downloading from https://forgeapi.puppetlabs.com ...
Notice: Installing -- do not interrupt ...
/home/vagrant/example
|--- puppetlabs-ntp (v3.3.0)
   |--- puppetlabs-stdlib (v4.24.0)
$ sudo puppet apply ./example/ntp/tests/init.pp -modulepath='./example' --noop
Notice: Compiled catalog for localhost in environment production in 0.74 seconds
Notice: /Stage[main]/Ntp::Config/File[/etc/ntp.conf]/content: current_value
{md5}7fda24f62b1c7ae951db0f746dc6e0cc, should be
{md5}c9d83653966c1e9b8dfbca77b97ff356 (noop)
Notice: Class[Ntp::Config]: Would have triggered 'refresh' from 1 events
Notice: Class[Ntp::Service]: Would have triggered 'refresh' from 1 events
Notice: /Stage[main]/Ntp::Service/Service[ntp]/ensure: current_value stopped,
should be running (noop)
Notice: Class[Ntp::Service]: Would have triggered 'refresh' from 1 events
Notice: Stage[main]: Would have triggered 'refresh' from 2 events
Notice: Finished catalog run in 0.67 seconds
```

The `puppetlabs/ntp` module includes a test manifest and supplies reasonable defaults for all of its parameters. There is no need to read the documentation to determine what inputs are mandatory, and there's no trial and error involved in a simple test application of the module. As a result, it's very easy to test, evaluate, and deploy this module.

Another case for which sane defaults are useful is during testing. If your module has mandatory parameters and may be invoked via an `include()` call from another module, you've implicitly created a dependency on Hiera (or another data binding). This can complicate the setup for your test cases because your Hiera data will not be available in this context.

Parameter default complexity. Puppet allows fairly complex generation of parameter defaults. The default can be a function call, nested function, selector, or a complex data structure.

As a general recommendation, if your default value is more than one line long, you should probably move it into the module's Hiera data, especially if it is not dynamic.

Although you can embed selectors and other complex logic in your parameter defaults, doing so makes the input section difficult to comprehend. The *data in modules* pattern moves complex logic outside the parameter default block without losing the benefits of parameterization. For more information, see "Hiera Data in Modules" on page 93 later in this chapter.

Parameter default limitations.   Until recent versions of Puppet, a parameter default could not contain the value of another parameter. To work around this, people often used confusing intermediary variables to test the value of the original variable. These were often suffixed with _real, like so:

```
class chroot (
  $root_dir = '/chroot',
  $prefix   = undef,
  $bindir   = undef,
) {
  # pick() returns the first defined value
  $prefix_real = pick($prefix, "${root_dir}/usr")
  $bindir_real = pick($bindir, "${prefix}/usr")
}
```

The module would then use the _real variable names in place of the original variable names.

This limitation has been removed in Puppet 5, and parameters can now use the value of any parameter declared before them. So you can now simplify all of the mess in the preceding example to this much more readable form:

```
class chroot (
  $root_dir = '/chroot',
  $prefix   = "${root_dir}/usr",
  $bindir   = "${prefix}/bin",
) { }
```

Parameter naming conventions.   A good parameter name has a few properties:

- It should be unambiguous.
- It should be consistent with your style guide.
- Its purpose should be fairly obvious.
- It should be memorable.

A good rule of thumb is to name the parameter after whatever will consume its value. For example, if your parameter will supply a DocumentRoot value for an Apache configuration file, the most intuitive name for your parameter will be documentroot. If your parameter provides a source for a package resource, the most intuitive name will be source or source prefixed with the package name when necessary to disambiguate multiple sources.

For example, the following parameter names would be fairly obvious to someone familiar with Apache:

- serverroot

- documentroot
- listen
- servername
- errorlog

If you're writing a module for a relocatable service, follow the GNU coding standards and use the directory naming conventions:

- prefix
- bindir
- sysconfidir
- localstatedir

In all of these cases, we attempt to conform to pre-existing naming conventions, with minimal transformation to meet Puppet's variable naming requirements.

When a parameter is to be passed to a puppet resource, we might simply reuse the resource's parameter name, possibly prepended with the resource name or resource title to remove ambiguity.

- ensure
- source
- package_httpd_source

Input Validation

Input validation is the act of testing input supplied to your module to ensure that it conforms to a specification and doesn't contain any nefarious data.

The design of input validation is important to consider and can be very environment specific. It is important to assess both the goals of validating input and the risks associated with invalid input.

Data supplied to your module will usually come from a trusted source such as from Hiera data from an internal data repository. In these cases, the goal of input validation is not so much about security as it is to generate useful failure messages when the input is malformed. When the data comes from an external source, the goal is to protect against not just invalid input, but also dangerous input.

Input validation should be designed to provide useful troubleshooting information, and you should avoid overly restrictive validation. Specifically, when you're designing input validation, be cautious that your tests don't reject inputs that are otherwise perfectly valid, such as nonfully qualified paths when your application will happily accept them. For example, unqualified paths are valid in most parts of an Apache configuration, and are interpreted relative to the ServerRoot directive. With Puppet, you can use variable interpolation in pathnames, allowing many paths to be relative to $confdir and other base directories.

The most common source of external untrusted data are facts generated by a managed node when working in a master/agent environment. Facts are simply data provided about the node, which can be used to customize the catalog. However, there is a risk of privilege escalation if a nonprivileged user can alter the fact values supplied to the Puppet catalog, which is implemented by the privileged Puppet agent process. You can protect against privilege escalation by preventing unprivileged users from modifying the environment or configuration used to determine fact values.

When using exported resources or other forms of shared node data, facts from one compromised node can be used to attack other nodes on the network. In these cases, input should absolutely be validated to help protect nodes from one another. The best way to protect against privilege escalation in an exported resources environment is to limit sharing to strictly validated values that can be tested for sanity before use. For example, ensure that only carefully validated hostnames are used in the load-balancer configuration built from exported resources.

We'll discuss available input validation functions and techniques in "Input Validation Functions" on page 64.

Data in the Module

Although all business and service-specific data will come from other data sources, it can be helpful to provide data within a module. For example, the names of the packages and the locations of the configuration files on different operating systems is well-known information that users of the module shouldn't be forced to add to their data. In a moment, we will examine two popular patterns for providing data in modules.

Regardless of the source of default data for a component module, the values should be component-specific defaults, not site-specific defaults or business logic. Module data default values should be true no matter where the module is deployed. You should use parameters from your roles and profiles to override these defaults when necessary to implement site-specific needs.

The params.pp Pattern

The *params.pp* pattern was designed to simplify the selection of platform-specific parameter defaults by moving default values into a dedicated manifest. For those familiar with Chef, the *params.pp* pattern was somewhat like cookbook attributes.

This pattern was necessary for now obsolete Puppet versions, but it has been replaced by the *data in modules* pattern of Puppet 4 and higher.

With this pattern, the logic to select the appropriate default values was moved out of the main class to, as you might guess, the *params.pp* manifest. Although Hiera could provide platform-specific values to a module, until Hiera v4 there wasn't any way for module authors to ship Hiera data inside their module. Adding component-specific data to an organization's global data was problematic for somewhat obvious reasons. *Please copy these values...*

The `params.pp` pattern violates several best practices. The pattern relies on the otherwise discouraged `inherits` feature of Puppet classes in order to enforce ordering between it and your module's main class. It also relies on fully qualified resource references to data outside the class scope. It's difficult to read and difficult to track variables in larger modules with many child classes, as demonstrated in Example 4-2.

Example 4-2. The main class declaration for a module using the params.pp pattern

```
class apache (
  $ensure      = 'installed',
  $config_file = $apache::params::config_file,
  $errorlog    = $apache::params::errorlog,
  $package     = $apache::params::package,
) inherits 'apache::params' { ❶
```

❶ `inherits` is mandatory. Otherwise, Puppet will throw an error complaining that we've referenced variables from a class that has not been evaluated. `inherits` ensures that the `params` class is evaluated before the `apache` class, as shown in Example 4-3.

Example 4-3. The params class declaration for a module using the params.pp pattern

```
class apache::params {
  case $facts['os']['family'] { ❶
    'RedHat': {
      $config_file = '/etc/httpd/conf/httpd.conf'
      $errorlog    = '/var/log/httpd/error.log'
      $package     = 'httpd'
    }
    'Debian': {
      $config_file = '/etc/apache2/apache2.conf'
      $errorlog    = '/var/log/apache2/error.log'
      $package     = 'apache2'
    }
```

```
      default: {
        fail("${facts['os']['family']} isn't supported by ${module_name}")  ❷
      }
    }
}
```

❶ This case statement declares platform-specific default values.

❷ Make sure the default case is good. Execute functions during data assignment, bad!

The *params.pp* pattern violates the tenents of both *data in code*, and worse yet, *code in data*.

Hiera Data in Modules

The *data in modules* pattern (see Example 4-4) allows a module author to embed a Hiera hierarchy within the module, allowing component-specific default parameters to be stored as YAML, JSON, or HOCON data in the module. This enables the author to keep functions in code, and data in text files.

 Hiera *data in modules* far exceeds the features of the *params.pp* pattern, which is now obsolete.

Example 4-4. Class declaration for a module with default values in Hiera

```
class apache (
  $ensure,
  $supported,
  $package,
  $config_file,  ❶
  $errorlog,
) {

  unless($supported) {
    fail("${facts['os']['family']} isn't supported by ${module_name}")  ❷
  }
  ...
```

❶ No default data in the code. This is safe because it's part of the module.

❷ Code decides what to do based on the data.

As you can see, the manifest now contains only actionable code. There are no data values embedded in the code.

So, where do these values come from? A component module should have a small hierarchy of data files containing platform-specific and default values, as illustrated in the following:

```
---
version: 5
defaults:
  datadir: data        # This path is relative to the module
  data_hash: yaml_data # Use the built-in YAML backend

# Default values
hierarchy:
- name: "OS-specific config"
  path: "%{facts.os.family}.yaml"

- name: "Defaults"
  path: "defaults.yaml"
```

Each of the data files shown in Examples 4-5 through 4-7 contains the exact same information in plain text.

Example 4-5. data/RedHat.yaml

```
---
apache::package: 'httpd'
apache::config_file: '/etc/httpd/conf/httpd.conf'
apache::errorlog: '/var/log/httpd/error.log'
apache::supported: true
```

Example 4-6. data/Debian.yaml

```
---
apache::package: 'apache2'
apache::config_file: '/etc/apache2/apache2.conf'
apache::errorlog: '/var/log/apache2/error.log'
apache::supported: true
```

Example 4-7. data/default.yaml

```
---
apache::supported: false
apache::package: 'unknown'
apache::config_file: '/etc/apache/apache.conf'
apache::errorlog: '/var/log/apache/error.log'
```

This code pattern provides a clear separation of code and data and is significantly easier to read and maintain than the inheritence pattern of *params.pp*.

Modularizing Classes

You can add classes beyond the main class, each in its own manifest file in the *manifests/* directory. Beyond keeping modules focused, as discussed in "Keep the Module Focused" on page 81, it is important to keep each individual class focused, too. This section covers managing the relationships between cooperating and dependent classes.

Dependencies

Module dependencies allow you to make use of classes, defined types, functions, and resource types and providers from other modules without reinventing the wheel within your own module.

It's very common for a module to have dependencies on other modules. For example, `puppetlabs/stdlib` is a nearly universal dependency due to the number of useful function calls it provides.

There are only three things necessary for safe, effective use of dependencies:

- List the dependency in `dependencies` of the module metadata and test fixtures.
- Use class relationships to indicate any ordering or notification requirements (described in the next section).
- Identify the relationship in the module documentation (covered in "Creating Useful Documentation" on page 108).

Class Relationships

Classes organize data and establish relationships between resources. If we were to write a `puppet_server` module, for example, we could establish a notify relationship between the *puppet.conf* and *auth.conf* `file` resources and the puppet `service` resource, or we could place these resources into separate classeses and declare relationships between the classes.

Building resource relationships this way then becomes a huge maintainability win. If we add a new resource to our module, we simply place it in the appropriate class and Puppet automatically establishes relationships between it and the rest of our resources, as demonstrated in Example 4-8.

Example 4-8. Resource-based relationships

```
file { '/etc/puppetlabs/puppetserver/conf.d/webserver.conf':
  notify => Service['puppetserver'],
}
```

```
file { '/etc/puppetlabs/puppetserver/conf.d/auth.conf':
  notify => Service['puppetserver'],
}

service { 'puppetserver':
  ensure => 'running'.
  enable => true,
}
```

Although this is suitable for simple cases, the number of relationships can grow exponentially as related files and services are added to the module. In this case, it's much easier to break each set of tightly related resources into a separate class and then set up the relationships between the classes, as shown in the following:

```
include 'puppetserver::config'
include 'puppetserver::service'

Class['puppetserver::config'] ~> Class['puppetserver::service']
```

Class relationships are also a huge win if we need to be able to uninstall an application. Removing an application from a node requires reversing the resource relationships so that things can be removed in the opposite order of installation. It's much simpler to reverse a small set of class-based relationships than a large web of direct resource relationships.

You can use these example relationships as a guide for how to break your module into classes. If you find a lot of relationships between two sets of resources, consider using classes and class-based relationships instead. It is not incorrect to create a module with three child classes for three resources. You can then add new things to the module without breaking existing relationships.

Class Containment

Containment causes relationships with a parent class to flow down to the contained classes. Let's take a moment to consider the code in Example 4-9.

Example 4-9. Class-based relationships

```
class java {
  package { 'openjdk':
    ensure => 'installed',
  }
}

class tomcat {
  notify { 'tomcat': }

  class { 'tomcat::package': } ~> class { 'tomcat::service': }
```

```
}

class tomcat::package {
  package { 'tomcat'
    ensure => 'installed',
  }
}

class tomcat::service {
  service { 'tomcat':
    ensure => 'running',
  }
}

include 'java'
include 'tomcat'

Class['java'] -> Class['tomcat']
```

In this example, the class java has a *before* relationship with the class tomcat and the resource Notify[tomcat]. tomcat::package and tomcat::service counterintuitively have no relationship with their parent class, tomcat, and thus no relationship with the java class.

Although the child classes are defined in the Tomcat module, the relationships with tomcat apply only to resources declared directly in the tomcat class and not to the resources in any of its child classes. In Example 4-9, the following relationships exist:

```
Class['java'] -> Package['openjdk'] -> Class['tomcat']
```

Unfortunately, the Tomcat class contains only Notify['tomcat'], whereas the following relationships remain freestanding:

- Class['tomcat::package'] contains Package['tomcat']
- Class['tomcat::service'] contains Service['tomcat']

To solve this problem, we need to either anchor or contain the classes.

Containment

The contain keyword includes a class and creates a relationship between the included class and its parent class. Example 4-10 presents our previous module but this time using containment.

Example 4-10. Class-based relationships using containment

```
class java {
  package { 'openjdk':
    ensure => 'installed',
```

```
    }
}

class tomcat {
  notify { 'tomcat': }

  contain 'tomcat::package'
  contain 'tomcat::service'

  Class['tomcat::package'] ~> Class['tomcat::service']
}

class tomcat::package {
  package { 'tomcat'
    ensure => 'installed',
  }
}

class tomcat::service {
  service { 'tomcat':
    ensure => 'running',
  }
}

include java
include tomcat

Class['java'] -> Class['tomcat']
```

By using `contain`, Example 4-10 now has the following relationships:

```
Class['java'] -> Package['openjdk'] -> Class['tomcat']
-> Class['tomcat::package'] -> Package['tomcat']
~> Class['tomcat::service'] ~> Service['tomcat']
```

Notice that `Class['tomcat']` now has a relationship with its child `Class['tom cat::package']`, whereas this relationship did not exist in Example 4-9.

Although the `contain` function automatically includes the class being contained, it can be combined with resource-style class declarations, as is illustrated in Example 4-11. Doing so is parse-order dependent, so you must declare the classes before you contain them (remember: you safely include a class previously declared with parameters, but not vice versa). Regardless, this approach is currently the best-practice solution to handling containment and is the officially documented approach to building good modules, as the preceding example shows.

Example 4-11. Contain with resource-style class declarations and chaining

```
class { 'tomcat::package':
  ensure => $ensure,
```

```
    source => $source,
  }
  class { 'tomcat::service':
    ensure => $ensure,
    enable => $enable,
  }

  contain 'tomcat::package'
  contain 'tomcat::service'

  Class['tomcat::package'] ~> Class['tomcat::service']
```

Anchors

The *anchor* pattern is the original solution to the class containment problem. Anchors are a resource type provided by the `puppetlabs/stdlib` module. Anchors themselves perform no actions, but they do offer an anchor with which to establish class relationships inside a module. They also pass along notify signals so that notification works between modules as expected.

> The `contain` keyword was added to Puppet in version 3.4. If you are writing modules for modern releases of Puppet, we recommend that you use the `contain` function in your classes rather than the *anchor* pattern.

Here is the `tomcat` class with anchors:

```
class tomcat {
  anchor { 'tomcat::begin': }
  -> class { 'tomcat::package': }
  ~> class { 'tomcat::service': }
  -> anchor { 'tomcat::end'}
}
```

Although this seems to be simpler than our containment example, it carries extra complexity to ensure that our resource relationships behave the way we expect. The `tomcat` class shown above contains a subtle bug: `Anchor['tomcat::begin']` does not have a notify relationship with `Anchor['tomcat::service']`. As a result, notifications sent to the Tomcat module would not cause the Tomcat service to restart. This might be an issue if, for example, you updated Java to patch a vulnerability using Puppet, and the Tomcat service continued running under the old release of Java because its service never received a notification to restart.

Beyond that, the *anchor* pattern creates some ugly resource relationship graphs that can be painful to read when attempting to analyze Puppet's graph output.

Intentionally uncontained classes

There are some cases for which you might want to intentionally avoid containing resources. Consider the following case for which we need to insert the deployment of one application after its dependent module has been installed and configured but before the service from its dependent service has been started:

```
include 'tomcat'
include 'my_tomcat_app'
```

```
Class['tomcat'] -> Class['my_tomcat_app'] ~> Class['tomcat::service']
```

This example will work only if Class['tomcat::service'] is *not* contained inside of Class['tomcat']. Otherwise, a dependency loop would be created, like so:

```
Class['tomcat::service'] -> Class['my_tomcat_app'] -> Class['tomcat::service']
```

Internally, the rest of the Tomcat module might have a notify relationship with Class['tomcat::service'] and a relationship loop will not be created. We could create such a module using this basic layout:

```
class tomcat {
  contain 'tomcat::install'
  contain 'tomcat::config'
  include 'tomcat::service'

  Class['tomcat::install'] -> Class['tomcat::config'] ~> Class['tomcat::service']
}
```

This works because resource relationships do not require that one resource be evaluated immediately after another when a relationship is defined. The relationship simply sets general ordering requirements and allows for other resources to be inserted into the order. Puppet maintains the relationship ordering internally using a dependency graph.

When using an approach such as this, remember that you lose the ability for the uncontained resources to generate notifications for the parent class; anything that wants to subscribe to Class['tomcat::service'] must do so explicitly now.

Because such module designs do not conform to the typical design pattern for a module, it's critical to test and document this special behavior and to treat the uncontained class as an interface into the module; not to be changed without planning for the break in compatibility.

Intermodule relationships like this are typically domain-logic handled in your profiles rather than hardcoded into your modules.

This approach is useful when complex relationships are necessary between arbitrary modules. In many cases, it's much better to use a defined type as an interface, as discussed in "Providing Clean Service Interfaces with Defined Types" on page 104.

Interfacing with Classes

There are three popular ways to pass data from the module's main class to its other classes:

- Use a resource-style class declaration with parameters.
- Declare classes using `contain` or `include`, with fully qualified variable references inside the class.
- Use class inheritance.

Let's consider what makes each of these solutions best for a given situation.

Passing data via parameterized class declarations

This is the preferred approach for passing data from a main class to another class. This approach, shown in Example 4-12, makes variable handling extremely explicit and causes immediate failures in the event of a typo or hasty change.

Example 4-12. Passing data using parameterized class and resource-style class declaration

```
class apache (
  $ensure  => 'installed',
  $package => $apache::params::package,
) {
  class { 'apache::install':
    ensure  => $ensure,
    package => $package,
  }
  contain 'apache::install'
}

class apache::install (
  $ensure,
  $package,
) {
  package { $package:
    ensure => $ensure,
  }
}
```

With this approach, if either the `package` or `ensure` parameter is missing or if there is a typo, the declaration of `apache::install` will throw an error. If the `apache::install` class does not accept a parameter that's passed to it from the main class, an error is also thrown.

This pattern is best-practice for several reasons:

- This is the most readable pattern. The main class knows which variables are used by child classes.
- Explicit parameter passing allows the main or child class to be refactored without breaking the other.
- This pattern can allow direct access to child classes from the outside, if desired.
- It can provide consistent variable names in the public interface, while refactoring at will internally.

The only downside of this class is the combination of a class declaration and a following `contain` function call.

Passing data via fully qualified variable references

With this approach, the `apache::install` class receives input directly from internals of the main class, as shown in Example 4-13.

Example 4-13. Passing data using fully qualified variables

```
class apache (
  $ensure  => 'installed',
  $package => $apache::params::package,
) {
  contain 'apache::install'
}

class apache::install (
  $ensure  = $apache::ensure,
  $package = $apache::package,
) {
  include stdlib
  assert_private("I'm an internal child class, don't offer me candy!")

  package { $package:
    ensure => $ensure,
  }
}
```

The benefit of this approach is that inclusion of the `apache::install` class and its containment are handled with a simple `contain` statement. The disadvantage of this approach is that the use of fully qualified variables means that the child class must be accessed from the parent class (enforced in the example with the `assert_private` function). In addition, the consumption of values by the child class is not visible to someone refactoring the main class. This somewhat mitigates the use of the main class to view the flow of a module.

Passing data via class inheritence

You can also pass variables using class inheritance. With this approach, shown in Example 4-14, variables local to the main class are available in the local scope of any class that inherits from the main class.

Example 4-14. Passing data using class inheritance

```
class apache (
  $ensure  => 'installed',
  $package => $apache::params::package,
) {
  contain 'apache::install'
}

class apache::install inherits apache {
  package { $package:
    ensure => $ensure,
  }
}
```

This approach carries the least initial development overhead, but it is the least readable and most fragile implementation. Variables are declared in the main class, and are automatically made available to any of the other classes as if they were declared locally. This effectively reimplements variable inheritance from the Puppet 2.x days within the child classes.

The major disadvantage of this approach is readability:

- You can't see the child class' usage from the main class.
- Any refactoring of the variables in the main class will likely break the child classes.
- It's easy to end up with complex inheritance trees that make it difficult to identify where a variable came from.

Even though this pattern is widely used, we recommend avoiding it if other choices would work, due to its impact on readability and the fragility of the module.

Reusing Defined Types

A *defined type* is a Puppet manifest that can be called repeatedly with different data to create unique resources of the type, similar to built-in or custom resource types. For example, you can create as many user resources as you like, as long as they have unique titles. Defined types operate in the same manner.

Defined types are commonly used in one of four ways:

- To create a list of resources from a list of input values
- To create interfaces in a module
- As a service to the outside world
- As the core purpose of a module

Providing Clean Service Interfaces with Defined Types

There are situations that will require complex relationships between modules. The principles of interface-driven design (discussed in "Interface-Driven Design" on page 42) advise against accessing internal data structures of other modules directly.

Defined types give a module the simplest interface for use in other modules. They read in the code exactly the same as any other resource type and automatically order the dependencies without explicit relationship markers. This makes them a preferable approach for handling intermodule dependencies.

Defined types provide a clean parameterized interface that you can define and test, allowing the internal structure of the module to change without breaking dependent modules.

In "Interface-Driven Design" on page 42, we provide the following example of the use of a defined type as an interface into an Apache module:

```
class myapp {
  include 'apache'

  apache::vhost { 'myapp':
    documentroot => '/var/www/myapp',
  }
}
```

In this example, the class `myapp` is interfacing with the Apache module using the `apache::vhost` defined type. It doesn't really matter what the internal structure of that defined type is; it manages the internals of that itself.

For example, that module might use resource ordering to ensure the virtual nodes requested are built in the right order, like so:

```
Class['apache::config'] -> Apache::vhost[$title] ~> Class['apache::service']
```

These relationships and references to the internal structure of the Apache module are contained within the defined type. The Apache module could be completely rewritten, and so long as the defined type exists and continues to provide the `servername` and `documentroot` parameters, the `myapp` class will continue to work.

By using a defined type as an interface into the module and having regression tests for the interface, we can safely rewrite or refactor our module without even knowing how others are using it. This flexibility is the huge benefit of interface-driven design. Without it, changes to one module often break code elsewhere.

In many cases your module might be able to provide a useful feature to the outside world via a defined type. The Apache module we've been looking at throughout this section is a great example of this—it provides a defined type that handles the OS-specific implementation details of configuring a virtual node such that our module will apply properly on any OS the Apache module supports.

This defined type doesn't prevent other modules from implementing their own vhost templates, but it does offer a simple way to define a virtual node that's integrated nicely into our module, and handles most common use cases.

The interface provided by the defined type is much better than creating virtual nodes in file resources because the defined type can establish relationships into the Apache module and access data from inside that module without violating the principles of SoC and interface-driven design.

Simplify Complex Operations with a Defined Type

There are often cases for which you can use a defined type to provide a clean and simple interface for complex operations.

Example 4-15 presents a defined type for managing network service names. It uses Augeas to manage /etc/services and a defined type to provide a clean interface around the Augeas resource.

Example 4-15. An Augeas resource wrapped in a defined type

```
define network::service_name (
  $port,
  $protocol     = 'tcp',
  $service_name = $title,
  $comment      = $title,
) {
  $changes = [
    "set service-name[last()+1] ${service_name}",
    "set service-name[last()]/port ${port}",
    "set service-name[last()]/protocol ${protocol}",
    "set service-name[last()]/#comment ${comment}",
  ]

  $match = "service-name[port = '${port}'][protocol = '${protocol}']"
  $onlyif = "match ${match} size == 0"

  augeas { "service-${service_name}-${port}-${protocol}":
    lens    => 'Services.lns',
    incl    => '/etc/services',
    changes => $changes,
```

```
      onlyif  => $onlyif,
  }
}
```

The defined type in Example 4-15 can declare service names without forcing the user to learn the Augeas syntax.

This approach helps a mixed team take advantage of experience. An experienced module creator or subject matter expert can create a defined type to manage a complex task. Less senior team members use the user-friendly resource declarations like any other Puppet resource, as shown here:

```
network:service_name { 'example':
  port => '12345',
  protocol => 'tcp',
}
```

Defined types of this nature can be so useful that a module might contain nothing more than defined type manifests.

Interacting with Other Resouces in the Module

When a defined type is included in a component module, it often needs to interact with the rest of the module.

Creating relationships with resources in the module

Because each defined type is a new instance, unknowable in advance, the best place to put relationships between the defined type and other classes and resources inside of your module is inside the defined type.

 Don't use collectors to indiscriminately set relationships against all instances of your defined type. Use tags on the defined type to avoid realizing virtual instances, as discussed in "Dangling relationships to unrealized resources causes breakage" on page 135.

Including other classes

It's best to keep your defined types as small and self-contained as possible. You should avoid resource-style declarations of classes or referencing out-of-scope variables.

In general, including any resource-style declaration with parameters will create parse-order-dependent catalog build problems that sometimes work until they suddenly don't. The problem symptoms will seem to defy the code as written, which make them very difficult to debug.

A class is declared (and parsed) only once. It is a singleton that exists in shared memory. A defined type is parsed for each and every declaration of it. If you're not scared of the parse order madness this creates, just wait.

Imagine a defined type that includes a class. Both of them have three resources. The defined type is declared five times. How many resources exist when you're done? 15? 30? How about neither? Let's examine this:

1. Defined type declared name *example1* declares three resources.
2. Defined type declares a class that declares three resources.
3. Defined type declared name *example2* declares three resources.
4. Defined type declares a class that has already been declared; no new resources.
5. Defined type declared name *example3* declares three resources.
6. Defined type declares a class that has already been declared; no new resources.
7. Defined type declared name *example4* declares three resources.
8. Defined type declares a class that has already been declared; no new resources.
9. Defined type declared name *example5* declares three resources.
10. Defined type declares a class that has already been declared; no new resources.

If you add them up there's 18 total resources. Now this a simplied example, but it highlights the differences between these two. Example 4-16 makes another problem clear.

Example 4-16. What value does this class receive?

```
defined example::defined_type (
  String $foo ❶
) {
  class { 'example':
    value => $foo, ❷
  }
}
```

❶ This parameter changes with every call to the defined type.

❷ The class accepts this parameter only on the first declaration. Any further declaration with a value will cause a catalog failure.

This pattern will work in any catalog with a single declaration of the defined type, but fail when a second declaration is added. The only safe class declaration inside a defined type is a parameterless `include` of the class. Defined types can safely include only classes that need no values from the defined type. Anything more complex is likely to create a parse-order problem that you can't read from the code.

This pattern works for one purpose only: to ensure access to resources and variables declared in a parameterless dependency class. This allows users of the defined type to declare it without having included the defined type's dependencies first.

Creating Useful Documentation

Documentation is an investment in the future. When you are in the middle of writing a module, the behavior of the module, its inputs and its quirks are self-evident. When you've moved on, it's easy to forget what each parameter does, what kind of input the parameters accept, and what quirks exist in your module.

Documentation of a module takes three forms:

- Inline documentation within manifests and other code
- Markdown documentation in the module's root
- `description` and other fields in the module metadata

The module skeleton provided by `pdk new module` includes useful examples of all three to kickstart your documentation.

README, REFERENCE, and Other Markdown

GitHub, GitLab, BitBucket, and other source-code repositories provide automatic rendering of Markdown documentation, making documentation committed to your software repository one of the most user-friendly ways of documenting the module.

It's a good idea to include a *README.md* file containing the following information:

- The name of the module
- Any dependencies your module might have, either internal or external to Puppet
- Example invocations of the module for common use cases
- Notes about bugs or known issues (if you are not using a public issue-tracker)
- Contact information

Usage examples

You should show some common usage examples of your modules. This can help the user test the module, provide ideas as to how to use your module, and help the user if they become stuck deploying the module, perhaps due to syntax errors in their input.

Usage documentation is also useful if you wish to highlight the most commonly set or modified parameters for your module. It's very common for a module to have several dozen parameters; this is the place your user will look for the most important parameters.

Dependencies

If your module has any dependencies or requires any setup, it's a good idea to provide an example of how to satisfy those dependencies, as well. You should do the following with dependencies:

- List them in the `dependencies` value of the *metadata.json* file.
- Add them to the *.fixtures.yml* file for automatic provisioning by tests.
- Document them in the *README.md* file.
- Use them in the samples placed in *examples/* directory.

The README should contain helpful instructions for how to satisfy the dependencies. If your dependencies are generic (this module requires a web server,) it's a good idea to mention the dependencies and show how a commonly available module can be used to satisfy the dependency. If the dependencies are very specific, noting the modules required, providing a link to those modules, and noting version compatibility is extremely valuable.

License information

If you plan to publicly release your module, it's a good idea to attach a license to it.

Enterprise users might have constraints placed on the code that can be deployed to their site. A license for the module might be required by their internal policies in order to permit use of the module. Some companies restrict what software licenses are acceptable for use internally, and might not be able to use code under more restrictive licenses such as GPL 3.

If you are writing modules for a business, you might want to clarify with your management or legal team regarding the license or restrictions that should be placed on the code. Some companies are fairly generous with their modules, releasing them publicly after they are scrutinized and sanitized. Others businesses will prefer to keep internally developed Puppet modules proprietary. You will save a lot of headache by making note of these constraints in your documentation.

If you plan to release the module to the public, a license is an essential way of communicating what other users can do with your code. Even if you are giving the code away for free, the license is what makes this possible. Use the helpful license selector at *https://choosealicense.com/* to find the most appropriate license for your needs.

REFERENCE Markdown

The *REFERENCE.md* file should contain full documentation for the classes, types, providers, facts, and functions provided by the module.

Parameter documentation

Documenting your input parameters is key to writing a usable module. Parameter names are often terse, tend to be numerous, and can often be confusing. When documenting an input parameter, it's good to provide the following information:

- The name of the parameter.
- A brief description of the parameters purpose.
- The types of data accepted.
- The structure of the data if structured data is accepted.
- The default value of the parameter.
- Any constraints on the data enforced by the application, module design, or input validation.

For example:

```
# @param document_root
#  The path to your site's document root. Defaults to '/var/www/html'
```

Document every input parameter. Internal or deprecated parameters can be marked with appropriate tags.

Inline documentation

Inline documentation is embedded into the code of your module. A number of Puppet tools including the `puppet doc` command (up through Puppet 3), the `puppet strings` command (Puppet 4+), and Puppet plugins for editors and IDEs can consume and display this documentation. A benefit of inline documentation is that the PDK and other tools can search for the documents in your module path, and IDEs can display the documentation alongside your code.

In most cases, the inline documentation can be reused to generate your Markdown documentation. `puppet strings` generates the *REFERENCE.md* entirely from inline documentation in your module. You can find some documentation for doing this well at *https://puppet.com/docs/puppet/latest/puppet_strings.html*.

Summary

In this chapter, you learned how to write clean modules that conform to the best practices discussed in Chapter 3.

Here are the main takeaways from this chapter:

- Install the PDK to install and test modules.
- Use an editor or IDE with syntax highlighting for Ruby and Puppet.
- Carefully design your module to limit its scope.
- Structure your module to make it easy to understand and simple to deploy.
- Design interfaces into your module and use them.
- Document your module for future maintenance.

Last of all, you should always test your modules. We've created an in-depth guide for testing modules in "Testing" on page 250.

## CHAPTER 5

Resources

Resources are the heart of Puppet's state management. Resources model a configurable entity on a node. The vast majority of resources model things you're quite familiar with, such as:

- Files
- Packages
- Package repositories (yum, apt, chocolatey, etc.)
- Users
- cron entries
- Databases
- Windows registry keys

Resource *types* declare the desired state (a model) of the resource, and resource *providers* converge the target to match the model. Put another way, types are the interface, and providers are pluggable platform-specific implementations.

This chapter reviews the built-in Puppet types and providers, along with popular custom types. We examine how to best use *virtual resources*, *exported resources*, *resource relationships*, and *metaparameters*.

Using Resources to Implement Change

Resources evaluate and manage state of their type on nodes. No matter how complex the codebase is, the manifests are ultimately compiled down to a *catalog* of resource declarations, which is what the Puppet agent uses to evaluate and converge a node. Resources are the only way Puppet can idempotently affect change on your nodes.

exec resources can also affect node state, but they create untracka-
ble, unknown changes that are antithetical to the purpose of Puppet.

Resource Types Abstract Implementation Details

A Puppet resource type is an abstraction layer and interface between Puppet and the underlying provider. You implement types in Ruby by declaring a child of the Pup pet::Type class.

Types attempt to model system resources in a common and abstract way. For example, even though there are dozens of different package managers available, the package provider attempts to implement a platform-independent model of a package, abstracting away the actual implementation details of managing that package, as illustrated in the following example:

```
package { 'puppet':
  ensure => 'installed',
}
```

The benefit of this abstraction is consistency. Code with this simple resource declaration works on every platform. Although the underlying package managers on Linux and Windows are wildly different, the package type has backend providers for every package manager. When asked to install this package, it will use the package manager appropriate for the current platform. This simplicity makes our intent clear and the code clean.

Use the Most Specific Resource Type

When declaring resources, consider the scope or impact your resource has, how the resource might conflict with other resources, and how the scope of a particular resource might affect your overall design.

For example, don't attempt to manage a file in its entirety when a resource with a smaller scope is available. To elaborate, in most cases you would manage */etc/hosts* using host resources rather than using a file resource. This allows multiple modules to add entries to the */etc/hosts* file without requiring all changes to go through one module that manages the entire file.

Many modern applications support reading configuration files from *service.d* directories, allowing you to build the configuration using multiple file resources. For example, you can add and remove configurations from Apache by writing to the */etc/httpd/ conf.d* directory. Modern releases of sudo support a *sudoers.d* directory using the #includedir keyword. In both cases, this allows multiple classes to drop in their own configuration files without the risk of creating conflicts. The configuration is built by reading each provided file. This allows multiple modules to affect the configuration without sharing a common file resource.

Choosing the appropriate resource type is key: the host resource is great for distributing entries for the critical nodes of your infrastructure. A half-dozen entries can reduce load on your DNS infrastructure and provide a bit of extra reliability. If you need to define thousands of hosts entries, it might be easier to declare DNS nameserver resources that configure the name servers that should be queried.

Examining a Naked Resource

A resource in the Puppet language is a data structure. The type name is data, the resource name is data, and the resource properties are data. Examples 5-1 through 5-3 look at the three most common ways you'll see resources described.

Example 5-1. The built-in file resource type declared using the Puppet Language

```
file { '/tmp/example':
  owner   => 'root',
  group   => 'root',
  mode    => '0444',
  content => 'This is an example.\n'
}
```

Any resource's attributes could be serialized into YAML.

 Serialization is the process of translating data structures or object state into a format that can be stored or transmitted and reconstructed later.

Example 5-2. A file resource seralized into YAML

```
file:
  - '/tmp/example':
    - owner:   'root'
    - group:   'root'
    - mode:    '0444'
    - content: 'This is an example\n'
```

To build the catalog, the Puppet manifests are parsed and resources are evaluated to build the Puppet catalog. Resources stored in YAML or JSON can be deserialized by create_resource and other methods to add to the Puppet catalog. Variables and conditional logic are evaluated into data values. Ultimately every resource declaration is rendered into a simple data structure in the Puppet catalog. Example 5-3 examines how that looks.

Example 5-3. A file resource from a Puppet catalog

```json
{
  "exported": false,
  "file": "/home/vagrant/example_file.pp",
  "line": 6,
  "parameters": {
    "content": "This is an example.\n",
    "group": "root",
    "mode": "0444",
    "owner": "root"
  },
  "tags": [
    "file",
    "class"
  ],
  "title": "/tmp/example",
  "type": "File"
}
```

What you see in Example 5-3 is the ultimate resolution of all conditional logic, variables, iteration, and all other code tricks. The catalog contains only explicit names and values. This is the final result.

Exploring Resources with Tools

There are a number of tools that you can use to test, document, and play with resources. Use Puppet on your workstation to experiment with types and providers in a safe environment. Let's take a look at a few of these tools.

puppet describe

The `puppet describe` command provides documentation for resources. `describe` is intended to be used as a command-line tool. `puppet describe --list` will list all installed resource types. `puppet describe` *type* will show documentation for a resource type that you specify.

`puppet describe` shows the inline documentation for both built-in and custom resource types currently installed. It can be invaluable when you have a lot of custom types and providers. It's also useful at sites running older releases of Puppet for which the latest online documentation might not be correct for the installed release.

 If the custom resource type is not in the `production` environment, you'll need to use the `--environment` option so that `describe` can find the resource.

---

puppet-strings

The *puppet-strings* gem provides automatic creation of formatted documentation from modules. You run the `puppet strings` command in a module directory to generate HTML documentation in *doc/* from the structured comments in your manifests, functions, types, and providers. You can find complete documentation at *https://puppet.com/docs/puppet/latest/puppet_strings.html*.

> The *puppet-strings* gem is not included by default, the purpose of which is to minimize package size in operational environments. Follow the instructions on the page listed in the preceding paragraph, or install it by using Puppet itself:
>
> ```
> sudo puppet resource package puppet-strings ensure=present \
> provider=puppet_gem
> ```

Of particular use, *puppet-strings* can autogenerate the module's *REFERENCE.md* in Markdown format. It will even inform you when the inline documentation doesn't match the code, as shown here:

```
$ puppet strings generate --format markdown
[warn]: Missing @param tag for 'service_name' near manifests/agent.pp:43.
[warn]: The type of the @param tag for 'value' does not match the
  parameter type specification near manifests/inisetting.pp:42
```

puppet resource

The `puppet resource` command allows you to interact with the Puppet resource abstraction layer from a command-line shell. It has two purposes:

- To query the current state of resources on the node
- To declare a puppet resource directly from the command line

This can be extremely useful as a learning tool, both for folks who aren't very familiar with resource syntax and for the investigation and exploration of a complex resource type.

Displaying a resource in Puppet language. When supplied with a type and a resource name, for example, `puppet resource host localhost`, the provider will query the named resource and return a resource declaration in the Puppet language with the resource's current properties. If you query a nonexistent resource, the result will show the resource as absent, as demonstrated in the following example:

```
$ puppet resource host localhost
host { 'localhost':
  ensure => 'present',
  ip     => '127.0.0.1',
```

```
    target => '/etc/hosts',
}

$ puppet resource host nothere
host { 'nothere':
  ensure => 'absent',
}
```

If you are using the resource command to generate resource statements, be aware
that some resources have read-only properties that will be returned by the resource
command but that should not be included in your resource declarations. For example, a file resource will include output like this:

```
$ puppet resource file /etc/hosts
file { '/etc/hosts':
  ensure  => 'file',
  content => '{md5}a3f51a033f988bc3c16d343ac53bb25f',
  ctime   => '2018-01-18 20:56:03 -0800',
  group   => '0',
  mode    => '0644',
  mtime   => '2017-06-29 20:42:42 -0700',
  owner   => '0',
  type    => 'file',
}
```

The content, ctime, and mtime attributes are read-only, and cannot be changed in a
resource declaration. It's a good idea to sanity check resources gathered by the
resource command and trim down attributes that are not of concern. If you don't
know whether you should include a parameter or don't know what it is, you should
default to leaving it out.

Another limitation is that you cannot pass parameters when performing a query. For
example, you cannot specify the *target* when performing a query. If you attempt to do
so, Puppet will interpret it as an attempt to declare a resource rather than to query a
resource.

Displaying all instances of a resource. Use of the resource command to identify an individual resource requires that the resource have a meaningful *namevar* attribute. The
namevar attribute is used to locate the resource and uniquely identify it. For example,
the *namevar* attribute of a file resource is the file's path attribute, which informs us
where the file can be found. This is equally simple for user, group, host, and package
resources because the *namevar* is their name.

Not all resource types have clear and obvious titles. For example, the *ini_setting*
resource title is an arbitrary index value used only for uniqueness in the catalog. You
won't be able to guess it from reading the target resource.

If you are not sure what a resource's title is, you can ask the `resource` provider to query the node. When supplied with only a resource type, the `puppet resource` command will determine the default provider for the type and ask it to provide all instances available, as demonstrated in the following:

```
C:\Program Files (x86)\Puppet Labs\Puppet\bin> puppet resource package
package { '7-Zip 9.38 (x64 edition)':
  ensure => '9.38.00.0',
}
package { 'OpenSSH for Windows 6.7p1-2 (remove only)':
  ensure => 'installed',
}
package { 'Oracle VM VirtualBox Guest Additions 4.3.18':
  ensure => '4.3.18.0',
}
```

Generally speaking, you can list a resource if there's a finite amount of all resources of that type. Not all providers provide that capability, in which case the query will return an error indicating that:

```
$ puppet resource file
Error: Could not run: Listing all file instances is not supported.
    Please specify a file or directory, e.g. puppet resource file /etc
```

You cannot query some resource types because the resource provider doesn't implement the method required to query the current resource state, either because it would be too costly to do so (every file on a node) or the resources are not something that can be queried in a practical manner, such as a list of all possible exec resources.

Declare a resource on the command line. As mentioned earlier, the `resource` command has the ability to declare resources on a node. Any time you supply attributes for a resource, you are declaring it rather than querying it. This can be extremely useful for one-off commands with simple attribute values, such as installing *puppet-strings* on your development host, as shown in the following:

```
$ sudo puppet resource package puppet-strings provider=puppet_gem ensure=present
Notice: /Package[puppet-strings]/ensure: created
package { 'puppet-strings':
  ensure => ['2.1.0'],
}
```

It can also be useful for experimentation; the `puppet resource` output includes the resource declaration for the resource defined on the command line. You can add the `--noop` option to generate well-formatted resource declarations.

puppet apply

If you're interested in performing more involved experiments, consider using puppet apply `--execute` with small snippets, as shown in the code example that follows. As this runs Puppet through the catalog building and application process, it's the best way to test out short snippets of puppet code.

```
$ puppet apply --execute "file { '/tmp/testfile': ensure => present }"
Notice: Compiled catalog in environment production in 0.12 seconds
Notice: /Stage[main]/Main/File[/tmp/testfile]/ensure: created
Notice: Applied catalog in 0.03 seconds
```

Using `puppet apply` in this manner is useful when you need to experiment with more complex resource types that tend to require a lot of trial and error. This allows experimentation without committing or pushing code until you're certain of the syntax.

You can use `puppet apply` with small manifest files for slightly longer examples:

```
$ puppet resource user jorhett > test.pp
$ puppet apply test.pp
Notice: Compiled catalog in environment production in 0.12 seconds
Notice: Applied catalog in 0.03 seconds
```

Because the manifest exactly matches the current state, nothing has changed. But you can now edit this manifest to try out changes. This allows you to test resource defaults, overrides, resource relationships, and any other features that are not available when experimenting with the resource command line.

Resource Declaration

Resource declaration is the act of adding a resource to the catalog. There are a number of ways to declare resources that can be useful in special cases, such as declaration functions, meta resources, virtual resources, and exported resources. In this section, we look at the different approaches to resource declaration and best practices for each approach.

Ensure states

The most fundamental property of a resource is whether that resource exists. Resources are *ensurable*; that is, they can be made *present* or *absent*. Some resources have additional ensure states, such as the `file` resource that can be ensured to be a file or a directory. A few irregular resources such as `exec` are not ensurable.

Although most resources have an explicit `present` or `absent` state, all resources have a third implicit *undefined* or *unmanaged* state. Understanding the unmanaged state is critical. When a resource is removed from our manifests, we intuitively think of that resource as being `absent`. But in fact, the resource becomes *unmanaged*; if the resource already exists it will continue to exist, and if the resource doesn't exist, it will not be created.

In all seriousness, when a resource is removed from the catalog the Puppet agent loses the ability to know whether the configuration managed by that resource exists or not. It has become Schroedinger's resource, the state of which is unknowable.

This unmanaged state is the number one cause of configuration drift. Machines that have been around for a long time tend to collect unmanaged resources that do not exist on fresh machines. This creates situations in which machines that should be identical are actually very different.

This unmanaged state complicates rollbacks. Intuitively, we assume that we can return to a previous state by simply reverting a change. With Puppet and other configuration management solutions, rolling back a change requires explicitly declaring the former state; for example, making a newly created file absent. The previous version of our configuration code didn't mention the new file at all.

Renaming resources in our manifests produces the same result; Puppet has no way to know that the new resource had a previous name. Instead of moving the resource from one name to another, it simply creates the resource with the new name. To make this change correctly, create a new resource and change the ensure value of the old resource to absent.

Use Variables for Data-Driven Declaration

Puppet code works best when the behavior is driven by Hiera data.

Static declaration

It is very easy to read a static declaration because all values are filled in, as shown here:

```
host { 'localhost':
  host_aliases => ['localhost.localdomain'],
  ip           => '127.0.0.1',
}
```

It is, however, rare that the Puppet developer will know the absolute values for a resource. This is more often a hint that you have *data in the code*, which should be avoided unless that data is absolutely, positively internal to the module and will never change.

Interpolation

The best way to write reusable code is to accept data input that instructs the code how to operate. For example, the package name, the configuration file location, and the user Apache runs under changes on different Linux platforms. You can keep the declaration clean and easy to read by using variables in the resource declaration. You can use variables in the resource title and any properties or parameters. These variables will be interpolated into values when the resource is added to the catalog, as illustrated here:

```
file { $apache_config:
  ensure  => $apache_file_ensure,
  owner   => $apache_user,
  group   => $apache_group,
  mode    => $apache_file_mode,
  content => template('apache/apache.conf.erb'),
}
```

This allows the platform-specific values to be acquired from the module Hiera data, which contains values appropriate for each supported platform. In addition, this allows the environment layer of Hiera to override the module data with a site-specific value, without changing a single line of code.

Use Arrays for Similar Resources

You can declare multiple resources in a single statement by passing an array to the resource title. This works best for very similar resources:

```
$web_directories = [
  '/var/www/',
  '/var/www/html',
]

file { $web_directories:
  ensure => 'directory',
  owner  => 'httpd',
  group  => 'webmasters',
  mode   => '2775',
}
```

Array-style resource declaration is a clean way to declare similar resources. However, there is a limitation; all of the resources must share the same attribute values. For simple resources such as packages and directories, this is typically not an issue.

In many cases, each resource will have its own properties: users have unique IDs, files have unique contents, and so on. In these cases, avoid using array-style resource declaration. Although it's possible to pass a hash of values to a function call or iterator block (each, map, ...) consider carefully whether this improves the readability of the code.

Using fancy but difficult-to-read code to declare resources has *no positive value* because the values are always expanded in the catalog. Easy-to-read code and difficult-to-read code will create the exact same catalog, so focus on making your code easy to read.

You can also use arrays in resource references to establish a relationship with every resource in the list, like so:

```
service { 'httpd':
  ensure   => 'running',
  subscribe => File[$apache_config_file_list],
}
```

This example showed how to have the `httpd` process track a data-driven list of configuration files.

Using Automatic Resource Relationships for Clean Code

Resources often contain code to automatically create relationships with related resources. For example, if you specify the owner of a `file` resource, it will automatically create a child relationship with the `user` resource for that owner, as demonstrated here:

```
user { 'testuser':
  ensure => 'present',
}

file { '/tmp/testfile':
  owner => 'testuser',
  require => User['testuser'],   # redundant and unnecessary!
}
```

Resource ordering might appear to be an issue with array resource declarations because the attributes are the same for each one. However, the resource's autorequire system will often handle ordering for you, as it does here:

```
file { ['/var/www/', '/var/www/html']:
  ensure => 'directory',
}

file { '/var/www/html/index.html':
  source => 'puppet:///modules/example/index.html',
}
```

In this example, */var/www/html/index.html* automatically requires resources */var/www/html* and */var/www*, because they are parent directories of the file. Autorequired dependencies allow for very clean and easy-to-read code, and leave the dependency management up to the provider.

Avoid complex structures in resource declarations

You should avoid embedding conditional logic such as selectors in your resource statements because doing so tends to produce difficult-to-read code. Assign the result to a variable and then use the variable as the attribute value, as discussed in the documentation (*http://bit.ly/2nYAyx7*). Here's what the code looks like:

```
# Long/wrapped lines
$motd = @("END")
Welcome to ${::fqdn}

This host is managed by Puppet.
Unauthorized access is strictly prohbited.
END

file { '/etc/motd':
  content => $motd,
}
```

This example uses Heredoc syntax (available since Puppet 4) for a multiparagraph string (unfortunately also demonstrating the *data in code* antipattern).

Resource Declaration by Functions

There are a number of functions that can declare resources. The most notable and common is `create_resources`, which you can use to create resources from hashes of data.

The create_resources() function

`create_resources()` is by far the most popular resource declaration function call. It declares resources from serialized data structures. The following example shows user resources serialized in a YAML hash:

```
example::users:
  'alice':
    ensure: 'present'
    comment: 'Alice'
    group: 'example_users'
    managehome: true,
  'jack':
    ensure: 'absent'
    comment: 'Jack'
```

The example that follows iterates over this hash of users and declares a new `user` resource from each entry:

```
# Get serialized user resources from Hiera
$hash_of_users = lookup('example::users', Hash, 'deep', {})

# Set default values
```

```
$user_defaults = {
  shell => '/bin/bash',
}

# Declare user resources with values from the hash
create_resources('user', $hash_of_users, $user_defaults)
```

For each entry in the hash, `create_resources` declares a user resource with the hash key as the title. The attributes for the resource will be taken from the hash of values behind the key, combined with any missing attribute values from the `$user_defaults` hash. For example, the first entry in the hash shown will be declared as a resource like this:

```
user { 'alice':
  ensure     => 'present',
  comment    => 'Alice',
  gid        => 'examplegroup',
  managehome => true,
  shell      => '/bin/bash',
}
```

The creation of resources from serialized data enables the separation of code from long lists of data. It enables us to create resources from lists supplied by other parts of our infrastructure, reducing duplication.

Whether this is best practice can be very situational. Here are some guidelines to help you discern:

Data in code?
A list of authorized users in Hiera data helps avoid putting changeable data values (the users to declare) in the code.

Code in data?
The code should never depend on essential parts of the code coming from data. The code should always operate with or without valid external data.

It's okay for a module to depend on platform-specific or default data included in the module.

The ensure_ functions

`ensure_packages()` and `ensure_resource()` are function calls that you can use to add resources to the catalog. Both function calls are included in the *puppetlabs/stdlib* module and are not available in a base Puppet install.

Unlike `create_resources()`, these function calls check whether a resource already exists before inserting the resource into the catalog. This would seem to be a good solution to the duplicate resource declaration problem, but you should use it with extreme caution because it's parse-order dependent. The following statement will compile and run fine:

```
file { '/tmp/example.txt':
  ensure => 'file',
}

ensure_resource('file', '/tmp/example.txt', { 'ensure' => 'file'})
```

This statement, however, will throw an error:

```
ensure_resource('file', '/tmp/example.txt', { 'ensure' => 'file'})

file { '/tmp/example.txt':
  ensure => 'file',
}
```

This parse-order dependence can create a huge problem; code that works in one situation can unexpectedly fail in another. A small change in the code can cause resource ordering to change, instantly creating problems not previously visible. As a result of the parse-order problem, you can safely use the `ensure_resources()` functions only where every instance is declaring that resource with the `ensure_resource` function.

 Functions are subject to parse-order problems, too. The only safe way to avoid the parse-order problem is to place the common resource in its own class. Then, `include` that class in each place that needs the shared resource.

The same problems are visible with resource declarations inside `defined_with_par ams()` and `defined()` conditional statements.

Resources Metatypes

Resources metatypes are resource types that declare other resources. Metatypes rarely have their own providers; instead, they declare instances of other resource types.

Puppet has two built-in resource metatypes: the `tidy` resource, which is responsible for removing files, and the `resource` type, which you can use to purge any type of resource for which the provider can provide a list. As shown in the following example, this is typically used to purge unmanaged users, groups, packages, and so on from a node:

```
resource { 'host':
  purge => true,
}
```

When a `resource` metatype is declared, the `resource` metatype declaration is added to the catalog and sent to the agent. When the `resource` metatype is evaluated by the agent, it uses the resource provider to acquire a list of all resources of that type. Any additional resources not already specified in the catalog are inserted into the client's in-memory copy of the catalog with the `ensure` value set to `absent`. The catalog is applied normally. The resulting report will contain the state of the resource metatype as well as the state of each resource it added to the catalog.

In the case of the `tidy` resource, the process is as follows:

1. The Puppet parser adds a `tidy` resource when building the catalog.
2. The catalog is sent to the agent.
3. The `tidy` resource uses the `file` resource provider to scan the named directory structure.
4. `file` resources returned by the provider are compared to criteria.
5. Each match causes a `file` resource to be added to the agent's catalog with `ensure => absent`.
6. The catalog is applied with the added file resources.

It's very important to note that there is no two-way communication between the agent and parser when evaluating resource metatypes. The parsing of the manifests has long been completed and the catalog build has finished. The evaluation of the resource metatype is handled entirely by the node's agent.

Because metatypes are evaluated after the catalog has been built, parse-order dependencies are not a problem. Unlike function-based resource declarations, resource metatypes will never add conflicting resources to the catalog. This means that if you explicitly declare that a resource should be present, a resource metatype will not attempt to remove it. For example, `tidy` will never attempt to remove a file that has been explicitly declared as present, and it will not generate a duplicate resource declaration. As a result, resource metatypes are a great way to remove everything except the resources you've declared in the parsed catalog.

 For more information, refer to the Resource Type: Tidy (*http://bit.ly/2LivIEw*) and Resource Type: Resources (*http://bit.ly/2Mn83YR*) documentation.

Resource Metaparameters

Puppet provides metaparameters, or attributes, that can be applied to any resource type. Metaparameters generally control the way Puppet operates rather than enforcing resource state. These are well documented in the Puppet reference materials, so, here, we concern ourselves only with practical uses that might not be obvious.

alias

The `alias` metaparameter allows you to specify alternative titles for a resource to provide a friendly name for a resource with a long and complex title, as shown here:

```
file { '/etc/httpd/conf/httpd.conf':
  ensure  => 'file',
  content => template('apache/apache.conf.erb')
  alias   => 'apache_config',
}
```

You cannot use aliases everywhere that resource titles can be. For example, you cannot use them as identifiers for resource chaining. The safer approach is to use a friendly name in the resource title and specify the longer *namevar* attribute explicitly, as demonstrated in the following:

```
file { 'apache_config':
  ensure  => 'file',
  content => template('apache/apache.conf.erb')
  path    => '/etc/httpd/conf/httpd.conf',
}
```

audit

The `audit` metaparameter accepts a list of attributes whose state should be tracked by Puppet. This has two purposes:

- It allows Puppet to report changes on resources that aren't managed by Puppet.
- It allows Puppet to generate notification signals when resources have changes outside of Puppet.

Audit works by recording the current state of the resource to an audit log. If the resource changes state after Puppet's evaluation of the resource, the differences from the current state of the resource will be reported. If a `notify` or `subscribe` relationship exists with another resource, a notification will be sent.

It's safe for some attributes of a resource to be managed while others are audited. Be aware that audited attribute notifications are indistinguishable from managed attribute change notifications.

You can use auditing to create triggers for resources changed by something outside of Puppet, such as when a file is replaced as shown in the following code:

```
file { '/uploads/myapp.tar.gz':
  audit  => 'contents',
  notify => Exec['extract_myapp']
}

exec { 'extract_myapp':
  command     => "/bin/tar -zxf ${myapp_tarball} -C /opt",
  refreshonly => true,
}
```

Ordering metaparameters: before and require

before and require allow you to specify dependencies and ordering between resources. They ensure that resources are processed in the correct order and that resources
are not processed if their dependencies failed to be applied.

before and require perform the same basic function in opposite directions. Use
whichever metaparameter will result in the most maintainable code.

In many cases, resource relationships are determined implicitly.
Puppet will automatically detect and autorequire dependencies
between related resources. You can take advantage of this behavior
to minimize the number of manually specified resource relationships. See the *autorequires* (*http://bit.ly/2MtRoD7*) documentation
for a resource to see what relationships are automatically created.

Notification metaparameters: notify and subscribe

Notifications allow a resource to signal other resources that it has changed during a
catalog application. The dependent resource receives a *refresh* event that it can act
upon, if relevant for that resource type. notify and subscribe implement the same
functionality as before and require with the addition of sending the refresh event
from a resource to its dependency.

Like their counterparts, notify and subscribe implement the same basic function in
opposite directions. Use whichever metaparameter will result in the most maintainable code. The code example that follows shows each:

```
file { '/tmp/foo':
  notify => Service['biff'],
}

file { '/tmp/bar':
  notify => Service['biff'],
}

service { 'biff':
  # redundant with the notify metaparameters
```

```
    subscribe => File['/tmp/foo','/tmp/bar'],
  }
```

In this example, when either declares file changes, the *biff* service will receive a refresh event, causing the service to be restarted before the same catalog application is completed.

Avoid tight relationships whenever possible

Relationships are best implemented observing the philosophy of *low coupling and high cohension*:

- Use relationships between resources only within a class (high cohesion).
- Use relationships between child classes within a module.
- Use relationships with the main class of unrelated modules (low coupling).

Beyond these simple rules, we can improve module reliability by doubling down on the philosophy:

High cohension
> Use resource relationships within a class even when manifest ordering is used. Manifest ordering is an unstated, implicit structure that is often broken by accident. Make a habit of testing classes with *random* ordering to help identify cases where a necessary relationship is missing.

Low coupling
> Resource relationships that cross class boundaries violate the principles of modular and interface-driven design. By creating relationships only with the main class, you can refactor each module without impact or risk to the other.

Wrapper Modules

There is one situation in which direct resource relationships between two different modules makes sense—and in fact, is a best practice. That is the creation of resource relationships between a wrapper module and specific resources in the wrapped component module.

The purpose of a wrapper module is to adjust or extend the functionality of the module it wraps. For example, a wrapper module might add a new authentication scheme to an application managed by a different module. Certain resources might need to happen after the component module's package is installed but before the service is started.

In a sense, the wrapper and the wrapped module function together as a single module. The code of the wrapper is already tightly integrated with the code of the wrapped

---

module. Therefore, the resources in both modules should have high cohesion, thus making it acceptable for direct resource relationships between the modules to exist.

You should do this only if the resource dependencies are unavoidable. If you can wrap another module while only using relationships with the main or child classes, your wrapper will be significantly less fragile. You should build your modules to allow others to wrap them without violating the class boundaries.

noop

The noop metaparameter allows you to explicitly enable or disable *no-operation* mode for a single resource, class, or defined type declaration. In noop mode, the resource will be evaluated and compared to the modeled state,; however, changes to the resource will not be applied. This allows you to report that a resource does not conform to your policy without changing the resource's state.

Setting this to false could cause resource states to change when the user wants to evaluate *potential* changes. Setting noop => false on a resource declaration might seem useful for partial enforcement of catalogs (e.g., security-related resources), but it removes one of Puppet's greatest strengths: the ability to safely simulate changes by running with --noop enabled. You run puppet apply --noop to review the changes, but the resource's hardcoded value wins over the command-line value, and a change to the resource is applied.

The converse problem exists for hardcoding noop => true in the code, which will cause an attempt to cause a change with --no-noop to be ineffective.

Because you cannot override this metaparameter on the command line or in the configuration, it is useless in general practice. Instead, use tagged runs for partial enforcement, as discussed in "tag" on page 133. This allows you to use the --noop command-line option or noop = true configuration value to prevent changes in a way that can be overridden when necessary.

Note that although Puppet will log the notifications and refresh events that would be created, it will not actually send those signals if noop is enabled. If you want to generate signals without enforcing state, consider using the audit metaparameter instead.

schedule

The schedule metaparameter allows you to assign a resource to be evaluated within a specific window, as defined by the schedule resource type. This attribute can be very useful for ensuring that a resource is applied only within a certain window. It can also limit the frequency at which a resource is evaluated. For more information, see Resource Type: schedule (*https://puppet.com/docs/puppet/latest/types/schedule.html*).

A schedule limits evaluation to the named window. It does nothing to ensure that Puppet applies the catalog during the same window. Creating a window that will intersect with Puppet convergence runs is an exercise for the implementor.

One surprising feature of schedule is that a resource evaluated outside of its schedule always succeeds for dependency purposes. If the resource has not been applied because Puppet has not yet run during the schedule window, the dependent resource won't have the resource it depends on. For this reason, it is necessary when you're first building a node or when you're deploying new features to disable the schedules so that the necessary dependencies are created. Thereafter, they will be updated only during the schedule window.

stage

You can apply stage only to entire classes, and it has a number of complications that make it unsuitable for most purposes.

- You must assign classes to stages using the resource declaration format, which prevents multiple classes from declaring the class and disallows the application of data-driven class assignment from Hiera.
- You cannot send notifications between resources in different stages.
- Class containment behaves strangely if any class resides in another stage.

Early Puppet users attempted to use stage for rough ordering; however, there are so many complications with stages that most sites have abandoned their use entirely. No matter how carefully you segregate resources into different stages, at some point during a minor change you're going to find that a dependency loop between the stages has been created. Fixing that problem will require a major refactoring, possibly of the entire implementation. There are no simple fixes to ordering resources that cross stage boundaries.

No Other Choice?

There are certain scenarios for which it will seem unavoidable to use stages. For example, if you want to apply a dependency to every package resource on updating the repository first, but you utilize virtual package resources that you don't want to realize by creating the dependency with a collector.

A number of patterns exist to handle large-scale dependency management, such as the binford2k/manifold (*https://forge.puppet.com/binford2k/manifold*) module, which can create bulk relationships in the catalog without collecting the resources.

> You should use stages only if there is truly no other way, and limit them to the smallest possible resource scope.

tag

Use tag to identify resources for collection (see "Avoid Parse-Order Problems by Using Virtual Resources" on page 133 and "Exporting Resources" on page 136), to perform partial enforcement of a catalog, and for reporting and review purposes with PuppetDB.

A resource acquires tags from multiple places:

- The tag metaparameter adds the specified values to the list of tags
- Tags automatically created for each resource, including the resource type, and each component of the class or defined type name
- Tags applied to the class containing the resource
- Tags applied to the class that declared the class containing the resource

If you recall the simple resource inspected at the beginning of this chapter, no tags were declared for the resource and yet tags existed on the resource in the catalog as seen in Example 5-3.

```
tag 'example_tag'

file { '/tmp/foo':
  tag => ['foo', 'bar', 'baz'],
}
```

In the preceding code, the resource File['/tmp/foo'] would have the tags ["file","foo","bar","baz","example_tag"]. If it was in a module class, it would have the class tag, too.

As you might imagine, it's easy to match resources you didn't intend to match due to this behavior. Use distinct tag prefixes to avoid collecting or acting on resources you didn't intend to.

Avoid Parse-Order Problems by Using Virtual Resources

When you declare a resource (such as a user), it is added to the catalog. Attempts to declare that same resource again in the same catalog build will generate an error. Therefore, if two different modules might need the same resource, but either one might not be declared for a given host, there needs to be a safe way for both to declare the resource if necessary—*virtual resources* fill that gap.

A virtual resource declaration adds the resource to the catalog, but marks it inactive. Modules that want to make use of that resource can realize that resource, which marks it active for convergence. Unlike normal resources, a virtual resource can be realized none, one, or multiple times safely.

 Unrealized virtual resources are in the catalog, but not available for dependency relationships. A resource relationship with a nonrealized/inactive virtual resource will cause a catalog failure.

The ability to realize resources multiple times dramatically simplifies cases for which resources are optionally added based on a set of rules. Example 5-4 demonstrates how to declare and realize virtual resources.

Example 5-4. Declaring and realizing virtual resources

```
@user { 'alice':
  ensure => 'present',
  gid    => 'dba',
}

@user { 'bob':
  ensure => 'present',
  gid    => 'web',
}

case $facts['role'] {
  'database': { realize( User['alice'] ) }  # realize a specific resource
  'web':      { User <| gid == 'web' |> }   # a collector realizes matching resources
}
```

In Example 5-4 if the role fact is database, the user alice is added to the catalog. If the role is web, users in the web group are added to the catalog. This logic can be applied multiple times in manifests without any concern about duplicate user resource declarations.

Virtual resources make it easy to create Don't Repeat Yourself (DRY), data-driven code that conditionally realizes resources from a list of possible choices. The alternative approach would be to maintain separate lists for every possible combination of users that might be applied to the system, dramatically increasing the probability of a conflict and greatly increasing maintenance overhead.

Virtual resources are not parse-order dependent. You can declare virtual resources late in your manifests and realize them early. They will work as expected without any explicit ordering. This allows considerable flexibility and avoids trying to manage manifest parse order.

Although virtual resources allow a resource to be realized multiple times, you should not use them as a way of handling shared resources and module interdependencies. Using virtual resources in this way violates the principles of modular design, the single responsibility principle, and separation of concerns. With this approach, two modules need to agree to use virtual resources and on how those resources should be defined. Splitting virtual resources between modules means that changes to the resource declaration in one module can break another module. In these cases, the creation of additional modules or classes to handle the commonality or dependency is recommended.

Dangling relationships to unrealized resources causes breakage

You should also take care when designing resource relationships with virtual resources. If you realize a virtual resource that has a relationship with an unrealized resource, a catalog compilation error will be thrown. You can use the before/require and subscribe/notify symmetry to work around the issue; if the unrealized resource declares the relationship, you're fine.

Instead, create relationships when realizing the resources with a collector.

Example 5-5 shows the `require` ordering (the -> chaining arrow) of the `yumrepo` resource being added as the collector realizes the list of packages.

Example 5-5. Declaring resource relationships when realizing virtual resources

```
@package { ['apache2', 'mysql-client']:
  tag => 'Debian',
}

@package { ['httpd', 'mysql']:
  tag => 'RedHat',
}

case $facts['osfamily'] {
  'RedHat': {
    Yumrepo['base'] -> Package <| tag == 'RedHat' |>
  }
  default: {
    Package <| tag == $facts['osfamily'] |>
  }
}
```

This technique is safe to implement with an empty list because a relationship to an empty collector will not cause an error, as shown here:

```
package {'filesystem':
  ensure => 'installed',
}
```

```
Package['filesystem'] ~> File <| title == 'nonexistent_resource' |>
```

Resource collectors can realize virtual resources based on any attribute of the resource. The `tag` metaparameter is commonly employed to realize virtual resources, but you should use it with caution. The compiler automatically assigns a large number of tags to each resource in the catalog based on calling class names, resource types, and many other considerations. If you use nonunique tag names to realize resources, you might find cases in which resources are realized unexpectedly. Tags are applied in a parse-order-dependent way, depending on the first class that declares another class, so the list of automatic tags for a resource is not stable. Use attributes other than `tag` to realize resources to avoid these issues.

Exporting Resources

Exported resources allow resources to be shared between nodes. Exported resources are implemented and treated very similarly to virtual resources. Resources can be exported without being applied, and must be collected in order to be added to the catalog. The syntax for exported resources is also very similar to that of virtual resources, only with a doubled **@@** prefix.

For example, a web server could export details of a web service for inclusion in a load balancer pool. The following code adds a `webserver` instance to a `haproxy` service pool using the `puppetlabs/haproxy` module:

```
@@haproxy::balancermember { $facts['fqdn']:
  listening_service => 'web',
  server_names      => $facts['hostname'],
  ipaddresses       => $facts['ipaddress'],
  ports             => '80',
  options           => 'check',
}
```

When a resource is exported, it is marked with an *exported* flag in the exporting node's catalog. A copy of the node's catalog is then stored in PuppetDB.

The node running `haproxy` would collect `haproxy::balancermember` exported resources using a search for the service, as shown here:

```
include haproxy

haproxy::listen { 'web':
  ipaddress => $facts['ipaddress'],
  ports     => '80',
}

Haproxy::Balancermember <<| listening_service == 'web' |>>
```

PuppetDB responds to the search with a list of exported resources that match the search, which are added to the Puppet catalog of the collecting node to flesh out the haproxy configuration.

 Exported resources are one method of implementing service discovery with Puppet. They allow nodes to supply resources for use on other nodes.

Exported resources satisfy a few common use cases:

- Configuring monitoring systems to monitor services on node
- Identifying nodes answering for a service pool or cluster membership
- Any other use case for which the services might scale up or down dynamically

You can export any resource, including exec resources.

Comparing virtual and exported resources

The similar syntax of virtual and exported resources is due to their very similar nature. In review:

Local resources
> Local node @virtual_resource collected by <| *search* |>

Shared resources
> Any node's @@exported_resource collected by <<| *search* |>>

Safely using exported resource

An important aspect of exported resources is that they have universal availability. A resource is unlikely to make sense outside the scope of its intended environment. An unexpected resource can cause catalog compilation errors, misconfiguration, or node failure if applied unexpectedly to the wrong environment.

Following are some guidelines for the safe usage of exported resources:

Exported resource titles must be globally unique across all nodes
> Because an exported resource could be collected by any node, and a resource title must be unique within a catalog, this requires each exported resource to be absolutely unique. Use a string unique to the node (certname, FQDN, serial, etc.) in the exported resource title to guarantee uniqueness.

A resource can be collected by any node in the infrastructure
> As of 2018, there's not yet any security controls to limit access to exported resources. Only the search parameter of the resource collector will limit the results.

Exported resources are not constrained by their Puppet environment
> It's possible for resources from a development branch to be applied to a production branch. If a Puppet server provides multiple environments that should not collect one another's resources, tag the resources with the environment and use it in the collector's search.

Exported resources should not contain resource relationships
> It is entirely possible that due to timing, one exported resource would be available and the other not yet processed. This will cause a catalog failure on the collecting node. As demonstrated in "Dangling relationships to unrealized resources causes breakage" on page 135, apply the resource relationships when collecting the resources, not when declaring them.

Exported resources could increase the catalog build time and size
> If many exported resources are collected, the time to build the catalog and its overall size will both increase. For example, if you have 10,000 nodes exporting their services, the time to build the catalog for a monitoring station collecting those services could be extreme. Use judiciously.

Exported resources provide slow but eventual consistency
> If you boot up a thousand new instances, it will take time for each node to run Puppet, build the catalog, and have their exported resources available in PuppetDB to be collected. This works well for eventual consistency, but is not suitable for quickly changing environments in which services might not exist for more than a few minutes.

The number of concerns listed here might concern you. The main benefit of exported resources is that they are tightly integrated and immediately available with Puppet. They solve many problems well, but they are not a solution for every service discovery need. Service registration services like Consul and orchestration services like Kubernetes, DC/OS, and Docker Swarm might be more suitable for highly dynamic services.

Overriding and Modifying Declared Resources

Resource declarations can be influenced or adjusted *off the page*, or outside of the specific Puppet language declaration. There are a number of ways in which you can specify a resource's attributes, relationships, or behaviors, both before and after the resource is declared. This section explores those capabilities.

Resource Default Statements

Resource default statements supply attribute values that will be used in any case for which the attribute is not explicitly declared on that resource type. For example, an Enterprise Linux node might want to set the `require` attribute of *package* resources to include a specific Yum repository.

This concept can be very useful for situations in which common values are used within a class or defined type. Here's an example that attempts to simplify a number of similar `file` resources:

```
File {
  mode  => '0440',
  owner => 'nobody',
  group => 'nobody',
}

file { '/tmp/foo.txt':
  content => 'Foo',
}

file { '/tmp/bar.txt':
  content => 'Bar',
}

include baz
```

Unfortunately, resource default statements apply to everything in the same scope, such as declared classes. This means that an inherited resource default will affect not just the `file` resources shown here, but also the `file` resources in the `baz` class.

It gets worse. Because classes are added to the catalog only once, if at a later time another class declares `baz` earlier the resource defaults will suddenly not apply. This parse-order dependency means that resource defaults can affect the behavior of included class resources without warning, and change suddenly due to an apparently irrelevent change far outside the scope of these two modules. In essence, the inherited nature of resource defaults violate the principles of modular design and SoC.

Resource default inheritence can affect the behavior of resources in unrelated modules without any intent on your part to do so. Many well-meaning operators add a default attribute to a given resource, only to discover that one or more modules was reliant on the default behavior. Such problems are often very difficult to track down.

To mitigate the problems associated with default inheritance, we recommend that you declare only resource default statements in *leaf classes*—classes that do not declare any other class.

Per-expression defaults provide a solution

Thankfully, there's a better way to provide default attributes that manages to be both safer to use and easier to read. Example 5-6 presents the code.

Example 5-6. Using a defaults hash to set file permissions

```
$my_file_defaults = {
  mode  => '0440',
  owner => 'nobody',
  group => 'nobody',
}

file {
  default:
    * => $my_file_defaults,
    ;;

  '/tmp/foo.txt':
    content => 'Foo',
    ;;
}

include baz
```

This example works by applying two techniques:

- It uses the splat (*) operator to assign the hash of attribute values.
- By assigning the hash to the per-expression resource default, it allows the resource to explicitly override any defaults.

This stacked resource declaration is a little longer, but it greatly increases readability by explicitly declaring which set of defaults values to use. Nothing happens *off the page* or through a parse-order-dependent inheritance. And the baz class is completely unaffected by this default, although it could explicitly use the same hash to provide default values if desired.

Per-expression defaults provide a way to avoid surprises

Although it's a bad idea to use resource default statements, it's a good idea to be tolerant of them when writing modules. There are two ways to avoid having resource default statements affect the functionality of your module:

- If your resource has specific attribute requirements, set them explicitly instead of relying on defaults you expect.
- Have your class set its own default for the resource. This default will be limited to your class and classes it declares.

- Have your class inherit from an empty class. An explicit `inherits` statement forces the parent class to one of your own choosing, blocking flow-down inheritence.

In contrast, being tolerant can also mean not fighting valid uses of the module. Let the user specify defaults if the values (such as file owner) aren't important for what the module does.

Resource Chaining

You cannot redeclare a resource relationship attribute, but you can add it after declaration, as shown in the following:

```
File['/etc/httpd/conf/httpd.conf'] ~> Service['httpd']
```

This particular chain adds a notification for changes to the *httpd.conf* file to the *httpd* service. This is exactly the same as adding `notify => Service['httpd']` to the file declaration, or `subscribe => File['/etc/httpd/conf/httpd.conf']` to the service declaration. The only difference is that we've done it after the fact. This is a very powerful technique for use in wrapper modules or profiles to create associations between resources in unrelated modules.

A good guideline is that chaining should be used only between single-line statements, as demonstrated in the line of code above. Using resource chaining on larger resources can easily be overlooked, as shown here:

```
package { 'httpd':
  ensure => 'installed',
}
-> file { '/etc/httpd/conf.d/httpd.conf':
  ensure => 'present',
  group  => 'httpd',
  mode   => '0440',
}
~> service { 'httpd':
  ensure => 'running'
  enable => true,
}
```

As this code demonstrates, the chaining arrows don't call attention to themselves. The `notify` and `subscribe` metaparameters would be more visible to the reader.

Resource Collectors

Resource collectors can also override resource attributes. Unlike resource chaining, resource collectors can override attributes for any matching resource, even if that attribute has already been defined. To illustrate this, in the next example, the file will contain the content `bar`, not `foo`.

```
file { '/tmp/example.txt':
  content => "foo\n",
}

File <| title == '/tmp/example.txt'|> {
  content => "bar\n"
}
```

Resource collectors can be very dangerous if used carelessly. The following code would cause every `notify` resource in the catalog to print *YOLO*:

```
Notify <||> {
  message => "YOLO\n"
}
```

Resource collectors will realize any matching virtual resources. Be careful to limit the search expression to resources that you want to add to the node's catalog. For example, the naive ordering implementation shown in the next example has unintended consequences:

```
Yumrepo <| |> -> Package <| |>
```

This example has a side effect of realizing every virtual `Yumrepo` and `Package` resource.

Resource Best Practices

In this section, we discuss a number of built-in types, custom types, and popular defined types for Puppet.

This section is not intended to be exhaustive; our focus is on best practices rather than just the usage of each resource type. Refer to the online documentation for each of the types referenced here to explore all the features of the type.

Spend some time reviewing the full list of built-in resource types as well as the list of Puppet *supported* and *approved* modules on the Puppet Forge. You will find many interesting custom resources and defined types among those modules.

Custom Resource Types

Built-in resource types are those that come installed with the Puppet agent. However, you should not limit yourself to using built-in types. Puppet long ago moved to a model of distributing new resource types in modules, and even spinning out built-in resources into their own modules. Built-in resources are not better in any objective way.

In this section, we reference a number of valuable resource types and providers that extend Puppet's functionality. We discuss both officially supported and community modules here.

The official type reference includes only built-in types. You can get a list of all installed resource types and their documentation by using puppet describe. Try out puppet describe --list in your development environment.

The ACL type

The ACL type and provider allow for the management of Windows access control lists (ACLs). This resource type provides much finer control than the file resource permissions. This resource type does not manage file content; you must use it as a supplement to a standard file resource. You use the ACL resource when simple read/write/execute permissions are not sufficiently granular.

This resource type is provided by the puppetlabs/acl module.

The anchor type

The anchor resource was an early fix for the problem of child class containment for class-based relationships. For the most part, it has been superseded by the contain function call. You might occasionally encounter modules that still use this resource type.

For more detail on the use and application of anchors, see "Anchors" on page 99.

Augeas providers

Augeas types are native resource types and providers that use the Augeas configuration editing tool to manage the underlying configuration files. Augeas providers is a set of modules written and managed by the Augeas team. These modules provide a number of new resource types for managing common files, a set of libraries for the creation of new Augeas resource types, and a number of Augeas providers for existing types.

These providers are more focused and user friendly than the built-in augeas resource type. We recommend using these modules rather than attempting to call Augeas directly.

You can deploy all of the providers by installing the herculesteam/augeasproviders module with the puppet module tool, or you can install them individually. You can best manage individual installations by using r10k to handle the long list of modules.

The datacat types

`datacat_collector` and `datacat_fragment` serve a function similar to the `concat` defined type discussed in "The concat defined type" on page 148. Instead of sending file fragments to be combined by the agent, `datacat` creates data structures in the catalog, which can be rendered into a template or utilized by other resources.

You can use this module to build very complex configuration files using templates. `datacat` works by merging data structures from the various fragment resources. `data cat` then generates a new resource based on the `target_resource` parameter given to `datacat_collector`, and passes the merged data structure to that resource.

Try to avoid crossing module boundaries with `datacat`. If you need to declare fragments from multiple modules, use a defined type in the module that contains the collector as the external interface for adding fragments.

Combining `datacat` and `concat` is where wizards tremble in fear. Generating the `datacat` fragments and collectors during the catalog build while leaving the `concat` fragments to be assembled by the agent will create a complex web of interactions to debug.

`datacat_fragment` and `datacat_collector` are provided by the `richardc/datacat` module.

The file_line resource type

You can use the `file_line` resource type to add or remove lines from arbitrary text files. This resource type is useful when you need to perform edits scoped more narrowly than the entire file but where a native resource is unavailable.

 Using this resource to adjust a file managed by a different module will create constant churn as the modules each attempt to fix the file. You should use this only for files that cannot be managed by another module.

This resource type is provided by the `puppetlabs/stdlib` module.

The match attribute. The `match` attribute allows `file_line` to modify existing entries in a configuration file, rather than simply adding new entries. By default, `file_line` simply checks to see whether the desired line is present, and adds it if not.

`match` expects a Ruby regex, and will throw an error if the expression does not also match the line to be inserted. This behavior prevents erroneous notification loops and the creation of duplicate lines. It is poor practice to try to trick the resource type

---

using regex *OR* matches. Instead, use one resource to remove the old line, and another resource to insert the new line.

The after attribute. The `after` attribute allows limited context awareness for the `file_line` type. You can use it to insert a line in a specific part of the file, immediately after the line matched by the `after` attribute. Normally, new entries are simply appended to the end of the file.

If you need more complex context awareness, consider using an `augeas` resource instead of a `file_line` resource.

Beware that not all versions of `file_line` support this attribute. If you are using an older bundled version of stdlib, this attribute might not be available to you.

Note that the `file_line` `after` attribute has no relationship[1] to the `before` and `require` metaparameters.

The gnupg_key type

This resource type allows for the management and distribution of GNU Privacy Guard (GPG) keys. GPG keys are widely used by installers to validate package integrity. This resource provider can help cryptographically validate `yumrepo` resources and other package downloads.

This resource type is provided by the `golja/gnupg` module.

The ini_setting and ini_subsetting resource types

These generic types allow granular management of specific items in INI files. Because the INI format is extremely common, you are almost guaranteed to find use for this resource type.

`ini_setting` provides per-line management of key/value pairs. Because you can declare the delimiter, spacing, and section(s), it is capable of managing virtually any file comprising simple key/value pairs. `ini_setting` is often used as a base for other resource providers. For example, it is the base provider for the `yumrepo` resource type.

 `puppetlabs/inifile` accepts parameters to specify delimiters and headers, allowing it to manage files that are not immediately recognizable as having INI syntax.

---

1 No pun intended.

`ini_subsetting` provides element-level management of INI values. The scope of the `ini_subsetting` type is extremely tight, allowing multiple modules to safely manage elements on a single line.

These resource types can help manage the following:

- */etc/sysconfig/* files containing Bash variables
- Java properties files
- *puppet.conf* and other puppet configuration settings
- Hashicorp HCL configuration files

These resource types are provided by the `puppetlabs/inifile` module.

The registry type

The `registry` type is invaluable for managing registry entries in Windows environments. This resource type is far more efficient and reliable than alternative approaches for editing registry keys.

This resource type is provided by the *puppetlabs/registry* module.

The reboot type

The `reboot` type allows Puppet to restart the node it is running on. Its primary purpose is to restart a system so that configuration changes can take effect. On Linux nodes a restart is usually required only to upgrade the kernel or install a kernel extension. Windows nodes might need to restart for routine software installation.

The `reboot` resource type is inactive unless it receives a notification signal. You can have multiple instances of `reboot` in your catalog, so long as each one has a unique resource title. It is safe to schedule multiple reboots from one or multiple resources.

If your Puppet runs are idempotent, only a single reboot should be required at the end of your run. The goal is to reach a consistent state during the run, rebooting only for the state to take effect. Ideally, no further changes should be pending when the system comes up. If further changes are needed after the reboot, your code is convergent rather than idempotent. On some platforms, this might be a necessary evil.

If you use `reboot` in a convergent way, it's a good idea to schedule a Puppet run at system startup. This can help to avoid a very long convergence cycle, and is useful for cases in which additional postreboot configuration tasks need to be performed. Without an immediate postreboot Puppet run, your overall configuration time can easily exceed an hour. Much of this time will be spent waiting for the next scheduled run.

Note that the `reboot` type will reboot the system only if it the `reboot` resource receives a notification signal from another resource. Consider how you contain and isolate the `reboot` resource in order to prevent an errant signal from inadvertantly triggering a reboot.

The `reboot` resource type is provided by the `puppetlabs/reboot` module.

The vcs_repo type

The `vcs_repo` type allows you to create and manage version control repositories. Its primary use is for cloning repositories to a managed system.

This resource type is useful for the distribution of files and data from repositories other than the ones that host your Puppet code. There are situations for which you might want to have Puppet deploy revision-controlled content but do not want to commit that content to your Puppet repository. Cloning your website to your web servers is one such example.

This approach helps to enforce separation of site content away from your site-logic and site-specific configuration data. It's also useful for enforcing access control requirements; each repository can have its own access rules.

Although you can use `vcs_repo` to distribute Puppet manifests, r10k provides significantly more deployment-oriented features. For more details, see Chapter 9.

This resource type is provided by the `puppetlabs/vcs_repo` module. It's a good idea to also check the available providers; as of this writing Git, Mercurial, SVN, Bazaar, Perforce, and CVS are supported.

The windows_env native type and provider

The `windows_env` type allows you to manage Windows environment variables. A surprisingly large number of applications use environment variables to modify pathing or other behaviors. This module is invaluable in Windows environments.

This resource type is provided by the `badgerious/windows_env` module.

Useful Defined Types

Defined types are not strictly speaking Puppet resources types. They are named collections of resources and logic bound together. They allow you to design a named abstraction layer that provides context for a group of resources.

We reference a few public-defined types here. These defined types extend Puppet's capabilities in useful ways. They are also dramatically simpler and more reliable than creating a new resource type to perform the same task.

The concat defined type

The concat defined type allows you to build files from fragments, combining multiple file resources into a single complete file. This resource provider is useful when you need to produce files from large multiline chunks. It retains most of the efficiency of the file resource, but it allows multiple classes or instances of a defined type to contribute fragments.

The downside of concat is that it is not always intuitive. Although it's much simpler to use than datacat, it is not nearly as simple as a conventional file resource. Like a file resource, concat must have complete control over the resulting output file. Ultimately, it's designed to share inputs, not outputs.

Another consideration is that fragments must be defined in a consistent way for each file. It can be a good idea to wrap the file fragments in defined types to simplify and control their interface.

The concat defined type is provided by the puppetlabs/concat module and is bundled with Puppet Enterprise.

The account defined type

When managing users with Puppet, it is often useful to abstract away the creation of user, group, and other associated resources in order to better organize your data in Hiera, to remove redundant data, and to simplify account creation.

There are several good account modules available, including the pe_account module bundled with Puppet Enterprise. You can use these modules as-is or extended in order to meet your site-specific requirements.

The camptocamp/accounts module is another popular account defined type. It does not conflict with pe_account.

Summary

Resources are the fundamental building blocks of state management. Understanding the capabilities of Puppet's resource types is invaluable for building comprehensive, scalable code. Understanding the ways in which you can declare, remove, and audit resources is invaluable for converting data about your environment into real configurations.

Here are this chapter's takeaways:

- Use resources to implement changes.
- Use the best resource type for the task at hand.
- Use resource types that provide context and demonstrate intent.

- Virtual resources allow for conditional inclusion of optional resources from a list.
- Understand your resource relationships and how a notification affects resources.
- Understand how a particular resource type will scale.
- Avoid implementations that will require thousands of resources.
- Understand what impact an approach will have as your site grows.
- Don't reinvent the wheel.
- Avoid `exec` resources whenever possible.
- Avoid creating long chains of fragile resources.
- KISS: there's no need to use `augeas` when a simple `file` will do.

## CHAPTER 6

Hiera Data

Hiera is a multilayered, hierarchical key/value lookup system for Puppet that provides data used to inform the code. In this chapter, we look at best practices for configuring Hiera backends, designing your hierarchy, and integrating Hiera into your Puppet code. We briefly review the features and functionality of Hiera before covering best practices.

Separating Code and Data

Hiera's most important capability and its greatest value come from its ability to separate your code and data. Separation of code and data is a fairly old idea as far as programming goes. You generally cannot use code that contains data without modification, whereas code that acts based on input data can be utilized repeatedly for different purposes. This abstraction makes it possible to assemble functionality from many reusable components rather than building a large monolithic codebase with a single purpose.

Conversely, the structure and storage of data is a well-studied and understood subject. There are frameworks and skill sets devoted to data management. Separating the code from the data allows the developer to focus on the code and data specialists to focus on data management.

There are many different guidelines and rules, but we've use the following three simple and easy baselines for clarity. When considering where some information belongs, compare it to these guidelines:

- Information that differs for each resource (user name, UID, etc.) is data.
- Code describes how to do something, whereas data describes what should be done.

- Data provides content, and code implements behavior.

Global, Environment, and Module Data

Hiera v4/v5 provides three independent layers where you can find data. Every query will proceed through the layers in the following order:

Global
> A hierarchy of site-specific data shared by all Puppet environments. Only globally shared values should exist here.

Environment
> A hierarchy of site-specific data for the Puppet environment. You will place the vast majority of data here.

Module
> A unique hierarchy for component-specific data in the module, usually only platform-specific data or module default values.

Each layer has its own unique hierarchy for data lookups. This provides considerable flexibility for management of data by different teams, as discussed in "Designing the Hiera Hierarchy" on page 153.

 Until the module layer was added to Hiera, it was necessary for module code to contain default values. The module layer of Hiera v4+ does away with that limitation, allowing for the creation of completely dataless modules.

Each query will proceed through the layers in order, checking each level of the hierarchy in each layer. You can configure each key lookup to return results using four different merge strategies:

First
> The lookup can return the first key found.

unique
> The lookup will return array values found from every layer, deduplicated and flattened into a single array.

hash
> The lookup will return the values of hash keys found under the query key from every layer.

deep

The lookup will return the values of hashes within hashes found under the query key from every layer.

Select the appropriate merge strategy based on your data structure.

Hiera Backends

Hiera can source data from built-in or custom backends, creating a pluggable interface between Puppet and any given data source. Hiera's built-in backends include YAML-, JSON-, and HOCON-formatted data files. Custom backends exist for HTTP sources, MySQL databases, MongoDB, Hashicorp Vault, and many other sources. It's quite trivial to create a custom backend for anything you want.

Data that differs for each resource should be stored in a Hiera datastore. Depending on the need, here are some recommended guidelines:

- You could store data that tends to change less frequently in YAML, JSON, or HOCON text files.
- You could store data that changes often in service registries or databases with low-latency lookup.
- Data that must be computed can be queried from functions and programs.

 We discuss the built-in text file backends in "The Built-In Backends" on page 166, and custom backends for database and service registries in "Custom Hiera Backends" on page 169.

Designing the Hiera Hierarchy

Each layer has its own hierarchy for data lookups. Each level of the hierarchy can select a different backend as a data source. This flexibility makes Hiera capable of sourcing data from innumerable sources.

The design of your hierarchy plays a key role in the organization of your data. There are several key considerations when designing a hierarchy. An ideal design should d the following:

- Reduce or eliminate duplication of data across the hierarchy.
- Reduce or eliminate the need to pass data between different teams.
- Group data according to the supplier of the data.

- Facilitate auditing and debugging.

Athough many of these concerns revolve around standard data management topics, we touch on concerns specific to Puppet in the sections that follow.

Variable Interpolation

The Hiera hierarchy contains interpolation tokens to select the appropriate data source for the current node. An interpolation token is special syntax that will be replaced with the value named. Hiera will recognize the interpolation token, look up the value, and then replace the token with the value found—just like interpolating a variable in a string.

You can interpolate any node fact or Puppet variable to customize a level in the hierarchy, as shown in Example 6-1. This flexibility can adjust hierarchies to suit each node, but it can also create problems if not designed well. In this section, we review best practices relating to interpolation of data in the hierarchy.

Node-provided facts

The most common interpolation is the use of node-provided facts to select the data source.

Example 6-1. Interpolate node facts

```
:hierarchy:
  - name: "Per-node data"
    path: "nodes/%{facts.hostname}.yaml"
```

The hierarchy level shown in this example will search a filename specific to the hostname provided by the node.

> Hiera uses the %{variable} token for interpolation and a period to access hash values. $facts['os']['family'] in Puppet language would be %{facts.os.family} in Hiera.

Use the facts hash to retrieve variables. Simple facts are available as top-level variables in Puppet (e.g., $hostname) but might be removed in the future. Sourcing facts from the $facts hash as shown in Example 6-1 guarantees it is a node-provided fact, and documents the source of data to the reader.

In contrast, %{some_name} could be a node fact, an ENC parameter, or a manifest variable. You'll need to analyze the code to determine the value's origin.

Viewing a node's facts.   You can run the `facter` command to see what facts are gathered about the node. You can also use `facter -p` or `puppet facts print` to get all of those facts plus the custom facts installed by Puppet modules. The `-p` option might disappear in future versions.

Use trusted facts when available

Using node facts is sufficient and necessary for most use cases, but it can be a security concern. You should prefer any fact available in the `$trusted` hash over node-supplied facts. There are few trusted facts, but they cover most essential use cases (*http://bit.ly/2N6ILKL*).

Example 6-2 demonstrates the use of the safer server-validated node certificate name.

Example 6-2. Interpolated trusted facts

```
:hierarchy:
  - name: "Per-node data"
    path: "nodes/%{trusted.certname}.yaml"
```

Any custom attributes from the node's signed certificate are available in the `$trus ted['extensions']` hash. For example, if the certificate was built to contain a customer name you can retrieve this and use it in the hierarchy as shown in the following code:

```
:hierarchy:
  - name: "Per-customer data"
    path: "customers/%{trusted.extensions.customer}.yaml"
```

To learn more about storing custom attributes in the node's certificate, refer to the documentation (*https://puppet.com/docs/puppet/latest/ssl_attributes_extensions.html*).

Remove environment interpolation

Hiera v3 (used in Puppet 3) had only a single layer, and thus only a single hierarchy. This led many people to develop complex environment interpolation in the global hierarchy to access environment and module data. Now that Hiera has separate layers for environment and module data, we can remove that unnecessary complexity.

Label node classifier-provided data

The hierarchy can and often should make use of data provided by a node classifier such as Puppet Enterprise Console or Foreman. Which values are provided by the ENC is specific to the implementation. Unless labeled clearly, they are indistinguishable from variables set in Puppet code.

To make the data source apparent to the viewer, place the ENC-provided data in its own bespoke hash, as shown in the following code:

```
:hierarchy:
  - name: "Site data"
    path: "sites/%{foreman.location}.yaml"
```

Avoid using Puppet variables

The hierarchy can make use of variables set by Puppet modules and manifests. You should avoid this in the *global* and *environment* hierarchies, because it ties the deployment or an environment to a specific module or manifest. It is also parse-order dependent, so any queries performed before the variable is defined will not resolve to the correct path.

This is useful and effective only when you use it to customize lookups within a certain module. For example, a service profile might use a mandatory parameter in the hierarchy layer for queries done within the profile.

To make the data source readily apparent to the viewer, place module-provided data in its own bespoke hash, as shown in the following:

```
:hierarchy:
  - name: "Data from service module"
    path: "services/%{service.cluster}.yaml"
```

As discussed in Chapter 1, use only variables explicitly documented as public by the module author. Otherwise, code refactoring of that module might rename, eliminate, or change the purpose and behavior of the variable used. It's best to avoid using module-sourced values whenever possible.

Use explain to debug lookup interpolation

As discussed in Chapters 3 and 7, it's easiest and most intuitive to follow variable references when those references strictly flow upward from your node's facts and the ENC data. By interpolating module-specific variables into higher-level Hiera hierarchies, the flow of data through your site becomes somewhat cyclical and difficult to debug and understand.

The puppet lookup --explain will get node facts from --node *hostname* or --facts *facts.yaml* and provide a detailed analysis of the Hiera hierarchy and in which level of which layer a specific value was found. This is an incredibly powerful and useful tool. The following example shows it in action:

```
$ puppet lookup --node node_name --explain classes --merge unique
Searching for "classes"
  Global Data Provider (hiera configuration version 5)
    Using configuration "/etc/puppetlabs/puppet/hiera.yaml"
    Hierarchy entry "Per-node data"
```

```
Path "/etc/puppetlabs/code/hiera_global/nodes/testy.example.om.yaml"
  Original path: "nodes/%{trusted.certname}.yaml"
  Path not found
...each level of each layer will be shown...
```

By keeping to the aforementioned recommendations, the puppet lookup command makes it trivial to debug. If any part of the hierarchy is interpolated from Puppet code, those values won't be available. You'll be forced to read and analyze the code yourself to figure out what happened.

You can read about how to use the explain feature at Using Puppet Lookup (*http://bit.ly/2OVtQDI*) and the Puppet Lookup man page (*http://bit.ly/2wg2H6D*).

This is by no means an exhaustive list; facts are arbitrary and treated as top-level variables. Any top-level variable can easily be spoofed unless it's defined explicitly by your Puppet code or ENC.

Facts are by default presented as top-level variables. Global variables and data from your ENC have priority over facts. However, values not supplied by your ENC can be spoofed using facts. For example, if your hierarchy uses a tier parameter from your ENC to provide production specific values and there is a case in which an agent can invoke a run without the ENC supplying a tier parameter, a malicious user might be able to recover data from that hierarchy using a static fact.

You should use caution with Hiera interpolation functions, as well. Although Hiera does provide the lookup() recursive lookup function, you should not use it as a hierarchy interpolation token because doing so might create an infinite recursive lookup loop.

Design Guidelines

Let's review some common design goals and best usage of them. These examples show YAML data files, but the principles apply regardless of which backend is used.

Most specific to general—top to bottom

Because first-found answers override lower answers, the Hiera hierarchy should always query node-specific files first, with each successive layer containing more general data. The final layer should contain fallback values common to all nodes. This allows overrides to be applied at the appropriate level for clarity and debugging. Example 6-3 shows a simple, flat hierarchy demonstrating the idea.

Example 6-3. Flat, data-focused hierarchy

```
:hierarchy:
  - name: "Per-node data"
    path: "nodes/%{trusted.certname}.yaml"
```

```
- name: "Per-site data"
  path: "sites/%{facts.site}/test.yaml"

- name: "Per-OS defaults"
  path: "os/%{facts.os.family}.yaml"

- name: "Common data"
  path: "common.yaml"
```

In this hierarchy, values for every node are applied in the *common* level. Values that are specific to the operating system (OS), site, and node are stored in their specific files. The first level is the most specific, and the final level is the most general. Even though most hierarchies will have more levels, this concept holds true regardless.

Avoid unnecessary deep hierarchies

In our experience, it's best to keep your hierarchy as flat as possible. In a flat hierarchy, levels of the hierarchy are near the root and have no children of their own. A flat hierarchy tends to improve data organization and tends to reduce the amount of duplicated data you need to manage.

A deep hierarchy is one shaped like a tree, where each node in the hierarchy is a child of a higher priority node. The example shown below was a flat hierarchy with a clear separation of data type. The best way to identify a problematic deep hierarchy is the use of unrelated data in subdirectories below data. The following type of hierarchy will create many layers of duplication:

```
:hierarchy:
  - name: "Node data"
    path: "%{facts.tier}/%{facts.location}/%{facts.os.family}/%{facts.fqdn}.yaml"

  - name: "OS data"
    path: "%{facts.tier}/%{facts.location}/%{facts.os.family}.yaml"

  - name: "Location data"
    path: "%{facts.tier}/%{facts.location}.yaml"
```

A deep hierarchy will increase data redundancy the deeper you look. In the preceding example, there is likely to be a lot of commonality in your os.family hierarchy, but because this is nested under location and tier, it will be duplicated in each location tree. If you have three tiers (dev, stage, prod) and four locations (America, Europe, Asia, Africa) you'll end up duplicating the same value in 12 places. Larger structures could have hundreds of duplicates.

When data is duplicated across many locations, there's more chances of inconsistent updates. An error in one copy might not be noticed during testing, simply because you're unlikely to test the data for every possible combination of choices.

Deep hierarchies should contain data relevant to the top level

The benefit of deep hierarchies is that they facilitate flexibility in your values. Because nothing is shared between branches of the structure, you are free to set whatever value you want in each branch.

For cases in which a deep hierarchy is necessary, the subsections should reflect most specific to most general. This will use Hiera's lookup functionality and decrease duplicate data. Here's what the code looks like:

```
:hierarchy:
  - name: "Per-node data"
    path: "nodes/%{trusted.certname}.yaml"

  - name: "Per-site data"
    paths:
      - "sites/%{facts.site}/%{facts.service}/%{facts.cluster}.yaml"
      - "sites/%{facts.site}/%{facts.service}.yaml"
      - "sites/%{facts.site}.yaml"

  - name: "Per-OS defaults"
    path: "os/%{facts.os.family}.yaml"
```

There are benefits and drawbacks to both approaches, but there's a simple golden rule for evaluating the need for depth in a hierarchy: *the branches should be refinements of their parent.* If the data is not related to the data higher on the branch, it should be stored in a more general location.

Useful Hierarchy Levels

There are a few other common levels that you might want to add to your hierarchy, based on your needs. These hierarchies (and any of the hierarchies listed earlier) are by no means mandatory, but they can be useful to solve a few specific problems.

The accounts hierarchies

Most organizations keep user account data separate from service data. Account data rarely needs to be platform, location, or tier specific, and it is often managed by a completely different team.

The example that follows will handle not only project-specific and shared-account lists, but also the few cases in which an account might be platform specific: your

Linux *root* and Windows *administrator* accounts will have platform-specific properties.

Example 6-4. Accounts hierarchy level

```
- name: "Account data"
  paths:
    - "accounts/%{facts.project}.yaml"
    - "accounts/%{facts.os.family}.yaml"
    - "accounts/common.yaml"
```

Data in the accounts hierarchy can be stored as serialized data in a form ready to be consumed by the `create_resources()` function or a defined type you've created for account management. For more details, see "Converting Serialized Hiera Data into Resource Declarations" on page 165.

Should You Use Puppet as an Authentication Database?

If you have a small site or a small numbers of users, it might make sense to manage your user accounts with Puppet. It's fairly easy to add an account hash to Hiera, and it avoids having to set up additional infrastructure.

As your site grows, managing large numbers of users can become burdensome data entry. A few thousand users could add tens of thousands of resources to the Puppet catalog. In those situations, a few resources to configure traditional directory services (such as FreeIPA (*http://www.freeipa.org/*), Active Directory, or OpenLDAP) for user management and authentication would be more effective. Directory services provide a centralized source of authentication data, removing user management from ongoing maintenance.

Directory services update faster: when you revoke access to a user, they'll be locked out of nodes immediately. With Puppet user management, the user account will be available until the next Puppet convergence interval.

Use Puppet to ensure the *root* and *administrator* accounts as well as any accounts used by running services are available on the node in the event that your directory services are rendered unreachable.

Packages hierarchy level

Some people create complex hierarchies to track package information for each OS. We recommend that you place this data as close to the relevant branch as possible. The following example shows a quite powerful example:

```
- name: "Service data"
  paths:
```

```
        - "os/%{facts.service}/%{facts.os.family}.yaml"
        - "os/%{facts.service}/common.yaml"

    - name: "OS data"
      paths:
        - "os/%{facts.os.family}/common.yaml"
        - "os/%{facts.os.family}/packages.yaml"
```

You can use this hierarchy with the `create_resources()` function call to install OS base packages and service-specific packages. You don't need to write platform-specific code for that purpose since the platform differences (data) are entirely contained in Hiera.

If multiple modules need to install the same packages, you can store the packages in a common hash and then create a list of packages used by each module. This ensures that all necessary packages are installed without platform-specific data (package names) in the code.

Team hierarchy level

In some cases, it can be useful to have a hierarchy to manage data based on the team that owns a particular node or the service it provides. This tends to be common in large environments that provide Infrastructure as a Service (IaaS) and allow self-service provisioning. This can be a useful hierarchy level for storing team-specific security data, tags for data gathering, and monitoring alarm recipient information.

Team is a property that is difficult to determine programmatically, and will usually be maintained as a node property in your configuration management database or determined from node configuration and provided as a fact as shown here:

```
    - name: "Team owner"
      path: "project/%{facts.project}/team.yaml"
```

This hierarchy has some overlap with the accounts hierarchy. Keep account data out of the owner hierarchy. Instead, use the owner hierarchy to list what accounts should be added to a particular host.

Eliminating Data

Not all data belongs in Hiera. If data is managed in another system, it should be output from that system in JSON format for Hiera, or you can use a custom backend to directly query it.

The following list contains common kinds of data stored and managed with Hiera. We'll review what the alternative approaches are and when it makes sense to source this data elsewhere.

Hierarchy design

We already discussed hierarchy design at length. It's important to emphasize here that a good design will limit, not cause, data duplication. Any design that makes copypasta problems more likely needs to be revisited.

Package management

A common use for Hiera is to store package version information. If your organization already uses a package management solution such as Pulp, Katello, or Spacewalk, use Puppet to configure that data source rather than recreate the same data in Hiera.

User management

Users are another common source of data lists in Hiera. Deploying a directory service provides security and usability benefits over maintaining user accounts as static data in Hiera.

Service discovery

Service information tends to make up the bulk of data in Hiera, and it tends to create the most change requests in a complex environment. Questions such as *what servers are currently available in my web pool?* are better answered by service registries such as Consul or etcd.

Accessing Hiera

Puppet provides three approaches to retrieving data from Hiera:

- Automatic parameter lookups
- The `lookup()` function call
- The `puppet lookup` command-line utility

All three of these approaches can make exactly the same queries. Let's review how each one is used.

Automatic Parameter Lookups

Puppet automatically queries Hiera whenever it encounters a class parameter that has not been explicitly declared by using resource-style class parameters, as demonstrated here:

```
class example(
  String $version = 'installed',
  String $ensure  = 'running',
  Boolean $enabled = true,
```

```
) {
  #...
}

include 'example'
```

In this code example, we declare our example class with three variables. When we declare the class without providing values, Puppet will perform an automatic lookup for the variables in the namespace of the class requesting them (e.g., `example::ver` `sion`). It will use only the default values provided if the Hiera lookups fail.

A major advantage of automatic parameter lookups is that they force a tight coupling between your data keys and the code that consumes those keys. Each parameter is keyed in the namespace of the module. Puppet would perform a Hiera lookup for the `example::version`, `example::ensure`, and `example::enable` keys. We can see at a glance that these keys are used by the `example` class to set the named parameters.

Automatic parameter lookups provide a simple guarantee: if a class has parameters, you can set the value of those parameters in Hiera by simply by adding the correct key/value pair to your Hiera data. Explicit lookups have no such requirements, and often result in the creation of arbitrary, sometimes undocumented, key names in your hierarchy as developers try to share keys between multiple classes.

Defined types

Defined types do not support automatic parameter lookups. This is because classes are singletons and use only a single set of parameters. Defined types (and any other resource type) can be called with unique parameters multiple times.

You can still get data from Hiera by interpolating a parameter within a lookup key, as shown here:

```
define example_module::example_type(
  id      => lookup("example_module::service_hash::${title}::id'),
  version => lookup("example_module::service_hash::${title}::version'),
) {
  #...
}
```

Hiera Function Calls

If you want to explicitly retrieve a specific value from another namespace in Hiera, use the `lookup()` function call.

Key naming conventions

When performing explicit Hiera lookups, it's a good idea to follow the same key naming conventions as the automatic parameter lookup system. To have profile-specific class parameters, you could use the following style:

```
profiles::apache {
  class { 'apache':
    docroot => lookup('profiles::apache::docroot'),
  }
}
```

This approach helps keep the key in Hiera tightly associated with the location that calls the key. Being able to quickly identify and review the context in which a value is being used is invaluable when attempting to update the key. In this example, we named the key as if it were a parameter within the `profiles::apache` class before being assigned to the `docroot` parameter of the Apache module. Even though no such parameter exists, the intent and context where the key is used is clear at a glance in our Hiera data. For a contrasting example, look at this key and value combination:

```
wordpress_docroot: "/var/www/wordpress"
```

Do you notice in this case how much context and clarity of purpose is lost by a simple change of key name? Although the variable appears to be named clearly, it would be difficult to determine where the value is being used without performing an exhaustive search of the code. With the `profiles::apache::docroot` name, it's immediately clear which class is using the variable, making it trivial to track down the code it might affect.

By carefully selecting key names, you can significantly ease troubleshooting and maintenance of your hierarchy data.

Hash and array data merges

When retrieving a value from Hiera using the `lookup()` function call or automatic parameter lookup, Hiera will normally return the first key encountered. For queries of `Hash` and `Array` values, you can choose a merge behavior. When a merge attribute is specific, Hiera will retrieve keys and values from every level of each hierarchy and merge all keys into a single data structure. The merge function selected controls how the results are combined into a single data structure.

Data-driven class assignment

You can pass a Hiera lookup that retrieves a unique array of class names to the `include()` function for Hiera-driven class assignment:

```
lookup('classes', Array, 'unique', []).include
```

This code looks up array of entries for `classes` from every level of each layer of the hierarchy, flattens the results into a single array, and removes duplicates. The results will be exactly the same as calling `include` *module_name* for each array entry.

Automatic parameter lookup ensures that each class' parameters will also be looked up from Hiera. This allows for great flexibility with design of your roles and profiles.

Converting Serialized Hiera Data into Resource Declarations

Earlier in this chapter, we mentioned that in some cases it makes sense to store resource definitions in Hiera. Here's an example of how you can accomplish that.

1. A hash of data for each resource needs to be available in Hiera.

2. An automatic or explicit lookup call to get that data must be made.

3. The hash must be iterated over by `create_resources()` or `each()` to declare resources with each hash entry.

Here's an example hash of packages to be installed or removed:

```
packages:
  emacs:
    ensure: absent
    tag: base
  vim-enhanced:
    ensure: present
    tag: base
```

`package` is a hash data structure inside Hiera. Each key in the hash is a resource title. The values under that key are the attributes for the package resource. This data structure serializes the title and attributes for the package resource type. The following code example will iterate over this data structure:

```
$packages = lookup('packages')
unless( empty($packages) ) {
  create_resources('package', $packages)
}
```

The `create_resources()` function call creates package resources to install Vim and remove Emacs based on the data in Hiera.

This example demonstrates the use of the `create_resources()` function call. Although this can empower DRY development principles, you can also use it to store code in data, which violates the KISS and SoC principles of software development. For a discussion of these concerns, see "The create_resources() function" on page 124.

We have seen many cases in which people build wacky, overcomplicated abstractions that do nothing but make their code difficult to understand. It's a nightmare to maintain, and it's a nightmare for their successors to decipher.

Interpolation in Your Data

Variable interpolation of Hiera data is somewhat safer than variable interpolation in your hierarchy configuration. The data indexed under a module key should be used only by the module, so problems will not be created if the module isn't included in the node's catalog.

Puppet variables can be interpolated into values, either directly or via the `scope()` Hiera function call. Use variable interpolation to do handy value adjustment like this:

```
my::source: "https://example.com/pkg/myapp-%{my::version}.%{facts.arch}.rpm"
```

In this example, we interpolate the app version and the node's architecture to select the appropriate RPM package name.

Hiera allows interpolation of Puppet functions in values. This enables dynamic lookup features such as inline lookup with lookup() (*http://bit.ly/2Lg1stM*) and referencing other values with alias() (*http://bit.ly/2OVhM5d*).

The Built-In Backends

Hiera v5 includes four built-in backends. Usage of these backends is well documented, so this section instead focuses on what makes each backend appropriate for different situations.

YAML

YAML Ain't Markup Language (YAML) (*http://yaml.org*) is a human-friendly data serialization standard for all programming languages. YAML is one of the most user-friendly and least syntax-heavy data formats, for the following reasons:

- It provides a simple syntax for creating complex data structures.
- It uses indentation to determine the data grouping.
- It allows comments at every layer.
- It supports every data type native to Puppet.
- YAML import and export is available in every programming language.
- YAML values can reference other values, avoiding duplication of data.
- YAML can be tested for validity, and will throw an error if a reference is broken.

YAML's native support for comments and data references make it the most human-readable format available. The reference syntax makes it very clear that a particular key is being consumed elsewhere in the YAML data. This greatly simplifies management of large and complex data files. These benefits make it the best choice for beginners as well as most situations in which data is not generated programatically.

YAML has a few major disadvantages over other backends:

- YAML's loose format is parsed somewhat slower than the JSON backend. If you have a huge amount of data or a large number of nodes consuming your Hiera data, you might see a performance gain by switching to JSON.
- YAML supports several string delimiters, and multiple folding methods. Flexibility for multiple valid formats is seen (by some) as less readable than strict formats.
- YAML that is loaded and dumped will rarely match the original file. References might be converted to strings, and comments will be dropped.
- YAML's syntax can also cause surprises for people who aren't very familiar with the markup language. For example, quoting strings is optional; however, the string *true* or *ON* must be enclosed in quotes to avoid being interpreted as a Boolean true value.

JSON

JavaScript Object Notation (JSON) is a lightweight, text-based, language-independent data interchange format that has long outgrown its JavaScript origins to become a de facto standard. Many applications use it as both a data-interchange format and as a configuration language. JSON is supported natively by Hiera and can be used instead of or in addition to the YAML backend. Following are some of the advantages of JSON:

- JSON's syntax is simple and very strict. This makes it one of the fastest data sources for code to parse.
- JSON's popularity makes it easy to find or develop tools for managing JSON documents.
- JSON that is loaded and dumped will match the original file.

Outside of the ease of writing out and reading JSON programatically, JSON has many disadvantages vis-a-vis other backends:

- All values in JSON are quoted or enclosed in braces, making it difficult for a human to read.
- JSON does not allow comments.

- JSON supports only basic data structures: Number, String, Boolean, Array, Hash, and null (this could be considered a security feature).

- JSON does not provide the ability to reference one value from another value.

- JSON's strict schema means that human editing errors and frustration are more common.

- The extra syntax required to escape special characters can be difficult to learn and read.

Because of these limitations, JSON is most suitable for programatic export of data for use by Puppet. Humans find manual maintenance of JSON data files to be frustrating and prone to error.

HOCON

Human-Optimized Config Object Notation (HOCON) is a superset of JSON and Java Properties that aims to utilize JSON's semantic structure while being easy to use as a human-editable config file format. HOCON provides many advantages over JSON:

- HOCON can parse any valid JSON file.
- It allows comments.
- It can reference other values, avoiding duplication of data.
- It can be retrieved as a flat properties list, like Java properties.
- The specification is far more forgiving, so there are many ways to represent different types of data.

HOCON has a few disadvantages when compared to JSON:

- HOCON's friendly format is parsed more slowly than the JSON backend.
- The specification's flexibility allows disparate ways to represent the same data.
- It is less common so there are fewer language bindings for integrations.

HOCON is the configuration file format utilized by all new Puppet tools and features.

eYAML

Encrypted YAML (eYAML) is the only encryption backend built into Puppet. It uses standard YAML format files with plain-text keys and encrypted values, allowing use of the same format and tools as used for unencrypted data. We cover eYAML implementation and security considerations in more detail in "Encrypted Key/Value Storage" on page 170.

Custom Hiera Backends

You can add custom Hiera backends to any level of the hierarchy. There are a large number of custom backends for Hiera. We cover just a few of them here.

Hiera backends are actually fairly simple to write. If your specific needs are not satisfied by an existing backend, it's straightforward to create something that will. For more information on how to do that, check out "Writing new data backends" (*https://puppet.com/docs/puppet/latest/hiera_custom_backends.html*).

Before writing a custom backend, review the use case to ensure that your needs aren't better met by an ENC or a service discovery tool. We've outlined some of the more common backends in this section.

Database and NoSQL Engines

Several database and NoSQL backends exist for Hiera:

- hiera-mysql (*https://github.com/crayfishx/hiera-mysql*) and hiera-mysql-backend (*https://github.com/Telmo/hiera-mysql-backend*)
- hiera-psql (*https://github.com/dalen/hiera-psql*) ad hiera-postgres-backend (*https://github.com/adrianlzt/hiera-postgres-backend*)
- hiera-mongodb (*https://github.com/mcourtois/hiera-mongodb*)
- hiera-redis (*https://github.com/reliantsecurity/hiera-redis*)
- hiera-http (*https://github.com/crayfishx/hiera-http*) connects to CouchDB
- hiera-rest (*https://github.com/binford2k/hiera-rest*) connects to any REST API

Database and NoSQL backends allow you to query existing databases and NoSQL backends in Hiera, with all the benefits and drawbacks that entails. This approach makes data from other applications and systems available without having to export it as JSON and transfer it to the Puppet parser.

Text file formats for Hiera data can be easily stored in version-control repositories to track the history of changes. Changes to the files can trigger automatic testing of the data. Database systems might not provide a way to audit who made a change, why the change was made, and what the configuration was before the change was made. This can be a major drawback compared to using the built-in text formats as a data store.

If the catalog depends on data from the database, an unavailable backend will cause catalog compilation to fail. Because Hiera is a read-only query system, the database backend can utilize read-only replicas to reduce the risk of service disruption.

Do not mask exceptions or otherwise allow a Puppet catalog to be built without results from a failed Hiera backend. This catalog failure will prevent incorrect configurations from being applied that can cause service disruption.

Even though a database can be updated every second, never forget that Puppet won't see the changes until the next convergence interval for your environment (30 minutes by default).

Service Discovery Backends

Service registration and discovery services are highly responsive to service changes, and contain near-instantaneous information about node and service availability. The ability to query service discovery services makes it possible to get data directly from the services for use in Puppet catalogs rather than duplicating or exporting it for use by Hiera. Here are just a few of the service discovery backends available:

- puppetdbquery (*http://bit.ly/2w1bdY1*) allows searches of PuppetDB data
- hiera-zookeeper (*http://bit.ly/2w1IkuR*) allows queries for Zookeeper keys
- hiera-consul (*http://bit.ly/2MoCBt2*) allows queries for Consul services
- hiera-etcd (*http://bit.ly/2N8ljgm*) allows queries of Kubernetes/etcd keys
- hiera-aws (*http://bit.ly/2N6hQyK*) and hiera-cloudformation (*http://bit.ly/2N6KcJ9*) allow you to query AWS infrastructure

You should not use any of these Hiera backends to replace these services. Data provided by them to Puppet is available only on the succeeding Puppet convergence interval for your environment (30 minutes by default), which makes it suitable only for eventual convergence applications.

All the same limitations and concerns regarding database backends for Hiera apply to these tools, as well. Make sure that you understand how service failure will affect your Puppet runs and compiled catalog.

If you use Hiera to query a service discovery tool, plan for the impact that this will have on Puppet reporting and simulation. Service discovery tends to create a certain amount of configuration churn. If you don't have a way to quiesce changes induced by service discovery, it can become somewhat difficult to compare the results of two simulated runs because it might be unclear if a change is induced by code or by service inventory.

Encrypted Key/Value Storage

The following backends use public key cryptography to encrypt Hiera data:

- hiera-eyaml (*https://github.com/TomPoulton/hiera-eyaml*)
- hiera-eyaml-gpg (*https://github.com/sihil/hiera-eyaml-gpg*)
- hiera-gpg (*https://github.com/crayfishx/hiera-gpg*)

These backends are incredibly useful when managing passwords and other sensitive data with Hiera. The primary benefit of a cryptographic backend is that you can safely store sensitive data in a Git repository without having to severely restrict access to that repository or accept risks of the data leaking.

With hiera-gpg, the entire YAML file is stored in encrypted form. With hiera-eyaml, the YAML is stored in plain-text form, and only the values are encrypted. Because of this, hiera-eyaml is much better suited to revision control; changes to a value affect only the lines in your data files associated with the value—no other lines are changed. In contrast, updating any value with hiera-gpg will result in the entire file changing, which will tend to break `git blame` and `git diff`.

Because these backends use public-key cryptography, you can give the public key to anyone to encrypt values for storage. This allows contributors to add encrypted values to your data without giving them the ability to see other encrypted values.

Encrypted Hiera is not filesystem security

When working with either of these backends, it's important to understand how the data is handled. Hiera's encrypted backends solve the problem of storing secrets in shared source-code repositories. They do not keep the value encrypted in all parts of the process.

hiera-eyaml and hiera-gpg only encrypt data in the hierarchy. The data is *decrypted during lookup and inserted into the node's catalog in **plain-text** form.*

When a request is made to Hiera, the value is decrypted and returned to Puppet for use in the catalog build. In many cases, the decrypted value will be inserted into a catalog, either as a class parameter, a resource parameter, or the contents of a file.

There are many situations in which your encrypted data is stored to disk and available in decrypted form, including at least the following:

- The node caches the catalog to the disk containing the decrypted values.
- The values might be written out by Puppet to files that contain the decrypted value.

- The values might be used to execute commands (and available in memory).

In short, you cannot keep encrypted Hiera values secret from someone who has root or administrator access to the node that uses the decrypted values.

This is not a complete data-security solution. Use these tools to facilitate revision control of your sensitive data, but do not expect them to provide anything greater than protection from people reading the secrets from your source tree. The value will not be logged or included in the Puppet report unencrypted. But it's not possible to prevent a user with access to a signed Puppet client certificate of the target node from accessing the decrypted values.

There are a wide variety of modules offering data encryption with different trade-offs. But unless the encrypted data can be decrypted by the application using it, the unencrypted value will end up being used or stored somewhere on the node unencrypted.

Summary

In this chapter, we explored best practices relating to Hiera hierarchies and data. Proper backend selection, effective use of each layer, and careful design of the environment hierarchy can greatly simplify site maintenance while providing great flexibility in the source of data.

Here are the takeaways from this chapter:

- Consider your backend selection based on how you maintain the data.
- YAML provides a user-friendly format for human-edited files.
- Be aware of the security risks associated with variable interpolation.
- Reduce the size of your hierarchy as much as possible.
- Build appropriate abstraction layers, but avoid the trap of over abstraction.
- Enforce strong naming conventions in your Hiera data.
- Avoid explicit Hiera lookups in your modules unless absolutely necessary.
- Avoid designing module interfaces around variable interpolation.
- Hiera data can be used to identify or inform the roles and profiles used on your nodes.

## CHAPTER 7

Roles and Profiles

Roles and profiles is a best-practice design pattern for Puppet that provides an interface between your business logic and reusable Puppet modules. Profiles are reusable groups of modules that configure applications. Roles utilize one or more profiles to implement business- or site-specific requirements. When implemented properly, this design pattern greatly simplifies node classification in large, diverse organizations.

Roles and profiles were not a feature provided by Puppet; they are a design pattern originally described in Craig Dunn's blog post, "Designing Puppet (*http://www.craigdunn.org/2012/05/239/*)–Roles and Profiles" (*http://www.craigdunn.org/2012/05/239/*). It described an evolution of Puppet usage that became a community standard and recognized best practice.

Back in Chapter 1, we discussed how the single responsibility principle enables creation of reusable building blocks for modular design. Those principles help create great modules, but reusable modules need to be combined together to deploy a complete service or application. A functional service often consists of different software components, each of which already has modules designed to configure it. A profile is the larger building block that encapsulates a specific build of that service.

Without using roles and profiles, a node would receive a list of classes from either a node statement or an ENC. This has some significant limitations:

- An ENC can provide only classes and parameters: it cannot declare resources or defined types.

- An ENC cannot declare relationships between modules.

- The ENC won't provide feedback about or dependency checking for modules that work together.
- ENCs are configured from a database, the data of which is rarely under change-control or versioned.

Let's begin by briefly defining what profiles and roles actually are:

Profiles
> A profile utilizes reusable modules to create a specific software or service configuration (*technology stack*). It implements component-specific code and logic to customize the delivery. For a metaphoric example: *Profile "omelette" uses components "eggs," "peppers," and "cheese" with a site-specific cooking style.*

Roles
> A role codifies a business-level configuration based on a selection of profiles to add to the node. The role will persist even if components of the role are switched out. For example: *Role "western_breakfast" uses profiles "omelette," "hashbrowns," and "coffee," but could become healthier with iteration.*

There's nothing intrinsically special about roles or profiles. There is no feature in Puppet called a *role* nor is there one called a *profile*. Roles and profiles are modules, classes, or external data implemented the same as anything else in Puppet. Their special purpose comes only from wide adoption of this convention as an abstraction layer.

Roles

A role provides the complete specification of a node by selecting and influencing profiles. Roles codify your infrastructure, making it simpler to reproduce configurations by eliminating ad hoc node classification.

A role is simply a declaration of profiles. It establishes relationships between profiles and provides the shared context for a specific implementation.

Creating Readable Roles

Roles should be easy to identify and easy to read. Because the role specifies only the profiles to be used to build it, roles should be easily readable by people with no programming experience, regardless of the profile implementation. Let's examine some readable role declarations in the subsections that follow.

Role classes

The original role implementation and perhaps the most widely documented is the use of a class to declare a role. Example 7-1 demonstrates a role as implemented by a class.

Example 7-1. Role class example

```
class role::web_frontend() {
  include profile::yumrepos
  include profile::antivirus
  include profile::mysql::client
  include profile::webserver
  include profile::firewall
}
```

This example demonstrates the value of well-named modules and classes. The list of descriptive profiles makes it easy to understand which pieces come together to create a frontend web server. Because the role is independent of the profile implementation, profiles can be completely redesigned without affecting the role.

 Roles should always be clear and easy to read. Any role with more than a page of code likely needs to have its profiles refactored for more effective use.

Hiera-defined roles

Because roles should contain nothing more than a list of profiles to be applied, it is entirely possible to provide a role definition in Hiera. This requires three components:

- Node facts or the ENC must identify the role for each node.
- Hiera must use the role provided in the hierarchy.
- The node must include() classes provided by Hiera data.

The Hiera hierarchy for the environment should contain a level that utilizes the role provided, as shown here:

```
- name: "Role data"
  path: "roles/%{foreman_data.role}.yaml"
```

Be cautious about the source of your data if the role provides access to security-conscious data. A trusted fact or an ENC-provided value will be more secure than a fact provided by an untrusted node.

The role-specific data file should contain the list of profile classes to be applied:

```
---
classes:
  - 'profile::yumrepos'
  - 'profile::antivirus'
  - 'profile::mysql::client'
  - 'profile::webserver'
  - 'profile::firewall'
```

Assuming that classes are loaded from Hiera with `lookup('classes', Array, 'unique').include`, this web frontend hiera data file implements the same web frontend role shown in Example 7-1.

Design Roles for a Singular Use Case

There's really only one rule for role design: it should implement a single, specific node configuration. The only things different on two nodes of the same role should be their hostname, IP address, and such forth.

Because roles are a manifestation of an organization's specific nuances, there are no hard-and-fast rules for what a role should and shouldn't do. However, there are certain things to look for (*code smells*) that imply the role isn't scoped correctly:

The role utilizes parameter input to make implementation choices
Are you sure this isn't two different roles?

The role implements logic or resources directly
It's likely that the logic or resources are general enough to be within a profile used by other roles.

The role is longer than a paragraph
If the role includes many profiles, it's likely to reuse groups of profiles that could be shared with other roles.

The role implements explicit ordering of the profiles provided
Avoid ordering relationships between the profiles contained in the roles unless they are absolutely necessary. Many profiles source common modules, creating ordering conflicts.

The same role is applied to nodes that don't provide identical services
If a role builds nodes that provide different services, it contains deterministic, not declarative logic.

Any one of these code smells isn't necessarily bad, but if multiple of these conditions are true, it's very likely that the role should be broken down into profiles and rescoped.

Provide the Role for Use in Data Lookups

You can assign roles in a multitude of ways, but the most common and flexible ways to do so are the following:

- A custom fact identifies the role.
- The ENC provides the role as a node parameter.

Identifying node roles in the ENC

The classic use of ENCs was to supply a list of classes for a node to apply. The ENC administrator would select the classes to apply to each node, but this has a significant number of limitations:

- Most ENCs provide no change history or versioning of the node configuration.
- The ENC interface doesn't display dependencies or relationships between the classes chosen.
- The ENC configuration isn't available for use in acceptance tests.

Due to limitations of interaction between the node classifier and Puppet, a human would need to manually input all dependency classes into the node data. This invariably led to many one-off *snowflake* configurations with no change history. In contrast, assigning a single role from the ENC provides numerous benefits:

- Roles and profiles are stored and versioned in your code repository, providing a history of changes for review.
- Roles and profiles can express complex relationships with the full functionality of the Puppet language.
- Roles can be independently versioned and tested without the ENC.

If your site utilizes an external node classifier, configure the ENC to provide the role as a node parameter. The ENC then focuses solely on identifying the appropriate role for each node. This keeps similar nodes controlled through a common source, minimizing drift between nodes of the same type.

Roles provide businesss-specific implementations that you can select from the node classifier without knowledge of the Puppet module structure.

A long-term benefit of roles is that they are portable between ENCs. If you switch from one ENC to another (i.e., from Foreman to Puppet Enterprise), there's no need to migrate the class grouping from one ENC's internal structure to the other. This simplifies upgrades and allows the flexibility to test and migrate to a different node classifier.

Identifying node roles using node facts

If an ENC is not used, node roles can be provided by custom facts. The custom fact would determine the role based on information available to the node. Following is an overly simplified example of a custom fact providing the role to be assigned:

```
Facter.add(:role) do
  setcode do
    if Facter.value(:hostname) =~ /^(\w+)[0-9]+/
      role = $1
    else
      role = 'unknown'
    end
    role
  end
end
```

This custom fact determines the role by stripping digits and anything after them from the node's hostname. Most node-naming schemes are more complex, but this shows the general idea.

Deconstructing the hostname assigned to the node is perhaps the most common, but a custom fact can use any information available on the node—network interfaces, data from files, a cloud provider's metadata—anything available to the node can be used in the logic for role selection.

Profiles

Profiles are the place for business logic. They instruct how to combine modules to build real-world applications, and they provide a bridge between node data, site data, and general-purpose code in a reusable component that roles can utilize.

Profiles should contain all the logic necessary to build site-specific configurations. By centralizing that logic in a profile, the component modules remain free of the weirdness inherent in a given implementation. With the implementation customized within the profile, you need only look at a single layer. It also becomes much easier to use community and vendor-provided modules.

Profiles facilitate the SoC by defining the relationship between modules for a specific implementation scenario. This helps manage or eliminate module interdependencies. Without profiles, modules would be forced to be more monolithic in nature, and `include` or `require` every possible dependent module. As a result, it becomes difficult to test the code without testing every module that it requires. It's tremendously difficult then to change the dependent modules because they are referenced in too many places. The web of interdependencies can severely hamper refactoring efforts, thus slowing your ability to respond to changing requirements.

Instead, you can declare module dependencies in a profile. Because your application stack logic is handled in the profile, modules can be focused on a specific component implementation. Dependencies are reduced to the absolute minimum needed for the module to be successfully tested.

As an example, imagine for a second that your site has a policy of blocking all incoming network connections to all hosts. A web server will need TCP ports 80/http and 443/https open. Most Puppet modules that configure web servers software would not change the firewall (*SoC*). Rather than write your own module to do both, you could create a profile that does the following:

1. Accepts input for which TCP ports on which to accept connections.
2. Uses a public module like `puppetlabs/apache` to configure the web server to listen on those TCP ports.
3. Uses a public module like `puppetlabs/mysql` to configure a database for WordPress to use.
4. Uses a public module like `puppetlabs/firewall` to configure the firewall to allow connections on those TCP ports.

With this profile design, site-specific data is provided to off-the-shelf modules to create a specific configuration pattern. The profile becomes easy-to-read documentation of how this technology stack is configured without getting bogged down in the implementation details.

A Sample Service Profile

Let's examine a sample profile for the aforementioned standalone WordPress service, as shown in Example 7-2.

Example 7-2. Example WordPress profile

```
class profile::wordpress (
  $wp_hostname = $facts['fqdn'],
```

```
  $tcp_port   = 80,
  $directory  = '/var/www/html',
) {
  include firewall
  include apache
  include apache::mod::php
  include mysql::client
  include mysql::server

  class { 'mysql::bindings':
    php_enable => true,
  }

  class { 'wordpress':
    install_dir => $directory,
  }

  apache::vhost { $wp_hostname:
    port    => $tcp_port,
    docroot => $directory,
  }

  firewall { '010 Allow Wordpress Access':
    action => 'accept',
    proto  => 'tcp',
    dport  => $tcp_port,
  }
}
```

This example follows the basic pattern of a profile. It is not concerned with basic system configuration or any other application. It is concerned only with configuration of a WordPress instance.

There are no strict ordering dependencies between modules, although a few resources establish autodependency relationships. There are one or two classes that are parse-order dependent, but they are contained entirely within the profile and are not sensitive to the structure of other modules or the order in which this profile is evaluated versus other profiles.

Providing Actionable Data in Profile Parameters

The profile in Example 7-2 passes in only the hostname, port, and docroot parameters. This is because these three parameters are the ones for which this profile has specific logic.

You should use profile parameters when the parameter affects the behavior of the profile or when the data needs to be modified before being passed to the module. Using input parameters this way increases the versatility and DRY-ness of the profile. Rather than creating multiple profiles that are basically the same, use a single profile that can adjust its behavior based on the input supplied. Used in this manner, profile parameters provide the business- or site-specific data for a bespoke configuration.

For example, Consul service discovery uses the same configuration file for both clients and servers. The difference between the two is established entirely based on data in the service. In this case, a Consul profile might pass the `bootstrap_expect` and `join_wan` parameters to the Puppet-approved `KyleAnderson/consul` module only when the server option (node- or role-specific data) is enabled.

Unlike component modules, it is acceptable to look up site-specific data in a profile. Profiles implement business logic, so it's perfectly alright to have unique and site-specific logic in the profile. The guideline to create reusable code is relaxed at this level: your profiles should be closely tied to your specific technology stack and its data.

Profile-specific defaults can be provided in the profile's data, thus keeping the business logic and business data close together.

Shared Hiera data

This profile relies on Hiera automatic parameter lookups for configuration of its component modules. The values for any parameter other than hostname, TCP port, and docroot parameters will fall back to a Hiera data lookup in the module's namespace. To change the database password, set `wordpress::db_password` in the Hiera data files.

This usage of default values from Hiera provides a DRY configuration that can be shared by multiple profiles without repeating yourself. Although DRY is good, it is less readable. Puppet recommends supplying all component module parameters from the profile to aid in readability. DRY is good; readability is good—you should carefully balance the two!

Implementing Business Logic in Profiles

Profiles are the appropriate place for business logic. You can use this logic to act based on input parameters or node facts to build the profile appropriately for a given node type.

The following profile installs the appropriate antivirus based on the node's OS:

```
class profile::antivirus {
  case $facts['kernel'] {
    'Linux': {
      include clamav
    }
    'windows': {
      include eset_nod32
    }
```

```
      default: {
        warning("No antivirus available for ${facts['kernel']}")
      }
    }
  }
}
```

This profile contains the conditional logic based on the OS, allowing you to include include 'profile::antivirus' for every node, regardless of OS type.

Firewall rules might be owned by multiple teams at a large or diverse organization. That breakdown would be specific to the organization, so this is the kind of logic that belongs in a profile. Let's assume that there are security rules provided by corporate security, site-specific rules provided by the operations team, and application-specific rules necessary to allow the application to work. Here is a fairly arbitrary example that generates a list of firewall rules from data provided by three different teams:

```
class profile::firewall(
  Hash $site_rules     = {},
  Hash $app_rules      = {},
  Hash $security_rules = {},
) {
  use 'stdlib'

  class { 'iptables':
    # merge rules from three teams, rightmost value wins conflict
    rules => deep_merge($site_rules, $app_rules, $security_rules),
  }
}
```

The number of cases for which this is actually required should be fairly minimal; in most cases careful design of your data hierarchy should avoid the need to perform a hash merge data lookup. But if it needs to get weird, a profile is the appropriate place to encapsulate that weirdness.

It's really when you put the combination of business logic and conditional logic based around the node type that you can create very readable, DRY profiles. The following example realizes virtual yum repositories based on the OS release and the application to be deployed on the node:

```
class profile::yumrepos(
  String $application = 'no_match',
  Hash $repositories  = {},
) {
  # Virtualize all hiera-listed repositories
  create_resources('@yumrepo', $repositories)

  # Realize all common repos
  Yumrepo <| tag == 'global' |>

  # Realize os-specific repos
  Yumrepo <| tag == "${facts['os']['name']}${facts['os']['release']['major']}" |>
```

```
    # Realize application repos
    Yumrepo <| tag == $application |>
}
```

This example demonstrates how to implement the business logic of a specific repository structure while tracking the needs of different operating systems, all while utilizing the common `yumrepo` resource.

Defining Module Relationships in Profiles

Profiles are the place to create relationships between modules and their dependencies. By creating intermodule relationships at the profile level, your modules neither need to be concerned with how their dependencies are satisfied nor how they relate to other modules.

Remember: profiles use site-specific data to assemble working services based on business logic. There is absolutely nothing wrong with creating relationships in your profiles when needed. If the installer for a component module requires Java, the profile should include Java and order it before the component module. This allows the component module's requirements to be satisfied differently for different use cases.

Just as with module development, it's a good idea to keep your profiles self-contained for a singular use case. Try to avoid creating relationships between profiles in your profiles; instead, try to make your profiles as self-sufficient as possible, and use roles to establish profile relationships where necessary.

Keep in mind that in many cases, it's not necessary to create relationships between modules. As we saw in "A Sample Service Profile" on page 179, it is often sufficient to simply add modules to your profile. Use relationships to identify dependencies, not to attempt to control the order. Attempts to specify ordering will only create unnecessary conflicts.

Creating Metaprofiles to Group Configurations

If you find that certain combinations of profiles are common, it's both reasonable and effective to create a *metaprofile* that connects the various profiles. Especially if there are a few parameters that would influence the implementation of each of those profiles, a metaprofile provides a great way to group together combinations by business logic.

The example that follows utilizes business logic for a standard web server build, making use of the profiles described previously. It provides a common technology stack without stipulating the specific usage details (e.g., WordPress, static content, whatever) that a specific profile can supply.

```
class profile::webserver(
  Boolean $external = true,
) {
  include profile::yumrepos
  include profile::antivirus
  include profile::apache
  include profile::mail::client
  if( $external ) {
    include profile::firewall
  }
}
```

This metaprofile provides a reusable combination of profiles that a specific application profile or role could apply. In doing so it provides a useful building block for role composition.

 A role is a metaprofile with a single use. This metaprofile isn't usable as a role because it doesn't include the unique part of the role— the actual application being served.

Let's next discuss the good and bad, things to do, and things to watch out for when using metaprofiles.

Avoid creating a base profile

It's a common rookie mistake to create a *base* metaprofile that will be assigned to every node. The expectation is that this base profile would handle all basic system configuration tasks, security policy, and postprovisioning tasks. Creating a metaprofile like this can definitely be useful, but it can also constrain you quite a bit.

The problem with base profiles is that because every node uses them, people tend to hack every one-off configuration into the base profile. Instead of having a reusable component that can be utilized, it quickly becomes a deep web of interlaced dependencies that are impossible to untangle. Yes, profiles are supposed to encapsulate the quirks of a specific implementation. Base profiles often quickly become the home for every quirk and one-off configuration. In short, it recreates the monolith that you were trying to avoid.

 A profile should provide a single implementation. If you have conditionals for wildly different use cases in the same profile, you should separate them.

Encapsulate one-off configurations in new profiles

Instead of hacking quirks for multiple use cases into a common base, you should create a new profile that contains the specific quirk. Allow each role or metaprofile to select which implementation to use.

```
class profile::webserver::nginx() {
  include 'profile::webserver'
  include 'nginx'
}
```

Designing an Appropriate Profile Structure

How do you structure your profiles when you have a lot of service profiles that share the same basic design patterns? By breaking them down into the smallest reusable components.

Implement the smallest usable component

The WordPress profile we created in Example 7-2 installs the web server and the database on the same node. In any realistic production service that functionality would be provided by multiple roles. By splitting the WordPress profile into its two major components, we can easily create three roles containing different combinations of those profiles. We have standalone MySQL and WordPress roles for larger scale production hosts, and and a combined role for test nodes.

Why Didn't We Create an Apache Profile?

There isn't a hard-and-fast rule as to what should be a separate profile. To support both Apache and NGINX instances, create WordPress profiles for each server type and have each of them include the appropriate web server. The main reason for this approach is that WordPress requires a fairly specific web server configuration to work correctly. As a general guideline, the more specific the dependency needs to be tailored to your profile, the more it makes sense to integrate the dependency into your profile.

Profile creation is an art, not a science. There isn't one single approach that will be correct for every site, every business, every need. What is important is that your profiles are easy to understand and reuse for multiple scenarios.

Handling multiple instances

Many profiles will need to implement multiple instances of something. Because a profile is implemented by a class singleton, you cannot declare it multiple times. Yet a single node can, for example, host multiple Java applications in a single Tomcat appli-

cation server. Each application will likely use additional `tomcat::instance` and `tom
cat::service` instances.

There are two different approaches you can use to solve this problem:

- Create a unique profile for each application instance that does the following:
  — Includes the Tomcat profile (which will occur only once)
  — Configures the application
- Accept array or hash input that specifies a list of instances to create so that a single profile can create the entire list of instances.

Each of these approaches has different advantages and disadvantages. Choose the one that is easier for you to maintain based on how you handle the data.

You can use both approaches together. For example, you could create different profiles that configure different database types. These profiles could all accept a list of nodes involved in database replication.

A profile for each service instance

With this structure, each service instance has its own profile, and each profile is independent of the other service profiles. Common dependencies can be implemented by a shared profile, whereas relationships are custom to the instance profile. This is the appropriate solution when you have a limited number of well-known service instances. Using Tomcat as an example, there would be a unique profile for each application instance, as demonstrated here:

```
class profile::tomcat::titleservice() {
  include 'profile::tomcat'

  tomcat::instance { 'titleservice':
    catalina_home => '/opt/tomcat',
    catalina_base => '/opt/titleservice/root',
  }
}
```

This approach tends to be highly flexible; each profile can have unique dependencies and logic. This provides a lot of flexibility while remaining fairly DRY. You can use resource-style class declarations in the profile. Each instance profile includes the shared service profile, which avoids duplicate resource declaration errors even with class-style resource declaration.

Creating instances from a data example

If your profile needs to create multiple instances of a service using a single profile, you can pass a list of instances as an array or hash using a `profile` class parameter, as illustrated in the example that follows. This approach works best when you don't know in advance what instances are needed and want to allow another group to specify them.

```
class profile::tomcat(
  Hash $instances = {}.
) {
  include 'profile::tomcat'

  $instances.each |$name, $values| {
    tomcat::instance { $name:
      catalina_home => $values['catalina_home'],
      catalina_base => $values['catalina_base'],
    }
  }
}
```

This approach tends to keep your code DRY—the same profile creates all of your instances from a single iteration loop. The disadvantage of this approach is that all of your instances need to be fairly generic. There's limited ability to customize each instance outside of the data attributes provided. Handling special cases with this type of profile will often result in *code in data* problems that are difficult to test and painful to debug.

Testing Roles and Profiles

Test cases can help ensure the stability of your profiles and catch common problems prior to the release of your code. Utilizing role-based node configuration facilitates testing without an ENC. It's fairly straightforward (and implemented automatically by development kits) to apply a role to a test node using the `puppet apply` command.

We don't cover how to implement unit and acceptance tests, because they are identical to the ones added to any component module. Instead, the following sections will provide guidance on the specifics of role and profile testing.

> For simplicity of language we refer only to profiles in the remainder of this section. Every statement made about profiles is true of roles (single-purpose metaprofiles), as well.

Validating Profiles by Using Unit Tests

Unit tests verify that each class, defined type, and resource used to build the profile are added to the catalog correctly. It validates that the Puppet catalog will contain resources to do what is expected. This primarily helps identify code mistakes and regression failures—where a profile change stops providing an expected feature.

Profiles should not reimplement all of the test cases created for the profile's component modules. Instead, it seeks to test that each of those modules is declared correctly.

The following example tests the WordPress profile built in Example 7-2.

```
context 'with default parameters' do
  # Ensure no parameters are supplied for this test context
  let(:params) do
    {}
  end

  # Declare the dependency classes with the profile's default values
  it { is_expected.to
       contain_class('mysql::bindings').with('php_enable' => true) }
  it { is_expected.to
       contain_apache__vhost(facts['fqdn']).with('port' => '80') }
  it { is_expected.to
       contain_class('wordpress').with('install_dir' => '/var/www/html') }
end
```

This example tests that a profile would invoke the component modules correctly, without recreating any of the tests of those modules. It can do this without knowing the internal structure of the modules that comprise the profile. Unit tests validate that the catalog will be built without error and ensure the stability of your profile interfaces.

Confirming Profile Implementation with Acceptance Tests

Acceptance tests apply the profile to the node and then verify that the expected changes are made. These tests measure the state before and after the test to confirm that the real-life expected results are visible on the node after Puppet has applied the profile.

You should supply each profile with an acceptance test specific to that profile. The goal of a profile acceptance test is not to reimplement all the tests created for the component modules. Instead, it should test the combined impact of the modules working together as a whole. The acceptance test provides end-to-end validation ensuring that the profile creates the model it was designed to implement.

At a minimum, test that the service is running as expected and that it responds as expected by creating a Beaker acceptance test for the profile.

The following example tests the WordPress profile built in Example 7-2.

```
# test that the profile applies idempotently
it 'should apply a second time without changes' do
  @result = apply_manifest(manifest)
  expect(@result.exit_code).to be_zero
end
```

```
# Make sure Apache is running with configured port
describe service('httpd') do
  it { is_expected.to be_running }
  it { is_expected.to be_enabled }
end
describe port('80') do
  it { is_expected.to be_listening }
end
```

This example tests that the httpd process is actively running and listening on the specified TCP port. This validates that the profile's parameters have been applied correctly, and it can do it without knowing the internal structure of the modules that comprise the profile.

You can refer to the documentation and guides for Beaker acceptance testing (*https://github.com/puppetlabs/beaker-rspec*) for more information.

Summary

The roles and profiles design pattern applies business logic to create site-specific configurations utilizing generic component modules.

The key takeaways from this chapter are as follows:

- Roles provide complete node configuration by selecting appropriate profiles.
- Profiles implement and encapsulate business logic.
- Profiles provide *opinionated* use cases for *unopinionated* component modules.
- Use class ordering and containment in the profile to ensure that modules are applied in the correct order.
- There is no golden rule for profile design: they should reflect the needs of your specific organization.
- Use SoC and single responsibility principle as guiding principles for profile design.

## CHAPTER 8

Node Classification

The term *node classification* refers to both the tools and process used to supply a role, individual classes, and node parameters used to customize the catalog for a node.

Classifiers take many forms. Large sites typically employ a database or console for node classification. Smaller sites will often use Hiera or the Puppet language to classify nodes. The best solution is always site specific.

In this chapter, we look at a number of classification strategies. The goal of this chapter is not to redocument all of the available classifiers, but to look at the available options and specific considerations and best practices behind each one.

What Data Should the Node Classifier Provide?

As we discussed in Chapter 1, node classification provides data used to customize the model to produce a catalog specific to a node. Let's take a quick look at the kind of data that is commonly set with a node classifier.

Roles and Profiles

Node classification's original and most common purpose is to declare classes to be applied on the node. This selection can be direct and explicit or indirect through the assignment of roles and profiles.

> A role doesn't need to be a class. The role could be used to alter the Hiera hierarchy appropriately for inclusion of classes from a Hiera array.

The recommended approach is to assign a single role class, as discussed in Chapter 7; however, a classifier can also assign individual classes or profiles a-la-carte if necessary. Direct class or profile assignment remains common in environments where responsibility for Puppet is split between multiple teams, such as when security has direct ownership of some Puppet data, or in environments that offer self-service node classification.

Node-Specific Data

You can use node-specific data provided by an ENC or node facts to customize the Hiera hierarchy or Puppet catalog. The most common use case for node parameters is to modify the Hiera hierarchy used for lookup. Some of the more commonly used values include the following:

- Hardware details such as node type, CPUs, interfaces, and storage
- Tier, such as whether it's a prod or dev node
- Site, the physical or virtual location of the node
- Contact information for node maintenance

Although data can be provided by either source, there are two points of concern for selection of the data source:

Information ownership
> Even though node information can be provided by either node facts or an ENC, you should take care to avoid having an external data source attempt to provide values that a node knows better, such as how many CPUs are available on the node. Databases will always have drift or replication issues that delay information updates. Source details of the node hardware and other fixed attributes come from node facts.

Security controls
> Node facts are provided by the node and can be altered by someone with superuser access to the node, whether approved or malicious. ENCs provide a centralized data source for security-sensitive values in environments in which superuser access to the node is shared, intentionally or otherwise.

Node Statements

Node statements are one of the oldest methods of classification for Puppet. They are simple classifiers based on the client certificate name, which makes them suitable for only the smallest sites.

The main benefit of node statements is their simplicity. They are available in a basic Puppet installation with no other infrastructure, as demonstrated in the following example:

```
node 'db011.example.com' {
  include roles::database
}
```

Node statements allow assignment of a block of code based on the node's name, which defaults to the certificate name, which defaults to the node's fully qualified domain name (FQDN). Typically, node statements are combined with semantic hostnames so that the purpose of a node can be derived from its name.

 Name-based assignment won't work well for any site that tracks nodes using serial number, MAC address, or other unique attributes. However, sites with complex tracking needs will have infrastructure available for an ENC to query, thus removing this need.

Although simple and easy to use, node statements have a large number of limitations:

- The node statement will match only a single value (usually the node FQDN).
- Only one matching node statement will be applied.
- Node statement blocks cannot use parameters except those provided by an ENC (which would obviate the need for node statements).
- Variables declared in the node statement are not available to top-level code outside the node statement (manifests in the *manifests/* directory of the environment).
- Variables used in the node statement are evaluated immediately and thus cannot be overridden by data lookups—a feature that's possible only in the delayed evaluation of declared classes.
- Node statements are all-or-nothing—enabling them requires that every node have a matching node statement (or node default definition).

As you will see through this section, node statements have a number of major limitations. Except when building small demonstration or isolated test environments, any of the other classifiers presented in this chapter will prove to be much more flexible and powerful.

Node Statement Matching

For review (because we touch on it in the sections that follow), nodes are matched by node statements in the following order:

1. Complete match
2. Regex match
3. Partial match
4. Default statement applied

Only the first match from this list is applied.

Default node statement

If any node statements exist, every node must match a node statement, or the catalog compilation will fail. Therefore, if you utilize even a single node statement, make certain to have a node default statement that will be applied to nonmatching nodes, as shown in the following:

```
node default {
  # this can be empty
}
```

Regular expression node statements

Node statements permit the use of regex statements to match groups of nodes. This is commonly used to classify nodes using a semantic hostname pattern. This can be useful for easily adding nodes of the same type without having to create node statements for each new node. The following example shows the code for this:

```
node /^web\d+[13579]/ {
  # odd numbered web servers are Blue pod
}
```

Because the regex language can be difficult to read, always put a comment in or above a regex explaining what you expect the regex to match.

> The behavior when multiple regex node statements match the same node is not guaranteed. One will be selected apparently randomly.

Because regexes are checked only after a complete name match is not found, create a node statement for a node's complete name to exclude it from a group that matches a regex.

Partial node match

Node statements permit the use of partial FQDN statements to match nodes. During this step, Puppet will strip the rightmost sections of the name (up to the next period) and then check for a complete match. This is commonly used to classify nodes using a hostname pattern where the domain name could differ, as shown here:

```
node 'puppet-server' {
  # will match 'puppet-server.example.com', 'puppet-server.example.net', etc
}
```

As a partial match intends to match against a missing part of the data, these statements are inherently unreadable. Always put a comment in or above the match reminding the reader that it is intended to match multiple domains. Otherwise, it might be either misunderstood as a mistake and fixed or copied when creating another node because the person copying it doesn't realize the consequences of a partial match.

Replacing Node Inheritance

Puppet versions prior to 4.0 allowed node statements to inherit from one another. You should avoid using node inheritance, even with older versions of Puppet. This was a source of significant difficulty and was made obsolete by the *roles and profiles* design pattern even for older versions of Puppet.

Let's review an example conversion of node inheritence to the *roles and profiles* design pattern.

Node classification with inheritance

The most common inheritance design pattern is to specify a base node, a series of node statements that extend the base with specific services (such as an Apache node, a Tomcat node, a MySQL node), and a node that performs the final service specific configuration tasks, as shown in Example 8-1.

 This older syntax has been deprecated and no longer works in any supported version of Puppet.

Example 8-1. Node inheritence example

```
# Base used by numerous profiles
node base {
  include 'ntp'
  include 'security'
}

# Web node profile extends base
node web inherits base {
  include 'apache'
  include 'php'
}
```

```
# Database node profile extends base
node db inherits base {
  include 'mysql'
}

# These nodes use existing node groups
node www1.example.com www2.example.com inherits web { }
node db1.example.com db2.example.com inherits db { }

# This node inherits web, but has to add db manually
node www-dev1.example.com inherits web {
  include 'mysql'
}
```

Even though this example was greatly simplified to keep it on a single page, in practice this often becomes a large sprawling mess of inconsistent updates. Besides becoming difficult to maintain, it has a few major limitations:

- Node definitions do not support multiple inheritance, so it isn't possible to create web and db profiles and include them both.
- Inheritance also affects variable lookup scope, causing node assignment changes to affect code evaluation unpredictably.

There is nothing worse than unpredictable variable values and resource defaults that leak in unpredictable manners. Seriously, you'd be staring at the same code applied to two identical nodes trying to figure out why they got different catalogs. It was always a rabbit-chasing exercise and never lent itself to being fixed permanently. That's why this approach has been abandoned.

Node classification using roles and profiles

The *roles and profiles* design pattern allows you to assign multiple profiles to the node without changing the code's scope or parent module. You can easily convert any node inheritence design to the *roles and profiles* pattern by following these steps:

1. Convert each node inheritence statement (something named `inherits` *name*) to a profile.
2. Convert each node matching statement (something that matched a given `cert name`) to a role.
3. Replace the node matching statement with a role selection.

So, the first thing we do is convert each inherited node statement to a profile:

```
class profiles::base {
  include 'security'
  include 'ntp'
}
```

```
class profiles::web {
  include 'apache'
  include 'php'
}

class profiles::db {
  include 'mysql'
}
```

Next, we convert each matching node statement to a role:

```
class roles::webserver {
  include 'profiles::base'
  include 'profiles::web'
}

class roles::devserver {
  include 'profiles::base'
  include 'profiles::web'
  include 'profiles::db'
}
```

With this approach you can simply apply `roles::devserver` to a node, making use of any other profiles. There's no linear map of single inclusion to maintain or work around. Each role implements a site-specific configuration by declaratively including the relevant profiles.

Finally, we use `node` statements to assign roles to the nodes to complete the conversion:

```
node 'www1.example.com', 'www2.example.com' {
  inlude 'roles::webserver'
}

node 'www-dev1.example.com' {
  inlude 'roles::devserver'
}
```

In several easy steps, you've just converted the old node inheritence pattern into the modern *roles and profiles* best practice. Further evolutions like removing kitchen-sink *base* profiles will be easy to accomplish after you finish this migration.

Node Parameters Within Node Blocks

When using node statements, node properties such as the location and tier of a host can be set as global variables within the node block. Because ENC properties are presented as top-scope variables, this offers a seamless way to transition to an ENC in the future.

If node properties are set this way, avoid adding any code that might rely on these properties outside the node statement. The rest of your site manifests are a higher scope than the node statement. Node properties will not be visible outside of the node scope. These properties will be visible to classes declared within the node scope, but not to classes declared within the top scope. This scoping restriction applies to Hiera lookups performed outside of the node scope, as well.

The practical implication of variables declared within the node scope is that top scope can be used for only very basic operations, such as setting resource defaults. You can no longer rely on it to include a base set of classes.

Fact-Based Classification

Facts are a simple way to pass node-provided data to a classifier and declared classes. They appear within the $facts[] hash and are available for interpolation in both the Hiera hierarchy and Puppet language modules.

Fact-Based Role Assignment

It's possible to declare classes in a manifest based on a fact supplied by the node, as demonstrated in the following:

```
if $facts['role'] {
  include $facts['role']
}
```

Because the include command accepts arrays as an input, a-la-carte profile provisioning can also be supported using this method:

```
if $facts['profiles'] {
  include $facts['profiles']
}
```

Although fact-based assignment can be powerful for environments where nodes self-select the Puppet model, it decentralizes node management in a way that will reduce your ability to restructure your code or change your interfaces in the future. This will also complicate attempts to migrate to other classification systems. This is only practical in environments in which Puppet is a smaller piece of a large node orchestration platform.

Security and Fact-Selected Roles or Profiles

Role and profile declaration from facts permits node owners to generate a catalog for any node type in your infrastructure. If you use this approach, you should carefully consider what data might be exposed.

This approach moves security and node classification out to the edges, to the nodes themselves.

For example, imagine a case in which Hiera stores database credentials for your web application. If a user was able to add the web application profile to their catalog, they could easily recover these credentials. Virtually any security-sensitive data is vulnerable to such attacks.

Mitigating the risk by using trusted facts

If you carefully control how node certificates are signed, you can employ the example shown in Example 6-2 to utilize a role stored in the node's signed Puppet certificate. This would be a very effective way to decentralize role assignment without an ENC.

If you make use of certificate authorities with autosign enabled, you'll gain nothing from this change. Anybody can generate a certificate with any role they want and get it signed.

Fact-Based Hiera Classification

A more powerful and more common approach is to classify nodes using Hiera data selected by node-provided facts. You can use this approach instead of, or in combination with, an ENC.

The implementation of a Hiera node classifier is fairly simple. A list of classes is stored in Hiera, a lookup is performed, and the classes returned by the lookup are applied to a node. This is typically used with a certname level in the hierarchy so that classification can be managed on a per-node basis.

Fact-based classification using Hiera is accomplished by the following steps:

1. Utilize node facts to adjust the Hiera hierarchy appropriately.
2. List classes to be declared in Hiera data.
3. Include classes from the Hiera data in a manifest.

Customizing Hiera hierarchy using facts

This topic was already covered in depth in Chapter 6, but let's refer to the following example that uses both default and custom facts:

```
:hierarchy:
  - name: "Node-specific data"
    path: "fqdn/%{facts.fqdn}.yaml"
```

```
  - name: "Role data"
    path: "roles/%{facts.role}.yaml"

  - name: "Site data"
    path: "sites/%{facts.site}.yaml"

  - name: "OS-specific data"
    path: "os/%{facts.os.family}.yaml"
```

Listing classes in Hiera data

We can add classes to the preceding example at multiple levels of the hierarchy.

1. Classes for the specific node in the *fqdn/* data file
2. Classes for the node's role (from a custom fact) in the *roles/* data file
3. Classes for the node's site (from a custom fact) in the *sites/* data file
4. Classes for every node of a given OS family in the *os/* data file

Following is the basic role definition in YAML format:

```
---
# classes for the webserver role
classes:
  - 'profiles::base'
  - 'profiles::web'
```

Declaring classes from Hiera data

The typical approach is to use the `include()` function call on the results of a Hiera lookup of `classes`, like so:

```
lookup('classes', Array, 'unique', []).include
```

Always supply a default value in case the `lookup()` call fails.

Node Parameters with Hiera Classification

Nodes are commonly given node-specific parameters during classification. It would appear that a circular dependency is created by storing these values in Hiera. Hierarchy lookups are based on these values, but these values are supposed to be sourced from Hiera lookups. How do you address this problem?

There are two solutions to this problem:

- Use only facts to customize the Hiera hierarchy.
- Provide the node values early in the classes being applied.

Let's review how this would work:

1. The class that retrieves these node parameters uses automatic parameter lookup or explicit `lookup()` calls to retrieve the node parameters.

2. The Hiera data file containing node data is read from a Hiera hierarchy level that uses node facts (such as `certname`).

3. Hierarchy levels utilizing the node data will be available after the node data values are read.

Let's look at an example that ties this self-referential lookup together:

```
:hierarchy:
  - name: "Node-specific data"
    path: "fqdn/%{facts.fqdn}.yaml"

  - name: "Role data"
    path: "roles/%{node_data::role}.yaml"
```

Within the data file accessible from node facts, we can define values to be used within the hierarchy:

```
---
node_data::role: 'webserver'
```

Finally, we use a module to source the node values and make them available for the Hiera hierarchy:

```
class node_data(
  String $role,
) { }

class roles::any_role() {
  require 'node_data'
}
```

Understanding the time-order nature of the lookups makes what would appear to be circular references easy to resolve.

Avoiding Node Data in Manifests

You should avoid using free-standing manifests (such as *site.pp*) to source and manipulate node data. Although this appears easy, you are creating an implicit interface that must be used by every module. Top-level manifests are shared by every node and every module in that environment. Any changes to that manifest will affect every node's catalog. You will find it difficult if not impossible to adapt this interface as needs change.

A node data module can be selected by a role, and it can be versioned. This allows multiple node data mechanisms to coexist.

The SoC philosophy makes it clear that a module whose purpose is to look up node data is the correct approach. The KISS philosophy applies here, as well. Contain all your application logic in your roles and profiles, and limit node classification data to one or more modules specific to that goal.

By creating a module that provides the interface for node data aquisition, you can tie the interface to the version of the module. You can test a new module and node data interface without breaking modules that depend on the older interface. Doing node data mapping in a single module (rather than spread out across manifests and classes) keeps it simple to debug, and easy to understand. This relegates your classification logic to the responsibility of determining what roles and profiles should be applied.

Serverless Classification

In a serverless Puppet environment, where the Puppet codebase and data are synchronized to every node, the node is responsible for self-classification. You can do this using any of the techniques used with a server or by passing the node classification directly on the command line:

```
$ puppet apply -e 'include roles::webserver'
```

This kind of implementation requires that each node is configured knowing what role to request. Using node facts to customize the Hiera hierarchy as discussed in "Fact-Based Hiera Classification" on page 199 provides a significantly more flexible and powerful implementation for self-classification.

ENCs

There are many ENCs available for use with Puppet. We review a few of them here and examine what makes them an appropriate choice.

The most important consideration for a node classifier are the benefits it provides to the teams managing the nodes; for example:

- GUI for node management
- Node inventory and reporting features
- APIs for automated node management
- Role-based access control (RBAC)

- Change management and history

These features make it possible for self-service provisioning and oversight by users who are not suitable for or capable of managing Puppet code.

What Data Can an ENC Provide?

The ENC can provide three types of data about a node. Let's take a quick look at these data types and how you can best use them in node classification.

Class list (node role)

The most common purpose of an ENC is to assign classes to a node. As the usage of ENCs has evolved with practice, the recommended approach is to assign a single role class as described in Chapter 7; however, a classifier can also assign individual classes a-la-carte if so desired.

Node parameters

There are often a number of node-specific properties that cannot be provided by node facts because they might not be available or knowable by the node. As with node facts, you can use these parameters for Hiera hierarchy and Puppet catalog customization. The more commonly used values include the following:

- Tier, such as whether it's a prod or dev node
- Site, the physical or virtual location of the node
- The state of the node for deployment purposes
- Contact information for node maintenance

You'll notice that most of this information is tied to inventory or resource management.

Puppet environment

The node classifier can override the Puppet environment requested by the node. This allows Puppet Enterprise or infrastructure management tools like Foreman to dynamically assign groups of nodes without making configuration changes on each node.

> It's important to be aware that the ENC-supplied Puppet environment is authoritative. If the classifier supplies *environment*, there is no way to override that from the node. This can complicate the use of Puppet environments for ad hoc testing.

There won't be a best-practice choice of whether to assign environments from the ENC because this will differ greatly depending on your infrastructure and tools available. Concerns about environment management and how to handle testing are discussed in depth in Chapter 9.

Puppet Management Consoles

Some ENCs are tightly integrated with Puppet and thus offer features above and beyond basic node management. Let's take a brief moment to review a few of the consoles available for Puppet.

Puppet Enterprise console

The Puppet Enterprise product offers the following capabilities:

- Provides both an ENC and a Puppet-supported console for Puppet node management. This is one of the prime differentiators between Puppet Community and Enterprise versions.
- Authorizes users based on granular RBAC that integrates cleanly with Active Directory and Lightweight Directory Access Protocol (LDAP) authentication.
- Uses a group model for node classification: classes and node parameters can be assigned to every node, to a group of nodes, to a subgroup, or directly to a single node. Additionally, a rules-based node classifier enables classification based on node facts or exported resources to assign classes.
- Generates a console overview of nodes in the infrastructure, including last run status and inventory. Node events can be inspected. Reports can be generated based on data from the Puppet convergence reports.
- Provides a robust RESTful API for managing nodes, making it fairly simple to integrate with external automation systems and node inventories.
- Includes a GUI for ad hoc execution and exploration of nodes using Puppet. The Puppet agent on a node can be invoked at any time from the Console.

With Puppet version 3, there were significant differences between the way Puppet Enterprise and Open Source Puppet were deployed to your infrastructure. Puppet 4 Unified Packaging uses the same basic installation layout as Puppet Enterprise, making conversion from and use of open source code much simpler.

We encourage you to consider licensing Puppet Enterprise. It's a great product, and purchasing a license helps to support ongoing development of Puppet for both Enterprise and Open Source users.

Puppet Dashboard

The Puppet Dashboard was an early proof of concept for what evolved to become the Puppet Enterprise console. Development was discontinued years ago, and community support has stopped as the ENC features no longer matched well with Puppet feature development. You should consider one of the other console solutions instead.

Inventory and Infrastructure Management ENCs

The following products are infrastructure management frameworks that happen to provide node data to Puppet through the ENC interface. Although these are less tightly integrated with Puppet, they provide features and functionality available both before and beyond what Puppet can provide to a node.

Foreman

Foreman is a complete lifecycle management tool for physical and virtual servers. In addition to providing an external node classifier for Puppet, Foreman provides inventory management, physical machine provisioning (PXE), virtual machine provisioning, cloud provisioning, and reporting services.

Its node classification system is robust. Foreman supplies a group-based class and node parameter inheritance model, similar to the model offered by Puppet Enterprise. Classes are autodiscovered but you can hide them. Parameterized class assignment is supported. You can pass array and hash data structures to the node. Unlike Puppet Enterprise, Foreman does not currently provide a rules-based classifier.

Because Puppet node management is just a part of what Foreman does, configuration is somewhat more complex than Puppet Enterprise or any Puppet-oriented ENC solutions. Foreman has a strong focus on provisioning, and provides PXEboot automation, DNS management, DHCP management, and an IPAM solution. As a result, its RESTful API is somewhat heavier than other solutions, though it is well documented and straightforward to use. Even though most of the components are optional, a full-featured environment management solution needs to integrate with your hypervisors, cloud providers, DNS, DHCP, TFTP, and Puppet infrastructure.

Foreman is a RedHat–supported project that works with community contributors, much as Puppet does. Upstream, it's incorporated into Katello and sold as part of the Red Hat Satellite product.

Cobbler

Cobbler was originally used as part of Red Hat Satellite provisioning services but was replaced by the more full-featured Foreman. Cobbler is a good choice if you're looking for a simple, lightweight provisioning system and ENC. It is not as full-featured as the other solutions, but it does provide platform-, group-, and node-based classification. You must supplement Cobbler with another console for reporting.

Cobbler's strength is that it's fast, well understood, and very simple to set up. Cobbler integrates with DNS and DHCP by writing templates for each. Its APIs are fairly straightforward, and KOAN provides a simple method to provision KVM and Xen virtual machines. It maintains a node inventory and provides an ENC for Puppet, but does not offer reporting features.

It stores node data in a simple JSON document, and supports a number of replication topologies out of the box. Using replication, you can easily scale out your DHCP and DNS infrastructure, as well. The storage backend is pluggable, and MongoDB, CouchDB, and MySQL are also supported out of the box.

Cobbler is a good choice if you need a simple provisioning solution for a small environment without node reporting requirements.

Build your own ENC

You can use virtually anything that stores node data as an ENC. The Puppet node terminus is fairly simple to extend using Puppet's plugin architecture, but if you're uncomfortable with that approach you can simply write an external node classifier to be invoked by the exec terminus.

Although we generally advise against creating anything from scratch when a suitable solution is publicly available, node classification logic can be incredibly site specific. The creation of an external classifier to use an existing configuration management database or inventory management database could be done fairly easily.

If you do decide to generate your own, be sure to consider the demand load from Puppet and reliability requirements. An ENC lookup failure will prevent the node catalog from being built. Here's some things to consider in an ENC design:

- The data source should be designed for availability not less than the Puppet servers.
- The data source must be capable of handling spiky bursts of traffic such as an orchestrated push, or every node restarting at the same time.
- Are read-only slaves available to handle traffic while maintenance is done on the database?

If you do implement your own ENC, it's a good idea to review Puppet's internal indirectors and termini and consider how your classifier can use them. In particular, the facts indirector and the report indirector can be queried for information about the nodes, such as the agent_specified_environment fact available on newer releases of Puppet.

Your console can also perform queries against PuppetDB, which makes a huge amount of node data available via the API. If your console relies on PuppetDB, be sure that it does so in a way that meets your availability and failover requirements because this approach can potentially create another point of failure.

Summary

Node classification provides data used to customize the Puppet catalog for a node. You can implement node classification in many different and overlapping ways, including node facts, ENCs, and node statements.

There is no single best-practice choice for a node classifier, because it depends on your specific needs and the tools available. The appropriate choice of a node classifier will vary or change over time depending on the infrastructure available to manage the nodes.

Here are the key takeaways from this chapter:

- A node classifier provides node-specific data not available from node facts.
- You can use node parameters to customize the Hiera hierarchy for data lookups.
- You can source classification data from existing inventory or infrastructure management tools.
- Assignment using `node` statements is suitable only for small environments without other infrastructure.

## CHAPTER 9

Release Engineering and r10k

r10k is a tool for deploying Puppet modules and environments based on a release specification. In this chapter, we review all the ways in which you can use r10k, with a focus on powerful features that are often overlooked. Because the use of r10k suffers from a lack of useful step-by-step instructions, we have included a walkthrough tutorial.

We then move on to designing release processes using r10k and the best practices for doing so. As such, we cover the following:

- How you can use r10k for change control in Puppet
- How r10k can simplify and enhance automated unit and acceptance testing
- How r10k can enable multiple teams to coordinate effectively
- How r10k can provide compliance auditing and controls without hampering development

Puppet Enterprise includes Code Manager (*https://puppet.com/docs/pe/2018.1/ code_mgr.html*), which has identical functionality and a shared parentage with r10k. Everything in this chapter also applies to Code Manager except for the *r10k.yaml* configuration file.

Further, there are several other tools that mimic r10k functionality and implement improvements for a specific need. All of the advice in this chapter applies to those tools, as well.

Although r10k is currently the best-practice tool to implement the workflows described here, it is not the only solution. This chapter covers testing, release, deployment, and CI strategies in general for Puppet. These topics are applicable to Puppet regardless of the deployment tool that you use.

Puppet Environments in Depth

Before discussing r10k's management of environments, let's step aside and quickly review the features and functionality provided by Puppet environments.

Don't skip this section because you already know what a Puppet environment is. The capabilities and usage of Puppet environments has evolved over time, and we discuss functionality based on key concepts presented here.

The term *environment* is commonly used to mean many different things. It can mean site, location, provider, tier of service, and even colloquially the political or logistical atmosphere in which something operates. For the purposes of Puppet, an environment is a specific configuration of Puppet modules (including manifests, functions, facts, types, and providers) and data utilized to build catalogs for one or more Puppet nodes.

Puppet Directory Environments

Puppet allows you to create, modify, and remove Puppet environments without making configuration changes to your servers or agents. You do this by adding or removing directories from Puppet's `$environmentpath` directory. Although you'd never do it manually like this, the following steps are all that is required to create a test environment:

```
$ cd /etc/puppetlabs/code/environments
$ cp -r production test
```

Seriously, never do this on a Puppet server unless sorting out the complications of mixed-merge catalogs built during a race condition sounds like fun.

The creation and removal of Puppet environments can be easily automated so that changes approved in source code management can be automatically deployed for testing. This ability to quickly create, update, and remove Puppet environments provides the foundation for enabling Puppet testing, release, deployment, and upgrade strategies.

Selectable Blocks for Catalog Building

Each Puppet environment has the components (code and data) necessary to build a node's catalog. All of the following can be distinct between environments:

- Manifests
- Modules, including:
  - Classes
  - Defined types
  - Custom facts
  - Functions
  - Resource types
  - Resource providers
- Hiera data, including:
  - Customized hierarchy
  - Custom lookup and merge policies on a per-key basis
  - Environment data providers
  - Encryption keys
- Files
- Caching (for performance)
- Catalog version provisioning

It's not required that each of these things differ: most of your environments will likely be very similar. But each of these things can be tuned distinctly for any environment.

Environment Configuration

Each environment contains a configuration file (*environment.conf*) that specifies the configuration of the environment. At the time this book was last updated, this file can specify the following:

- A directory containing Puppet manifests (replacing the historic *site.pp*)
- The directories from which Puppet modules (and their facts, functions, types, and providers) are loaded
- Whether the data should be cached for performance
- An optional program to provide the catalog version number

Every parameter in this configuration is optional and falls back to the global default.

Environment Independence and Isolation

One of the often-overlooked features of Puppet environments is that they operate independently. When you deploy a new environment, you don't need to modify any other environment to enable its existence. When you remove an environment, no changes are required in anything that the other environments use. This complete independence greatly simplifies testing and deployment without any risk of impact to uninvolved environments.

Because each environment can have a unique module path, this means that each environment can have different versions of functions, resource types, and resource providers of the same name. And because Puppet 4.6 environments can safely utilize these conflicting versions by generating type metadata for each environment, this greatly simplifies development and testing of improved resource types and providers.

Deploying with r10k

As a deployment tool, r10k creates Puppet directory environments based on the branches in a repository. It populates modules and data into those environments based on the *Puppetfile* specification found in each branch.

Even though r10k's role appears on the surface to be fairly simple, it makes possible powerful development and release workflows. In this section, we quickly review the features and functionality so we can refer to them in the sections that follow, in which we review best practices for deployment.

 In our consulting experience, r10k is one of the least understood and minimally deployed tools we see. Imagine walking into a kitchen and finding a fully functional *Star Trek* food synthesizer capable of building entire meals being used exclusively to provide hot coffee.

What Does r10k Actually Do?

Although our introduction touched on the benefits of deploying r10k, we didn't really explain how it works to support those goals. r10k has two primary commands:

deploy
    Deploy Puppet environments based on code branches in one or more control repositories.

puppetfile
    Install modules and data in an environment from a *Puppetfile* specification.

The most common use of r10k uses both commands together to deploy a complete environment in two phases. Let's review how to configure each of these phases.

The Control Repository

r10k deploys environments based on a configuration stored in what is commonly called a *control repository*. A control repository contains multiple branches, one for each Puppet environment available to be deployed. Each branch contains the minimum necessary files and metadata used to deploy the entire environment.

The concept of a control repository is not specific to r10k. This is actually a design pattern around which r10k's features and functionality continue to evolve.

The control repository needs to have a branch named for each Puppet environment. Even though it would not provide much value, the simple steps presented in Example 9-1 would create a fully functional control repository.

Example 9-1. Creating the smallest possible control repo

```
$ mkdir environments
$ cd environments
$ git init
Initialized empty Git repository in /home/you/environments/.git/
$ git checkout -b production
Switched to a new branch 'production'
$ git commit --allow-empty -m 'empty production environment'
[production (root-commit) cd1cde6] empty production environment
$ git remote add origin https://git.example.com/puppet/environments
$ git push -u origin production
```

You might have noticed that this creates a default branch of production rather than master. Every Puppet environment must have a production environment (whether you use it or not) so this is commonly used as the default branch. The default branch can be anything you want, so long as you keep it mind that name will be deployed as a Puppet environment.

Control Repository Branch Contents

There is no requirement for any file to exist in a branch of the control repository. An empty branch (as created in Example 9-1) will simply deploy an empty environment directory. However, there are a number of files within a Puppet environment and design patterns that enhance and empower usage of r10k. The following are the most common default files.

Files expected by Puppet

These files are used by Puppet, irrespective of the environment deployment method:

environment.conf
    The Puppet environment configuration file.

`hiera.yaml`
> The Hiera hierarchy for this environment.

`manifests/`
> The manifests directory used by Puppet unless otherwise configured. This is generally used for site-specific manifests, and may contain node statements.

`modules/`
> The module directory used by Puppet unless otherwise configured in `$module` `path`.

`.resource_types/`
> A hidden directory containing metadata about functions, types, and providers. Its existence enables environment isolation.

All other environment files are optional.

Files used by r10k

The following files are used by r10k to provide metadata for deployment of data and modules in the environment:

r10k.yaml
> This file specifies the repositories that should be scanned for environment branches.

Puppetfile
> This file specifies a list of modules and data that should be deployed into this environment.

Alternative file and directory conventions

There are a number of standard file or directory names that have no default usage by Puppet or r10k but have been found to be useful design patterns:

- `Rakefile`: Rake tasks for test, build, and deployment.
- `README.md`: Documentation for the environment.

`data/`
> Hiera data files for the environment. You must specify this in *hiera.yaml*.

`site/`
> A single-repository monolithic deployment of site-specific modules such as roles and profiles. You must add this to the `$modulepath`.

dist/
> Modules sourced from external repositories that are bundled into the control repository. You must add these to the $modulepath.

spec/
> Unit and acceptance tests for the environment.

These are common conventions, but you can choose to ignore or change them to meet your needs.

r10k Configuration File

r10k has a configuration file, */etc/puppetlabs/r10k/r10k.yaml*, that contains only the things required to access the control repository and Puppet module sources, including the following:

cachedir
> The directory where r10k caches repositories it has downloaded.

proxy
> The proxy required to access the control repository.

forge
> Configuration required to access the Puppet Forge (or a mirror).

git
> Configuration required to access the Git server hosting the control repositories.

sources
> A hash of control repositories that should be checked for each environment deployed.

The use of r10k and the parameters in this file are well documented by Puppet at *https://github.com/puppetlabs/r10k*, although we do refer to some of these settings when we discuss multiteam cooperation in "Enabling Multiteam Coordination" on page 239.

Puppetfile

The *Puppetfile* contains the specification for Puppet modules and data to be installed in the environment.

 If you are familiar with Bundler and its *Gemfile* for Ruby development, or Pipenv and *Pipfile* for Python development, you already understand the purpose and usage of *Puppetfile*.

Modules

The *Puppetfile* lists each Puppet module that you should install in the environment, what version, and from where it should be sourced. We won't bother replicating the documentation, but Example 9-2 provides a glimpse of how detailed the specification can be.

Example 9-2. A Puppet module in three different stages of development

```
# Get released version 3.1.0 from the Puppet Forge
mod 'puppetlabs/apache', '3.1.0'

# Install puppetlabs/apache from Github and track the 'docs_experiment' branch
mod 'apache',
  :git    => 'https://github.com/puppetlabs/puppetlabs-apache',
  :branch => 'docs_experiment'

# Install puppetlabs/apache from GitHub and pin to the '83401079' commit
mod 'apache',
  :git    => 'https://github.com/puppetlabs/puppetlabs-apache',
  :commit => '83401079053dca11d61945bd9beef9ecf7576cbf'
```

The clean, clear specification makes it possible for each environment to manage risk according to its own needs, which could be anything from the tested and approved public release version to a specific Git commit that provides necessary functionality.

Hiera data

Although r10k was originally intended to deploy only Puppet modules, it has become obvious that using r10k to deploy Hiera data is both practical and powerful. r10k version 2.4 added the ability to specify that the checkout branch of a repository should match the control repository's branch, which makes it possible to test module changes alongside the environment's data changes that would be deployed at the same time.

The example that follows deploys Hiera data in the *data/* subdirectory of the environment. It will use the branch matching the control repo if it exists, or *production* if not.

```
# Install Hiera data
mod 'data',
  :git => 'https://git.example.com/hiera_data.git',
  :branch => :control_branch,          # Track control branch name
  :default_branch => 'production',     # Default if no matching branch
  :install_base => ''                  # Install in the root of the environment
```

r10k Deployment Walkthrough

r10k's installation and configuration is quite elegant, despite appearing to be fairly complex at a glance. Lets take a look at a very simple configuration that you can use

---

for learning, experimentation, and testing. For this example, we use the default user environment for Puppet, allowing you to experiment in your home directory.

 This section is for those who are not experienced with r10k. If you are already using r10k at your site, you can skip ahead to "Uses for r10k" on page 219.

The most basic use case of r10k involves deploying modules using a *Puppetfile*. This is commonly used during testing and development and requires minimal effort to use. Here are the steps for this deployment:

1. Install r10k and create an r10k configuration file.
2. Create a control repository as shown in Example 9-1.
3. Create a new *test* environment branch.
4. Populate it with an *environment.conf* and and *Puppetfile*.
5. Use `r10k deploy` to deploy the test environment.

Installing r10k

The simplest way to install r10k is to use the Ruby provided by Puppet, as shown here.

```
$ sudo puppet resource package r10k ensure=present provider=puppet_gem
```

Now that you've installed r10k, let's create a basic r10k configuration file in your home directory (you'll need to customize this file with your own Git repository and where your Puppet environments are located, naturally):

```
sources:
  main:
    # where will the control repo be stored?
    remote: 'https://git.example.com/puppet/environments.git'

    # run Puppet as normal user for this exercise
    basedir: '/home/username/.puppetlabs/etc/code/environments'
```

You have now configured r10k with a source pointing at where your control repository will be. Next, let's create that control repository.

Creating a test branch

It's time to create a *test* environment. Simple and easy:

```
$ cd environments
$ git checkout -b test
Switched to a new branch 'test'
```

You need to give the environment a basic environment configuration file. Let's copy it from the default one installed with Puppet:

```
$ cp /etc/puppetlabs/code/environments/production/environment.conf ./
```

Now create a basic *Puppetfile*, installing some common dependencies for module development.

```
mod 'puppetlabs/stdlib', '4.25.1'
mod 'ipcrm/echo', '0.1.5'
```

After you've created your *Puppetfile*, you can validate it and then commit it to the repository:

```
$ /opt/puppetlabs/puppet/bin/r10k puppetfile check
Syntax OK
$ git commit -am 'small test environment'
[test (root-commit) 641da544] small test environment
$ git push -u origin test
```

At this point, you have created a fully functional, albeit minimal, control repository for r10k to use. You are now ready to deploy an environment.

Deploying with r10k

Before you attempt any commands, use the deploy display command to verify that r10k is configured correctly:

```
$ alias r10k=/opt/puppetlabs/puppet/bin/r10k
$ r10k deploy display
---
:sources:
- :name: :main
  :basedir: "/home/user/.puppetlabs/etc/code/environments"
  :remote: https://git.example.com/puppet/environments
  :environments:
  - production
  - test
```

Finally, invoke r10k to build your Puppet test environment:

```
$ r10k deploy environment test --v info
INFO    -> Deploying environment /home/user/.puppetlabs/etc/code/environments/test
INFO    -> Environment test is now at 641da544b4df4bb14a48928ae71065f6736de4c7
INFO    -> Deploying Puppetfile content
           /home/user/.puppetlabs/etc/code/environments/test/modules/stdlib
INFO    -> Deploying Puppetfile content
           /home/user/.puppetlabs/etc/code/environments/test/modules/echo
```

As you can see, deploying an environment the first time does both phases: it creates the environment and then deploys the *Puppetfile* content. To update the environment you need to use the `--puppetfile` flag for the *Puppetfile* to be parsed and deployed, as shown by the following commands:

```
$ r10k deploy environment test --verbose info
INFO    -> Deploying environment /home/user/.puppetlabs/etc/code/environments/test
INFO    -> Environment test is now at 641da544b4df4bb14a48928ae71065f6736de4c7

$ /opt/puppetlabs/puppet/bin/r10k deploy environment test --puppetfile --v info
INFO    -> Deploying environment /home/user/.puppetlabs/etc/code/environments/test
INFO    -> Environment test is now at 641da544b4df4bb14a48928ae71065f6736de4c7
INFO    -> Deploying Puppetfile content
           /home/user/.puppetlabs/etc/code/environments/test/modules/stdlib
INFO    -> Deploying Puppetfile content
           /home/user/.puppetlabs/etc/code/environments/test/modules/echo
```

Now that we've deployed our control repository using r10k, we can make use of the installed module using Puppet apply:

```
$ puppet apply --verbose --environment test --execute 'echo { $environment: }'
Info: Loading facts
Notice: /Echo[test]/message: test
Notice: Compiled catalog for testnode.example.com in environment test
Info: Applying configuration version '1523171606'
Notice: Applied catalog in 0.02 seconds
```

With everything working, you can add more modules to the *Puppetfile*, add manifests to the control repository, and test to your heart's content from your home directory.

Uses for r10k

r10k's primary use case is code deployment. It is commonly run in three different deployment situations, but the total number of use cases just within these three can be far greater, such as:

- On a developer's workstation for testing local development
- By a test framework for evaluating repository changes (Jenkins, Gitlab CI, etc.)
- On a Puppet Server instance to deploy changes to the environment

Although r10k's features appear on the surface to be fairly simple, it makes possible powerful development and release workflows. This section reviews those workflows and identifies important concepts for use in the discussion of best practices for each.

Build Development Environments

One of r10k's strengths is its ability to build and deploy development and test environments. You can use this to reduce iteration time, reduce the risk associated with new deployments to production, and perform small-scale test upgrades to production infrastructure.

Introducing new, potentially breaking, features can be a huge risk. The common three-way split of dev/stage/prod does not provide sufficient testing to minimize this risk. Every one of us who work in production environments has seen the drift problems created by too simple of a split. If the dev environment is preparing for next month's release, and the stage environment is load-testing this month's release, but a critical break-fix needs to be deployed to production ASAP—you need something more flexible for testing.

With on-demand creation of Puppet directory environments, you can introduce changes as separate *feature* branches. The ability to create arbitrary Puppet environments provides a lot of flexibility when implementing dangerous changes, significantly increasing the agility of the development team. Instead of testing against whatever is deployed in stage today, an exact replica of production with only the single change to be tested is made available. This ability to introduce one change at a time to a subset of nodes implements and simplifies CI practices.

The benefit of this approach is that you can apply new Puppet environments quickly and easily, allowing developers to test changes to environments as needed. The ability to quickly deploy new releases will encourage testing in live nonproduction environments and will tend to increase development agility. This approach is also somewhat simpler to implement than a package-based solution.

For testing purposes, you can think of feature branches as *versions of code*. This concept is very important to understand. Puppet directory environments allow the safe release of new code without applying it. Only when a node is configured to use that branch/version/environment will the new version be applied.

Simplifying Acceptance Testing

In acceptance tests, all of the modules and data are brought together to build out the complete solution (as opposed to unit tests, which are intended to be run in isolation). This kind of testing needs a complete Puppet environment mirroring what you have today (to provide a starting point) and another environment providing what you intend to deploy.

 Within Puppet and community documentation, integration tests covering multimodule interactions and end-to-end testing of complete solutions are grouped together under *Acceptance Tests*.

r10k is an invaluable tool to deploy environments for acceptance, integration, and end-to-end testing. If you are using r10k to build your production environments, you need to do nothing more than copy the production branch and insert the one change you'd like to test. The following example shows how to change one module's version number to create a test environment:

```
$ cd environments
$ git checkout production
$ git checkout -b try_new_stdlib
Switched to a new branch 'try_new_stdlib'
$ sed -i'' -e 's/\(^mod 'puppetlabs\/stdlib',\).*$/\1 '4.26.0'/" Puppetfile
$ git commit Puppetfile -m 'stdlib version 4.26.0'
[production 7d1c3e6] stdlib version 4.26.0
$ git push -u origin try_new_stdlib
```

Your testing framework could deploy the new environment using r10k, and perform existing acceptance tests to ensure that nothing is broken by the change.

Implement Continuous Integration, Delivery, and Deployment

Continuous integration (CI), continuous delivery (CD), and continuous deployment refer to the process of automating the testing and deployment of your code. Each of them builds upon the previous one as follows.

CI involves automating your unit and acceptance testing in such a way that it can be triggered every time new feature code is available. The value of such a process is that it can catch a lot of problems before the code reaches a live environment. This immediate feedback improves the quality of code and can help improve the deployment process.

CD is more of a release mindset: it involves ensuring that every feature being merged back to the main branch is ready for deployment. r10k simplifies this process by making each branch available as a Puppet environment for testing by the admin, developer, or user waiting for that change. The fast roundtrip for testing the change and integrating it to the main branch improves the quality of the main branch. We find this to be crucial to avoiding drift between development and production environments.

Continuous deployment is a release methodology that might not be suitable for all environments. It involves immediately testing a CD branch (usually after a new feature is merged) and deploying it immediately if the test succeeds. Although this isn't usually suitable for application development, it works rather well with website deployments, and you guessed it, Puppet configuration management changes.

Development and release processes are usually broken down into a number of deployment stages, from feature branch creation to release candidate creation to final production deployment. Automating these steps individually and independently creates a short-circuit feedback loop on integration problems. This in turn results in much faster turnaround times for overall and combined delivery efforts. A huge benefit of r10k is that it provides a simple, unified way to deploy development, test, and production environments. This helps improve consistency and simplifies the process of setting up a CI solution.

As CI/CD processes are general-purpose release management strategies well documented elsewhere, we refer to them here only when applicable to Puppet and related technologies. We cover a number of these deployment methodologies and how they relate to Puppet and r10k in "Release Management Strategies with r10k" on page 224.

Learning More About CI/CD

Numerous books and training courses have been and will be written on these subjects. We recommend starting with *Continuous Integration vs. Continous Delivery vs. Continous Deployment* (*http://bit.ly/continuous-integration-vs*) and then proceeding on to books or tutorials more specific to your needs.

In addition, you might find the following search queries useful:

- Safari Books: continuous integration (*http://bit.ly/2KyNmTR*)
- Video Training: continuous integration (*http://bit.ly/2vLG0XK*)

Deploy Production Environments

Production deployment is the final step of a release-management process, and typically takes place only after the build has passed all other validation steps.

You can use r10k on production nodes to deploy changes. How you use it depends on how catalogs are built in your environment.

Puppet Server
> r10k is invoked on the Puppet server to deploy the new or updated environment for all agents using that server.

Puppet apply
> r10k is invoked on a destination node to deploy the new or updated environment in the local filesystem.

Regardless of the approach, r10k checks the control repository with each invocation, and populates one or more environments based on the branches available in the control repositories. Repositories are locally cached, thus limiting the load created by new deployments to only the differences (e.g., *git pull*).

The requirement of this approach is that each node invoking r10k must be authorized to fetch your control repository and every module referenced by the control repository. A failure to fetch any repository or module can cause the update to fail. This is most commonly used in Puppet server environments where a relatively small number of servers need to invoke r10k to service a large number of Puppet agents. Standalone environments might need to scale out their Git infrastructure to support a large number of nodes.

All of the standard best practices for deployment apply to Puppet. None of the following are specific to Puppet, but r10k makes a lot of them easier to implement:

- Employ a canary deployment to evaluate problems whenever possible.
- Spin up a production clone automatically to compare scaling characteristics.
- Deploy changes in pods, allowing instaneous cutover and rollback from one version to another.
- Implement error-tracking variance to signal or initiate an automated rollback.
- Utilize parallel orchestration tools (e.g., MCollective/Choria) to minimize version drift when deploying to large clusters.
- Prototype resource changes in a release to tag whether the change is *low*, *medium*, or *high* risk.
- Automate creation and testing of a rollback commit that reverts the state of every resource modified by the change.

Build and Package

You can use r10k as a build tool. Puppet code can be bundled together, versioned, and packaged for use in detached or embedded environments. A major benefit is that you can use your existing package management for the release of Puppet code.

This process is nothing more than combining the steps we just outlined with a testing framework and packaging solution. The process would generally look like this:

1. The new release changes are placed on a new branch in the control repository.
2. r10k is invoked to deploy the new version.
3. r10k or another tool kicks off acceptance testing of the solution.
4. If testing is successful, the r10k-deployed environment is packaged up.

We recommend this approach with standalone, black-box, or embedded Puppet nodes, especially when included with published software or black-box deployments in other environments. It scales very well, and requires that only your CI infrastructure be authorized to pull from your code repositories.

A hybrid approach

You can absolutely mix the build and deploy approaches together. Most sites using r10k as a build tool will still gain value from using it as a deployment tool for development purposes. The hybrid approach generally works like this:

1. Development branches are deployed automatically by r10k (usually on the dev Puppet server) for testing.

2. Release branches are deployed automatically by r10k for QA and acceptance testing.

3. Release branches that pass testing are bundled for deployment in preproduction and production environments.

Release Management Strategies with r10k

Release management is the process of determining how and when new code should be published to your systems. With Puppet, this tends to be dictated by your revision control system workflow. The foundation of most release strategies is rooted in the branching and merging strategy that you choose to employ. The good news is that Puppet has few constraints here; you can almost certainly apply your existing code management strategies to Puppet. With a few exceptions, you can pretty much use any strategy supported by your revision control system.

Although this chapter focuses on Git, you can apply most of these strategies to other revision control systems, including SVN and Perforce. The caveat is that certain strategies are much less common with those tools and can require more effort to implement. SVN, for example, is not nearly as elegant in its branch management.

Revision control is about answering the five Ws. *Who* made this change? *What* was the change? *Where* does this change apply? *When* was the change made? *Why* did they make the change? Being able to track down the author of a change or cross-reference changes and events can be an invaluable troubleshooting tool. Without a code repository, it can become very difficult to answer these questions. At best, you're reliant on access logs, timestamps, file ownership, and code commentary.

Good commit messages, and single-purpose commits are incredibly valuable when you're trying to understand a bit of code. Commit messages and the context provided offer a huge amount of information. These things can be invaluable for correlating events, especially when combined with monitoring and logs.

If you aren't using a revision control system with Puppet, now is a good time to start. Even a single, local, nonreplicated Git repository is a huge improvement over a simple directory containing a bunch of *.bak* files.

Stage/Production Branches

With this strategy, multiple branches are maintained, allowing flexibility in what code is released to staging hosts, and then when that code moves to production hosts. Production follows stage, lagging behind as needed. Changes are initially merged into the stage branch, which is deployed to stage nodes for testing. After testing, the changes on stage are merged onto the production branch.

In theory, this approach has the following benefits:

- All changes are tested in a working environment before going to production.
- Stage and product have their own current HEAD and revision history.
- It's easy to test with postcommit hooks to a testing framework that utilizes the existing stage nodes.

In practice, this theory falls down due to the following real-life implementation issues:

- It doesn't cope with overlapping short-term and long-term deliverables.
  - Locking stage for release testing holds up hotfix testing, and vice versa.
  - Hotfix changes might be merged to production without implicit dependencies left on the stage branch.
- It requires a strong skill set with source code tools to manage production merges.
  - Identifying and cherry-picking codependent changes is a highly skilled practice.
  - Any mistake would merge changes being tested in stage to production early.
- Drift over time and abandoned efforts left in stage must be cleaned up manually.
- Long-lived testing branches invariably are abused by developers for conditional execution.

That last bullet item can be far more risky than it might seem. `if stage: do X`, `if prod: do Y` leads to testing different code than what is deployed in production. When all tests are done on (effectively) random branch names, these kind of mistakes can be caught and removed.

Nutshell version: managing stage branches in this fashion is much more complicated than it would seem, and will require an expert release management skill set to manage. Consider using the layered approach provided by "GitFlow" on page 226.

Single Branch (GitHub Flow)

This release strategy avoids the complications of managing multiple development and release branches. Each and every change flows back to a single branch for use in deployment. Although this is likely unsuitable for large-scale application release strategies that have overlapping periods of new and maintenance releases, this is often perfect for configuration management purposes.

The single branch deployment model is often called *branch-per-task* or *branch-per-issue* but the best guide we've seen is the GitHub Flow introduction (*http://bit.ly/2M6acXH*).

This model has the following benefits:

- All deployed code is committed on a single `master` branch.
- All other branches are feature branches for testing purposes.
- It is easy to learn by team members who have minimal experience with revision control systems.
- It is easy to test with precommit hooks, does not require a testing framework and infrastructure (although it works well with them, too).
- Changes implemented in single, whole pieces are easy to revert.
- Abandoned efforts aren't left in a shared branch.

The major advantage of this approach is simplicity; teams need only understand the fundamentals of creating a new branch, and are less likely to make mistakes when merging efforts together. This makes it suitable to employ in a team of system administrators unfamiliar with complex release management practices.

Even though the production infrastructure follows a single branch, you still create and deploy feature branches with r10k. This allows an opportunity to test dangerous changes before merging into the master branch.

GitFlow

The GitFlow strategy takes advantage of Git's branching and merging capabilities to maximize flexibility. You can view it as an implementation of the single-branch practices on a dual-branch (stage/prod) model. This deployment model is well documented at A successful Git branching model (*http://bit.ly/2MlwDoR*).

With GitFlow, each feature change starts with its own feature branch. From that point the process diverges:

- Feature branches are forked from and merged back to the `develop` branch.
- Automatic nightly builds and acceptance tests are built from `develop` branch.

- Some infrastructure might consistently run from `develop` (e.g., stage).
- Release branches fork from `develop`.
- You can deploy release branches in specific environments.
- Release branch changes are merged back to `develop` for ongoing integration.
- Release branches are merged to `master` as a complete change.

 Only teams that are very comfortable with Git and release management should use this process. Particularly large organizations should seriously consider an investment in employee training in order to adopt this workflow.

In a GitFlow model, production nodes utilize one of the *release branches*. This model has the following benefits:

- All deployed code is merged to a single `master` branch.
- People with limited release management experience manage only their own feature branches.
- Release management or QA practices (whether manual or automated) control the creation of release branches.
- Automated test frameworks can be triggered based on the GitFlow branch names.
- Changes that involve multiple dependent changes can be safely tested in isolation from other release efforts.
- Release branches can be used to test alternate implementations, with only one merging to master after a successful deployment.

The major advantage of this approach compared to GitHub Flow is that it enables layered processes:

1. Developers create and test the concepts on feature branches before merging back to `develop`.
2. Release management or QA (automated or manual) runs tests and creates release branches.
3. Hotfixes can be created from a release branch, and merged back to `develop` after testing.
4. The concept of a release branch and a Puppet environment are effectively identical. Changing the Puppet environment of the node changes the release version.

5. Flexible and partial upgrades are possible, because you can roll out changes node by node, or group by group.

If you are already familiar with GitFlow, you might ask why we maintain release branches rather than rely on tags. This is an intentional design decision; tags are not intended to be removed. Puppet environments are created only for branches. Tags can be used for multirelease association and long-term archival, allowing your release branches to be pruned without the risk of losing history.

There are only two disadvantages to this approach:

- It requires an experienced release management skill set to perform the release and master branch fork and merge tasks. This works well in organizations that already have significant release management talent and infrastructure, but it can be difficult to implement without those skills and tools.
- The GitFlow model was built around Git's strengths in decentralized development. Although you can apply this workflow using other revision control systems, it requires one with a low cost of effort for branching and merging.

Invoking r10k

r10k is a fairly simple process; it checks that the environment matches the specification, it runs a postrun task if configured, and then it exits. It performs its tasks entirely independent of Puppet; as a result, it needs to have its own invocation strategy.

r10k is not a gate or policy enforcement mechanism. It deploys code available on the branch when requested. Code reviews, mandatory processes, and other gating should be handled within the toolkit provided by your development environment or code management tools (GitHub, GitLab, Bitbucket, etc.). It should be safe to run r10k at any time on any system, without fear that doing so could result in unintended changes.

So long as you do not rely on r10k as a release gate, any invocation strategy is viable. The one you implement will be a matter of preference.

Puppet Prerun Command

It is possible to invoke r10k as a prerun command using the `prerun_command` configuration setting. Serverless nodes can use this to update the code stored locally, thus ensuring that each Puppet run is performed with the latest available release of code. The infrastructure affected by this benefits from Puppet's built-in concurrency protection and splay timing.

This is suitable only for on-demand test configurations that would update a single environment prior to running a test in that environment.

Deploying on Receipt of a WebHook

By far the most common implementation of r10k utilizes a WebHook from the source repository to indicate that new content is available in a given branch. Every source code management system contains this capability.

This approach is handy because it ensures that new code is deployed immediately after it has been pushed to the Git repository. This reduces the latency between pushing a change and the change becoming available to agents. This allows developers to push code and then immediately invoke Puppet to test that the changes worked as desired.

Another benefit of using a postreceive hook is that you can build intelligence into the hook. For example, the hook can do the following:

- Deploy only the branch that has changed instead of synchronizing all environments.
- Deploy appropriate branches: feature tests in dev, releases in production.

 Unless you already manage home-built webhook automation, don't reinvent the wheel. There are dozens of implementations for every deployment model: *http://bit.ly/2nmxZFb*. We recommend *http://bit.ly/2vFFxXb*.

Puppet Enterprise: Code Manager WebHook

Puppet Enterprise includes a WebHook for notifications to Code Manager (PE's bundled r10k). No additional software is required. You can find instructions at *http://bit.ly/2vHSeAS*.

Orchestrating Deployments with MCollective/Choria

Among other useful tools, Vox Pupuli's puppet/r10k (*https://forge.puppet.com/puppet/r10k*) module includes an MCollective plug-in that can invoke r10k on demand. This approach allows automation tools to run r10k on many remote nodes at the same time.

Here are just a few of the benefits of using MCollective to trigger r10k deployment actions:

- New nodes automatically subscribe to the channel (versus static WebHook list).

- Requests can be filtered by many different criteria.
- Execution can be ordered, timed, and handled serially or in parallel.
- Access is validated against signed Transport Layer Security (TLS) keys and logged for auditing purposes.

r10k deployment via MCollective requests is far more robust and secure than Secure Shell (SSH) or source code repository WebHook notifications.

Invoking r10k in Testing Frameworks

You can configure whatever testing framework you use to invoke r10k as part of its features and operations. Due to how r10k derives its actions from the existence and content of source-code branches, few if any options are necessary to be passed when invoking r10k. This makes it easy to use in multipurpose test scripts.

The following are just a few of the testing framework plugins available to utilize r10k:

- The Puppet Development Kit (*http://bit.ly/2OPIKwf*)
- Rake tasks related to r10k and *Puppetfile* (*http://bit.ly/2OaNjzK*)
- A puppet provisioner for Test Kitchen (*http://bit.ly/2KyIu1j*)
- Autogenerate *Puppetfile* for r10k and *.fixtures* for rspec testing (*http://bit.ly/ 2LVwBIj*)
- Use AWS CodeCommit as a Puppet r10k Remote Control Repository (*https:// amzn.to/2M4ufG9*)
- (Gitlab) Workflow automations for deploying Puppet modules with r10k (*http:// bit.ly/2vnAZp9*)
- Jenkins Plugin: Puppet Enterprise Pipeline (*http://bit.ly/2KvZeWU*)

Combining Multiple Invocation Methods

None of these processes are mutually exclusive. It's not uncommon for a wide variety of implementations to be used within a single organization, like so:

- Local r10k deployments on developer workstations
- Automated r10k invocation by the testing framework on feature branch update
- WebHook notification to dev Puppet servers for r10k invocation on merge
- MCollective-based deployment to all production sites on release branch cut

The possibilities are endless. The most important aspect of your invocation process is that it works well with your development strategies. r10k should facilitate development rather than impede it. Because r10k works quickly and immediately, any blockage will come from delay of code changes reaching it. If your team is routinely blocked waiting for changes to arrive, you should improve or streamline your code release pipeline.

Concurrency

Whatever mechanism you use to invoke r10k should prevent parallel deployments on the same node. How to configure this will differ based on your deployment instructure. If necessary, you can use `flock` or a similar tool in a shell script for lockfile management.

Migrating to r10k

There's a good chance that at this point you already have an existing installation of Puppet with directory environments. These have been available for four years, and enabled by default for three years now. If you are already using directory environments, it's quite straightforward to adapt your existing repositories to work with r10k. This section goes over the issues to be addressed as you migrate.

Repository-per-Module Benefits

Repository-per-module means that each module resides in its own source-code repository. The opposite approach is to create a monolithic repository, containing all of your modules, manifests, and Hiera data. There are major benefits to the modular approach:

SoC

The repository-per-module design strategy encourages modular development. Rather than pulling your entire site for development, you develop in the context of a single module. This approach encourages modular design and discourages violation of important design principles.

History of changes in each Puppet module

A clean history for each module makes it easy to develop, deploy, and revert each module independently. This means that change logs will pertain to the module at hand rather than being spread across every module in your code. This also means that there will be less simultaneous development in each module's repository, reducing the likelihood of a merge conflict.

Tight specification of dependencies

A specified version for each module makes it possible to easily test and revert small changes. If all modules' changes happen in a large group, rolling forward or back one change requires rolling back all changes.

Simplifies use and development of public modules

A huge benefit of maintaining separate histories comes into play when you need to use and contribute back to a public module. With a repository-per-module structure, your changes can simply be a fork of the public module. If you maintain your changes as an independent branch, you can often rebase those changes onto upstream improvements. This approach also makes it very simple to see how your fork differs from the upstream repository, which can be invaluable in troubleshooting and upgrades.

Allows common core upgrades; avoids forced collective upgrades

When every role and profile needs to share a single common core, an upgrade to the common core forces every profile to upgrade immediately. In practice, this means that improvements in the core require agreement and investment from every team that uses them. With unique versioning of shared components some teams can upgrade to the latest version, whereas other teams can stay with their last tested version until ready to update.

Configuring an Environment in the Control Repository

If a monolithic repository contains environment configuration or other files in the environment directory, you should add these to the branch of the control repository named for the environment, as demonstrated here:

```
$ cd environments/
$ git checkout stage
$ cp /monolithic/environments/stage/environment.conf ./
$ cp /monolithic/environments/stage/hiera.yaml ./
$ git add environment.conf hiera.yaml
$ git commit
...
$ git checkout production
$ cp /monolithic/environments/production/environment.conf ./
$ cp /monolithic/environments/production/hiera.yaml ./
...
```

You should try to avoid copying other files to the control repository, for the reasons outlined in this section.

Enabling Monolithic and Per-module Hybrid Deployment

It's entirely possible to deploy r10k with an existing monolithic repository. Once it is deployed, r10k simplifies the process of moving your modules into their own repositories. This section outlines the steps to enable a hybrid deployment that will make it easier to iteratively move other modules as needed.

Adding r10k deployment of monolithic repo

Although r10k gives you options to mix monolithic modules with *Puppetfile*-managed modules in the same directory, it can be painful to maintain. It's much easier to simply put the monolithic repository in its own directory, as illustrated here:

```
# old repo with many modules
mod 'dist'
  :git => 'git://github.example.com:puppet/monolithic.git'
  :install_path => ''
```

 The *dist/* directory is a common convention used to store modules that would normally reside in their own repositories, but have not or cannot for one reason or another. The following code snippet shows the code to do this.

Modulepath adjustment

The next step is to create or update the environment's *environment.conf* file (in the control repository). You need to ensure that it has an entry in your `modulepath` for the monolithic repository modules *after* the directory for modules deployed via *Puppetfile*. Relative paths are evaluated within the environment directory.

```
modulepath = modules:dist/modules:$basemodulepath
```

Place the r10k-managed modules directory before the *dist/* modules directory. This allows you to test a migrated module in a few environments without removing it from the monolithic repository. If the monolithic module path is first, you'd need to remove the module from the monolithic repository for it to find the new one—which would affect all environments.

Adding r10k to existing deployments

The final step is to modify each script or process that would deploy the monolithic repository and replace it with an r10k invocation. r10k will deploy the old monolithic repository alongside the per-repo modules as soon as they are available. No further changes to the test or release processes are necessary as modules migrate from the monolithic repository over time.

Moving Modules to their Own Repositories

After you use r10k for deployment, you can begin the process of moving your modules to their own repositories. You do not need to move all modules at once; you can perform this process iteratively.

The easiest moves to migrate are those that have no dependencies and are not a dependency of any other module.

Moving public modules

If you have a monolithic repository, it might contain Puppet-supported or community-maintained modules that were copied as-is into the monolithic repository. puppetlabs/stdlib is a module often installed in this manner. You can move public modules that have been copied unchanged into your control repository by simply adding them to the *Puppetfile*. To avoid unexpected changes, pin the module to the version that was in use previously:

```
mod 'puppetlabs/stdlib', '4.12.0' # last version before deprecations
```

You can easily test later versions of the module whenever you are ready.

Moving dependency modules

Next, move dependency modules—modules required by other modules that do not have their own dependencies. Because these are self-standing, nothing will break.

For each module, you should create a new repository and move the module to that repository. It's a good idea to preserve the history of your module during this migration process. The --subdirectory-filter flag of the filter-branch Git command can be useful for extracting just one module's history.

Moving dependent modules

Finally, move modules that depend on the modules that you've already migrated. Use the same process that you used for the dependency modules.

Be sure to resolve any intermodule dependencies. Although r10k should make module migration seamless where it is used, you will need to update your local test fixtures manually. These are modules that will be installed in the testing sandbox. Add the dependency modules to the *.fixtures.yml* file within the module, like so:

```
fixtures:
  repositories:
    depends1: git://git.example.com/puppet/depends1.git
    depends2: git://git.example.com/puppet/depends2.git
```

For each migration iteration, it's a good idea to run your full test suite, just in case you missed a dependency.

While your site is in transition, the module might require fixtures from the monolithic repository in order to satisfy dependencies. The simplest way to satisfy these dependencies is to clone the entire monolithic repository into your module as a fixture and then create symlinks for each module of the monolithic repository on which the module depends. You can automate this by configuring the *.fixtures.yml* file with these details, as shown here:

```
fixtures:
  repositories:
```

```
    monolithic: git://git.example.com/puppet/monolithic.git
  symlinks:
    dependent: "#{source_dir}"
    depends1: "#{source_dir}/spec/fixtures/modules/monolithic/modules/depends1"
    depends2: "#{source_dir}/spec/fixtures/modules/monolithic/modules/depends2"
```

During the transitory period, you can pull the migrated modules into your control repository using r10k. This can be handy for testing purposes. As each dependency is moved to its own repository, replace the module in the symlinks hash with the module repository location in the repositories hash.

Placing Roles and Profiles in the site/ Module Directory

The *site/* module directory is often used for site-specific modules, most commonly your roles and profiles. It differs from *dist/* in that it contains modules that are *very* specific to your organization and will never be shared with the outside world. Site modules are typically tightly coupled to the module set deployed at your site and to your site-specific data.

The most common layout for your roles and profiles within the site directory is to create a module called *roles* and another called *profiles*. The actual roles and profiles are child classes within these modules. Using this design pattern avoids the risk of a collision between your roles, profiles, and other modules. This is important because your roles and profiles are often named after the services they manage. Here's an example of creating the site *modulepath* structure:

```
$ cd /etc/puppetlabs/code/environment/environment
$ mkdir site
$ cd site/
$ pdk new module profiles --skip-interview
$ cd profiles
$ pdk new class apache
repeat for each profile
$ cd ../
$ pdk new module roles --skip-interview
$ cd roles
$ pdk new class wordpress
repeat for each profile
```

You would then need to prepend the *site/* path to the environment's *modulepath*, like so:

```
modulepath = site:modules:dist/modules:$basemodulepath
```

If you use this design pattern, your *webserver* role would be named roles::web server, and your *mysql* profile would be named profiles::mysql. This avoids a namespace collision with the *mysql* service module.

$modulepath is a search path; it does not provide namespaces. A module named *apache* in the site directory will be loaded first, and the module named *apache* in your modules directory will be ignored.

You might instead prefer to create individual modules for each role or each profile. In that situation, prefix the role and/or profile with role_ or profile_, respectively. This will avoid name-space collisions with other modules. For this design pattern, your *webserver* role would be named role_webserver, and your *mysql* profile would be named profile_mysql. Using a prefix groups your roles and profiles together when viewing a list of site modules.

This isn't an either/or decision: you can mix and match these two approaches as necessary. Use whichever method or combination thereof is clear and understandable for your team.

Remove Fully Qualified Paths

The key to the r10k adaption process is that Puppet uses relative paths and module search paths to locate module components. For example, when you include a class, the Puppet autoloader searches $modulepath for the appropriate manifest. You do not need to specify the location of the class file. So long as the class is in your *modulepath* and its module has the appropriate structure, it will be located and loaded. Files and templates use the same basic process; templates are referenced by module name and sourced from the module's directory. Because all of these objects are located using configurable reference points, you can reorganize the underlying file structure at will.

It's a good idea to scan your codebase for the following:

- import statements that might use absolute paths
- prerun or postrun scripts in the Puppet configuration file
- generate statements

import was removed in Puppet 4. Put the manifests previously imported in the manifest directory specified in *environment.conf*.

Even though this cleanup requires some effort, it will pay down technical debt and make future upgrades much easier.

Moving Shared Tools to Their Own Repository

With monolithic repositories, it's fairly common for modules to centralize and share tools in the large repository. These tools might be used by many modules and might be included or invoked from qualified paths that need to be addressed.

We recommend packaging any shared tools as a versionable component that can be installed with the module:

- Modules should be given their own repository and version.
- Ruby tools should be packaged as gems.
- Scripts can be given their own repository and version.
- Compiled tools should be added to the native package system (RPM, dpkg, etc.).

 The *puppetlabs_spec_helper* gem contains tools and code that can be shared between multiple modules. Compare the complexity of installing this gem against the complexity of maintaining the same code spread across many module repositories.

Implementing Test Cases

With the hybrid deployment described in the previous section, the process of moving your modules is fairly low risk. As you move modules to their own repositories, take a moment to refactor the modules to modern practices, including doing the following:

- pdk convert the module for use with the PDK (*http://bit.ly/2vIvrou*)
- Ensure that the module uses modern standards by validating the module (*http://bit.ly/2LY4aZZ*) code.
- Add units tests if they don't exist already, and test the module (*http://bit.ly/2OPIKwf*).

Unit tests are small and easy to write. Acceptance tests can be more difficult but can catch significantly more real-life problems. Take the time to create or improve the acceptance tests.

Best Practices for Puppet Deployments

In this section, we touch on a number of best practices for deploying Puppet code, with or without r10k. Although we have discussed some of these practices elsewhere in the chapter, this section brings some additional focus to them.

Using Repository Access Control to Enforce Deployment Policy

As a general rule, anyone with the ability to modify your configuration management repositories also has the ability to modify and control the hosts managed by those configurations.

It is much more difficult, if not impossible, to limit access to code and data that has been widely shared. It is thus very important to set up appropriate controls early in the process.

A code collaboration system will provide tools that simplify peer-review, commentary, bug tracking, change control, and other workflows. Each collaboration system has its own access control and release management models. Puppet is no different from any other code tree in this sense, and you should give Puppet code the same careful code review process that you would apply to any other development project. The choice of source code management and release process has the same needs. Workflows for Puppet and r10k require only a source code system that enables easy creation and merge back of short-term feature branches.

 Did you burst out laughing when you read the words *careful code review process* in the preceding paragraph? If so, perhaps it's time for you to lead. Show the development team how it can be done well!

Don't get too wrapped up in security controls. The security of code branches should ensure that release management processes are followed. It should not inhibit developers from deploying feature branches to development and test hosts.

Security of the control repository

In order for developers to push out feature branches for feedback and testing, they need to be able to create new branches in the control repository. This generally means giving every developer a high level of control in the control repository. There are two methods for protecting production environments that deploy changes with r10k:

- Implement per-branch permissions on the production branches that ensure the release is tested and approved.
- Implement a release process that copies production-ready branches to a tightly controlled production repository after approval.

Either of these processes will work. Choose the one that works best with the tools and processes you have today.

Hiera data in the control repository

In most cases, data will be closely coupled to your site-specific module set, meaning that the choice of data sources will be tightly tied to the modules used. As a result, the control repository's *Puppetfile* is by far the most appropriate place to identify the data sources, maintaining cohesion with the module specification that uses them.

You can store the data in the control repository with the module specification, or it can reside in its own repository. As always it will be a balance of the trade-offs, mostly around how the data is structured.

If all environments are test environments that share a single, small dataset, putting the data in the control repository makes it downright easy to test module changes and their related data. In a small shop, keeping the code and data together can simplify updates when the modules and data are maintained by the same team. If you're using this approach, purge the environments and recreate them early and often to avoid drift from the production dataset. In larger enterprises, it can be impractical for a number of reasons:

- Very large datasets can be unsuitable for replicating into each environment.
- Levels of the hierarchy might be sourced from external data, which is not easy to deploy on demand to alternate locations.
- If environments segregate different projects, teams, or applications, they will likely require unique data sources.
- It might be necessary to store parts of the data hierarchy in different repositories to give teams ownership of their data without giving them control of the module specification.

In our experience, choosing how to structure the data is rarely a difficult decision. The choice will likely be obvious, and will need to be reevaluated only when team restructuring and code or data ownership changes. As is often the case, a blended approach can work, so long as it is well documented.

Enabling Multiteam Coordination

No matter how small the team using Puppet is today, you should prepare and plan for coordination between multiple teams. In larger organizations, it's not unusual for Puppet code to be written and maintained by multiple teams: infrastructure, security, and application teams will all have a part to play, and we recommend that you plan for this from the start.

Such an approach is valuable because it allows your subject matter experts to automate their own applications. This is especially valuable when teams are horizontally layered: one team is responsible for node provisioning, another for security policy, and another for application deployment. Allow these teams to maintain their own code and data while sharing access to modules developed for common use throughout the organization.

It's not uncommon for a tools, release, or automation team to take on the role of a service provider to delivery-oriented teams. These organizations can still develop, review, and approve modules, but a lot of the individual delivery goals might be handled by teams directly involved in delivery.

r10k facilitates multiteam development by allowing each team to control their own modules and even their own environments. If necessary, each team can utilize distinct control repositories to provide a secure method to control what is ultimately deployed.

Deployments for multiple team modules

In "Control Repository Branch Contents" on page 213 we discussed how to organize a control repository. In "Repository-per-Module Benefits" on page 231 we discussed how a *Puppetfile* can allow your control repository to pull modules from multiple teams. But what if you need to allow other teams to contribute to the control repository itself, without granting those teams full control over the repository?

In smaller sites, it might be sufficient to simply use a pull request model. Any team can submit pull requests for desired changes. One team is responsible for reviewing, approving, and merging changes. Many large public projects use this model successfully.

Multiple control repositories providing Puppet environments

The conventional approach is to have r10k source multiple control repositories. Environments from each are deployed with their own unique prefix. This provides the greatest flexibility, allowing each team to create feature branches with any name without conflicting with other teams. This is often combined with a release management strategy that has production branches in a control repository maintained by the QA or release management team.

Multiple control repositories can cohabituate in a single environment path if each repository is prefixed with a unique identifier to help avoid environment name conflicts. This capability allows you and your users to maintain organization-specific control repositories. This capability can be useful when the needs of various teams are dramatically different, but you'd still like to share infrastructure.

You can also run r10k multiple times with different `environmentpath` directories. As with the *modulepath*, the *environmentpath* is a search path: if the same environment name exists in multiple directories, the first entry found in the path will be used exclusively; others will be ignored. If you are pulling environments from multiple repositories, be sure to take this into account. If you are not prefixing your Puppet environments, consider using the *modulepath* to prioritize specific sources.

Multiple module directories within a single Puppet environment

It can suit teams to place different modules in different module directories. Although this is often deployed for external (*dist/*) modules versus internally developed modules, it can also be employed to segregate multiple teams' modules, as well. r10k allows this by setting the `install_path` parameter separately for each module, as demonstrated in the following example:

```
# Puppet Forge Modules
mod 'apache',
  :git => 'https://github.com/puppetlabs/puppetlabs-apache'

# Security team
mod 'security'
  :git => 'git://github.example.com:security/profiles.git'
  :install_path => 'security'

# Platform team
mod 'role_webserver'
  :git => 'git://github.example.com:platform/webserver_role.git'
  :install_path => 'site'

mod 'role_database'
  :git => 'git://github.example.com:platform/webserver_role.git'
  :install_path => 'site'
```

Puppet sees only the first module directory of a given name. Having multiple directories might be mistaken for the ability to reuse module names, which will fail in difficult-to-debug ways.

Pinning Module Versions

Modules listed in the *Puppetfile* can optionally specify a tag, branch, or ref that should be checked out. If not supplied, r10k will deploy the latest version of a module, or the HEAD revision of a Git repository.

Using r10k with pinned versions guarantees consistent tests and deployment. When you deploy the same versions of every component, they will operate in the same way. You can pin versions of modules to packaged versions, repository tags, and Git hashes. When you pin a module to a commit hash or release tag, you can be confident that you are getting exactly the code you expect.

This guarantee of consistency can be the cornerstone of your change review and release process. By pinning dependencies to a specific version, the team who originally developed that module is free to continue development with minimal risk to your production infrastructure. Conversely, you can easily test new versions simply by changing the version number.

For testing purposes, it is possible to select a branch name or `:latest` as the version to deploy. This is useful for automatically testing the latest updates to public modules, but it introduces considerable risk in deployed environments. A release-ready branch should always specify explicit versions or Git hashes.

 Only repositories that provide hashes of the entire repository state are guaranteed to be consistent. Although you can pin to an SVN revision or Git tag, you cannot cryptographically validate the integrity of these sources.

Always pin each repository-sourced module to a specific commit hash. Unlike refs and tags, or even short commit hashes, a full commit hash is cryptographically secure; you get exactly the code you expect, and there's no way for the repository owner to accidentally break you. Pinning dependency modules this way prevents both malicious and nonmalicious changes from reaching your production environment. The following code shows you how to pin a module:

```
mod 'apache',
  :git    => 'https://github.com/puppetlabs/puppetlabs-apache',
  :commit => 'f7946501ddb68e0057b5dc3272657bea891639e5' # Pin to specific bugfix
```

It's a good practice to document inline the criteria used for the selection of tag or version used. This will make life much simpler for anyone attempting to update the *Puppetfile*, debug a problem, or investigate version-specific features. This also simplifies the process of identifying out-of-date modules.

Being able to pin to a commit hash is a Git-specific feature; other revision control systems might not provide equivalent functionality. In those cases, you should pin to the specific branch or commit that is likely to remain unchanged. Pinning this way allows your team to continue improving the head revision of the module without the risk of breaking production nodes. Alternatively, mirror from the other repository into Git and thus make Git hashes available.

Isolating Puppet Extensions

Native Ruby extensions to Puppet are handled using Ruby's built-in autoloader. New resource types and functions can be encapsulated in modules because Puppet adds the module's `lib` directory to Ruby's load path. Without enabling environment isolation, after a native extension is loaded from one environment, Ruby will not attempt to load the same extension from another environment.

This hasn't generally been a problem for short-lived, ad hoc Puppet applications, but it can prevent testing of improvements in long-lived Puppet server environments. This is not an issue for agent-side extensions such as facts and resource providers, because the client process terminates at the end of each application—even when the agent is daemonized.

For years it was necessary to work around this by using a long list of environment separation practices, including physical separation of development Puppet servers. Depending on how far you were willing to go, crazy monkey-patches that attempted to adjust the Ruby load path of active instances were available. If you have any of that hackery in your Puppet deployment today, **get rid of it**.

After an environment is deployed, run the following command in the environment to enable environment isolation:

```
$ puppet generate types --environment production
```

That's it. No separation of development components. No crazy hackery. Just unique metadata within each environment identifying a unique load path for each extension.

Utilizing Standard Environment Configuration Practices

The following are all practices that have become so commonly used that the tools all assume you'll be using the same approach. Take advantage of these conventions unless you have a really good reason for not doing so.

Keeping Hiera configuration within the environment

Because the mapping of modules and the data they use is critical for testing what you're deploying, you should store the *hiera.yaml* file in the control repository with the *Puppetfile*. These two files are integrally tied to building the environment consistently. This approach avoids confusion, and simplifies the process of testing hierarchy changes.

> The unwritten consequence of testing consistency is that you can't have Puppet making changes to the Hiera configuration. This was never a good idea, because you have to deploy the Puppet code and data in order to utilize Puppet to manage the data…a bit late, no?

Global modules

You can configure Puppet to use a fallback module path for modules shared between all Puppet environments.

The modulepath environment configuration setting allows you to specify a set of module directories that should be available to the environment. You can use this to add a directory from outside the environment (such as */etc/puppetlabs/code/modules*) that is searched for shared modules.

 The $basemodulepath is appended after the per-environment modulepath by default. It contains directories with modules distributed and maintained by Puppet and should not be overridden. Customize the modulepath only within the environment configuration.

Environment manifests

Each Puppet environment specifies a single manifest file, or a directory containing manifest files, to be read as top-level manifests. The *manifests* directory replaces the classic *site.pp* manifest as the entry point for all Puppet applications. These manifests are always evaluated when compiling a catalog for each node in that environment.

Environment manifests are the appropriate place for the following:

- Hiera-driven class assignments
- Role assignment
- Node statements
- Global resource defaults
- Top-level variables

As we covered earlier in this book, the last four bullet items are practices that have been deprecated in favor of better approaches. In an ideal scenario, the only thing you want in top-level manifests is a lookup() to get classes to be applied from Hiera, as discussed in "Data-driven class assignment" on page 164.

For a more through discussion on node management, including alternative approaches to node classification, see Chapter 8.

The modules directory

The *modules* directory is the default location where r10k will deploy modules, and the default location that Puppet expects to find them. In the control repository, it should be empty. You should specify modules in the *Puppetfile*, instead.

If you are migrating from an existing monolithic modules repository, place it in the *dist/* directory, as mentioned previously. This will allow you to slowly deploy the modules with r10k, until finally the monolithic directory can be removed.

Test tools, rake tasks, and other utilities

The control repository is a good place for test configurations that test the environment as a whole, such as Rakefiles and Travis configurations.

The control repository is not a good place for helper code used to perform the testing. Avoid placing site management scripts, code maintenance scripts, and other utilities within the control repository. All of these should be version-pinned in the *Puppetfile* for deployment, as discussed in "Moving Shared Tools to Their Own Repository" on page 237.

Environment documentation

It's a good idea to place a README file in each branch of the control repository. This will be available for anyone testing the environment. Limit environment documentation to the unique use case for the environment and testing instructions.

Use whatever documentation is standard for your code collaboration tools to display. Markdown is by far the most common documentation format found in code collaboration tools.

Git Best Practices

There are no Puppet-specific best practices with regards to Git or any other version control system. That doesn't mean you don't need to apply them, but you should employ the established best practices in your Puppet release management strategy.

> The number one practice that every Puppet person should focus on is clear, well-written commit messages. For more information on this, read How to write a Git commit message (*http://bit.ly/2vIAOEa*).

Deployment Practices

Each control repository branch contains the contents of an individual environment. Do not attempt to overload this practice to supply configuration files to copy down to the node.

The Puppet server, Puppet agent, and r10k configurations should be managed by Puppet using modules and data, the same as any other application. The advantage of this approach is that it will allow you to apply your change control procedure to Puppet configuration updates.

If you are a Puppet Enterprise user, a number of bundled modules are included to manage the Puppet infrastructure. They are installed in */opt/puppetlabs/puppet/modules* and should not be moved into the control repository. These modules are managed as part of the Puppet agent or server all-in-one installation.

Concurrency protection

If you are running r10k on a frequent interval or if r10k is triggered externally, there is a risk of r10k being invoked again while it is already running. Although r10k will usually tolerate this, you can end up with a situation in which r10k processes are being spawned faster than they can complete, overloading the system.

The voxpupuli/puppet_webhook module implements concurrency protection. If using a deployment tool or WebHook receiver that does not have the ability to limit concurrent invocation, use Flock or a similar tool to provide concurrency protection. Flock automates the process of creating, checking, and removing lockfiles, as demonstrated in the following:

```
flock -w 360 /var/lock/r10k -c '/opt/puppet/bin/r10k deploy environment -v warn'
```

Don't go cowboy on shared infrastructure

You should never edit Puppet code on shared infrastructure. Save that for testing on your development workstation. All of the release workflows we discussed expect developers to create a feature branch of the code, edit and test it offline, and then push back the feature branch for testing.

Summary

r10k is an invaluable tool for deploying Puppet code, whether you want to build packages or deploy directly to your systems. Hopefully, this chapter has helped you evaluate the strengths and weaknesses of your current deployment strategy or helped you to design a new strategy.

Keep in mind that it can take quite some time to implement a comprehensive CD process. Plan iterative improvements in the current process, rather than a huge project to build out a complete system. Many of these components are useful in isolation; start small and build toward an end goal.

 If you try to boil the ocean, you might just drown first.

Here are the key takeaways from this chapter:

- r10k deploys Puppet environments based on code branchs in a code repository.
- r10k is a tool to be used in a release workflow such as GitFlow or GitHub Flow.
- The *Puppetfile* provides a specification to rebuild a complete environment.

- Best practices for r10k are best practices for Puppet environment configuration.
- Select code collaboration tools with flexible and powerful code review and gating controls.
- Puppet release management is very similar to other code deployment practices.
- These practices grew from many users sharing experiences—steal from the best!
- CI can leverage CD for improved feedback.
- CD can use continuous deployment to speed change delivery.

## CHAPTER 10

Extending Puppet

One of Puppet's strengths is its extreme extensibility. Even though a basic deployment of Puppet includes a fairly comprehensive set of resource types, facts, and function calls, it's fairly simple and incredibly common to extend Puppet's functionality.

This chapter is not intended to provide detailed API documentation for Puppet; instead, we look at a lot of the approaches, best practices, and pitfalls of extension development.

The Cost of Extending Puppet

Before writing custom extensions for Puppet, it's a good idea to consider the ongoing costs associated with creating and maintaining in-house customizations to Puppet.

Although all code (including Puppet manifests) carries some maintenance costs, native Ruby extensions to Puppet carry somewhat higher overhead than the Puppet language code.

Minimizing Development Costs

Development of extensions beyond basic facts is generally considered a specialty skill that many Puppet users will not have. Creating Puppet extensions requires a higher degree of familiarity with Ruby and Puppet's internal APIs than is required by simply using the built-in language features. Although the new resource API will make developing extensions easier than ever before, choosing to build your own extensions has an unavoidable effort cost that can only be borne by senior developers. It can be difficult to find developers capable of maintaining internally built extensions in the long term.

The cost of developing extensions is not specific to Puppet. Everything said here holds true for any tool you might want to modify or extend.

Documenting your extensions, writing good unit and acceptance tests, and following general development best practices can mitigate this cost. You should pay special attention to the concepts discussed in Chapter 3, especially the KISS principle, the single responsibility principle, and the interface-driven design principles. Most of all, remember YAGNI: *You're Not Google* and it's likely that *You Ain't Gonna Need It*.

Reducing Upgrade Costs

Puppet maintains a strong degree of backward compatibility between releases. Even though Puppet features introduced in the latest release of Puppet will not work on earlier versions of Puppet, code that worked in earlier minor versions (5.1, 5.2, etc.) should work cleanly in the latest minor release of that version.

Although Puppet's APIs are stable, not all of the internal libraries are guaranteed to provide backward compatibility. This is especially true when inheriting and extending Puppet's internal Ruby classes. If you have written Puppet extensions that rely on Puppet behavior or internals that are not part of the API, especially those that rely on Puppet's less commonly used internal classes, it becomes increasingly important to test your code against new releases before attempting to upgrade. As a result, writing Ruby-native code that peeks into Puppet's internal libraries tends to create upgrade-related overhead.

Even if you don't have a lot of Puppet extensions, it's a good idea to build automated upgrade testing into your pipeline. By deploying your standard tests on each new version, you can identify code that will break on the latest releases of Puppet. This type of testing will give your team visibility into compatibility problems, help scope upgrade work, and will ensure that your upgrades go smoothly.

Testing

Although deploying code and watching for explosions is a form of testing, it can hinder development speed and trust between teams. Testing, like documentation, is an investment in the future of your module. Testing outside the scope of your overall site is a good way to identify assumptions about your module, and to catch unexpected dependencies. This section covers best practices for testing Puppet code before it burns down something in production.

Static Code Analysis

Static analysis is the process of evaluating code without actually executing it. The PDK runs a number of static analysis tools to quickly identify flaws, coding inconsistencies, and validation against a chosen style. You can use this at any point in development, even for situations in which the code is partially implemented or missing dependencies.

The benefit of static analysis is that it is extremely fast and can be performed against code in any state of development. You do this by running `pdk validate` within a module directory, like so:

```
$ pdk validate --list
pdk (INFO): Available validators: metadata, puppet, ruby

$ pdk validate
pdk (INFO): Running all available validators...
```

Let's review the validators that run against the module's code.

Puppet metadata

The metadata test analyzes the *metadata.json* for conformity to Puppet tool expectations and module deployment requirements.

Puppet code lint

The lint tool analyzes code for conformity to Puppet style guide. It can catch a number of common coding errors that might otherwise hide bugs, and it will tend to improve the readability of your code.

Common problems caught by lint include the use of nonqualified variables, variable inheritance, documentation problems, embedding of selectors where they don't belong, use of bare values that should be quoted, and use of double quotes where single quotes are more appropriate.

Lint is especially useful for testing upgrades between major releases of Puppet. It can catch variable inheritance and variable naming issues that would break a Puppet 3 or Puppet 4 upgrade, respectively.

Ruby code cop

Much like Puppet lint, the Rubocop tool analyzes Ruby code for conformity to the Ruby style guide. It can catch a number of common coding errors that might otherwise hide bugs, and will tend to improve the readability of your code.

Unit Testing

Unit testing is a process in which small units of code are individually and independently scrutinized for proper operation. The code is typically built and tested in a sandbox environment sufficient only to evaluate the code structures. *No resources will be harmed during unit testing of the code.*

Even though the lint and validate commands will ensure that your module parses, unit testing actually exercises the functions, logic, and resources in your module. Where validate might not catch a typo in the parameter of a resource, unit testing will. It tests that your changes have not altered your module's interfaces, broken support for other platforms, or created a regression in the module operation.

The PDK runs unit tests on a module when the command pdk test unit is run in the module directory:

```
$ pdk test unit
[✓] Preparing to run the unit tests.
[✓] Running unit tests.
  Evaluated 28 tests in 4.17108 seconds: 0 failures, 0 pending.
[✓] Cleaning up after running unit tests.
```

Although not as fast as static code analysis, unit tests generally run very quickly, as seen in the preceding example (4 seconds for 28 tests). Unit tests are small and fast. Units tests are performed entirely within the constructs of the Ruby interpreter, with no impact outside of bundling Ruby gem and Puppet module dependencies into the module directory. They can run quickly on your local workstation, and can safely be configured to run on every commit to the repository.

With few exceptions, rspec can run tests for any platform locally. For example, puppet-rspec can test a module targeted for Debian and Red Hat systems on a MacOS node without issue.

 Unix/Linux/Mac tests will often fail on Windows workstations, and vice versa, unless mocks for the platform-specific resources have been set up. It's getting better all the time, but it's safest to run unit tests for Windows on Windows nodes.

The PDK now autogenerates validation and catalog parsing tests for you. It will fall to you to add the following tests:

- Test input validation and proper handling of both good and bad input.
- Validate that the output of your module matches your expectations.
- Prevent regression problems (old behavior failing to work after a change).

Unit tests do not need to validate the internal state of your module and need not be absolutely strict about the output. Overly strict testing with heavy focus on the internal structure of your module will needlessly slow the development process.

> The limitation of unit testing is that it tests the units within your modules; it doesn't validate external dependencies or interactions between them. We cover this in "Acceptance Testing" on page 255.

Dependencies

There are two places that dependencies must be listed for testing to be successful. The PDK autogenerates suitable starting points, but you need to add any new dependencies:

- The module's *.fixtures.yml* contains a list of Puppet modules that must be installed to test the module. Always update the fixtures when a new module is added to dependencies in the metadata.

- The module's *Gemfile* contains a list of gems that must be installed to test the module. Always add gems used by the module's Ruby types, providers, functions, or facts to this.

The module skeleton created by `pdk new module` includes an appropriate *Gemfile* and fixture starting points.

Input testing with rspec

Input validation ensures compatibility with your documentation and ensures that changes do not break compatibility within a major release of your module. Writing good input validation tests provides the freedom to modify the module with the confidence of knowing that any changes that break compatibility will fail the test.

Perform the following tests for each documented parameter of your module. Start with default values, as shown here:

```
context 'with document_root => undef' do
  it { is_expected.to contain_file('/etc/httpd/conf/httpd.conf').with({
      :content => %r{DocumentRoot /var/www/html}
    })
  }
end
```

Then, test valid and appropriate values being passed to that resource:

```
context 'with document_root => /tmp' do
  let :params do
    { :document_root => '/tmp' }
```

```
      end

    it { is_expected.to contain_file('/etc/httpd/conf/httpd.conf').with({
        :content => %r{DocumentRoot /tmp}
      })
    }
  end
```

Finally, test for some known bad input. Get creative about mismatched data types:

```
context "with document_root => false" do
  let :params do
    { :documentroot => false }
  end

  it { is_expected.not_to compile }
  it { is_expected.to raise_error(Puppet::Error, /not an absolute path/) }
end
```

If you test all of these situations for every resource, you can have complete confidence that a breaking changes won't pass the tests.

Resource validation

In most cases, input validation will by its nature check the output of the module. However, there are often resources in your module that are not affected by input parameters. You should test those resources explicitly, as demonstrated here:

```
it { is_expected.to contain_service('httpd').with({
    :ensure => 'running',
    :enable => true,
  })
}
```

This test has confirmed that the Apache service is configured to run in the catalog.

Testing input validation

Test the module's input validation to ensure that it behaves as expected. Nothing is more frustrating than having valid input data rejected because of a poorly designed test.

For input validation, we recommend using Test-Driven Development (TDD) practices; write your test cases before you write the module code to implement them. Always test both good and bad input, and positive and negative outcomes. You are much more likely to build the code for input validation correctly if you have a good list of tests available for immediate feedback. Example 10-1 presents some sample input validation code.

Example 10-1. Example input validation

```
# Positive tests
good_ports = [ 80, 443 ]
good_ports.each do |port|
  context "with port #{port}" do
    let :params do
      { :port => port }
    end

    it { is_expected.to contain_file('/etc/httpd/conf/httpd.conf').with({
        :content => /Listen #{port}/
      })
    }
  end
end

# Invalid data tests
bad_ports = [ -1, 65536, 'monkey' ]
bad_ports.each do |ports|
  context "with port #{port}" do
    let :params do
      { :port => port }
    end

    it { is_expected.to raise_error(Puppet::Error, /expects an Integer/) }
  end
end
```

This basic good/bad value-testing pattern is easy to read and comprehend, and the list of values to be tested can grow significantly without adding any new lines of code.

Acceptance Testing

Acceptance testing is done to ensure proper behavior of a product for the intended use, generally expressed as an example or a usage scenario.

Acceptance tests provide a quick way to apply your module to a real running system, and can catch issues related to ordering, idempotence, undeclared dependencies, and external resources that cannot be reliably tested in any other way.

Acceptance testing is done by creating (and destroying) virtual nodes or containers to test how all of the code will behave when deployed as a complete solution. This is especially important to ensure that your code applies idempotently, but it also allows you to perform experiments to identify limitations in your code. Acceptance testing can utilize a wide variety of platforms for testing interoperability.

Use containers or virtualization for acceptance testing

The following platform tools are commonly used to provide node creation and destruction for acceptance testing.

Vagrant

Vagrant is a tool for managing ephemeral virtual machines (VMs). Vagrant focuses on simplifying VM distribution, provisioning, and postconfiguration tasks. Vagrant supports most virtualization and cloud platforms, including AWS Elastic Compute Cloud (Amazon EC2) instances, Openstock Compute nodes, VMWare Vsphere clusters, Microsoft Azure Compute nodes, and desktop virtualization such as VMWare Workstation, VMWare Fusion, and VirtualBox.

Vagrant streamlines the process and reduces it to a repeatable configuration. Postprovisioning configuration tasks such as configuring port forwarding, mapping shared directories, and invoking Puppet are declared in the *Vagrantfile*. It's simple enough that a developer otherwise completely inexperienced with virtualization should be able to bring up and use a VM for testing.

Packer

Packer is a tool for building VM images, cloud provider images, and containers. These capabilities make it possible to automate the creation and maintenance of versioned and tested images. You can run Packer-built machines through the same CI systems as your Puppet code. You can even use them as part of the Puppet CI process.

Packer provides a simple way to create and maintain Vagrant boxes that mirror production deployment standards. Although Hashicorp's Vagrant Cloud provides a large number of boxes from reputable sources, there are many cases for which a locally built box might be necessary to test site-specific code. For these cases, the Box Cutter project (*https://github.com/boxcutter*) is an excellent starting point for the creation of custom boxes built entirely in-house.

Docker

Docker and other containerization solutions are an excellent option for the creation of development nodes. Containers are light on resources, easy to manage, and offer extremely high performance. Containers are ideal for testing applications or services without (waiting for) deployment of an entire operating system (OS), or when large number of nodes are needed for testing or experimentation within a small footprint. If you need to test multiple application or service interactions without utilizing signficant test resources, a container offers significant benefits over conventional VMs.

Even though containers do allow you to bring up machines with a different distribution or library set, they are not ideal for testing your application on multiple platforms. Containers share the kernel of the base OS, and cannot easily host a

32-bit kernel on a 64-bit host OS, host different kernel releases, or bring up instances with completely different operating systems. There are solutions (such as Docker for Mac) that utilize a VM running Docker that can deploy containers for the VM's OS.

Resource validation

With acceptance tests, verify the functionality of the applied module and the return codes from applying the module. For example, with an `apache` module, you might want to ensure that the Apache package is present on the system and that the service is running and responds with the boilerplate site when queried.

It's also valuable to ensure that Puppet returns an exit code indicating that it modified system state with no errors upon initial invocation and that further invocations produced no change. These tests will quickly ensure that your module is idempotent when applied to a live system:

```
apply_manifest('include myapp', :catch_failures => true)
apply_manifest('include myapp', :catch_changes => true)

describe package('httpd') do
  it { is_expected.to be_installed }
end

describe service('httpd') do
  it { is_expected.to be_running }
end
```

Beaker supports multiple backends for acceptance testing. The most commonly used backend is Vagrant, which is compatible with your existing boxes. However, Beaker can build and invoke tests on Docker, OpenStack, VMWare, AWS, Azure, and many other cloud providers. We cover these tools in "Acceptance Testing" on page 255.

When writing Beaker tests, it's important to begin with a base system image, free of debris from earlier tests, to ensure that your module is not implicitly dependent on some system state left behind by other tests. If your site uses a custom base image, use a fresh copy of that image base for Puppet testing. Local security policy can create restrictions that are not present on public images. The testing will also be more relevant if the base image has preconfigured package repositories for your site.

If you intend to publicly release the module, you should test the module against a publicly available base image to ensure maximum compatibility.

Creating Facts

On the target node, Puppet provides a number of facts about the node. The facts are available from the `$facts` hash for use while building the catalog. This works exactly the same in server-based or serverless uses of Puppet; the only difference is whether the catalog is built by a Puppet server or the node itself.

The supplied facts will be sent to Puppet's facts terminus, which can store or analyze them. They are usually stored in the Puppet server's cache directory in a file named for the node, and submitted to PuppetDB for use in queries and reporting.

In this section, we review different kinds of facts and the best practices for fact development.

Distributing Facts in Modules

Facts placed in modules will be automatically synchronized to the node at the very beginning of the process. The node will install the custom facts, evaluate all facts, and then provide the resolved facts for catalog compilation. This works exactly the same regardless of whether `puppet apply` is used locally or `puppet agent` is communicating with Puppet server.

Ancient releases of Puppet (many years out of support) did not synchronize external facts or require configuration options to be enabled for fact synchronization. This led to Puppet developers using Puppet to deploy facts directly into Facter's directories on the node using file resources. This approach worked, but it meant that the external facts were not available on the first invocation of Puppet, thus rendering the first few Puppet runs nonidempotent.

Facts have been synchronized automatically in server-based and serverless deployments of Puppet since the mid-Puppet 3 release cycle, a full year before Puppet 4 was released. A Puppet module is the only place to put custom facts. Any facts being written to the node using a file resource should be simplified into an external fact.

Custom facts

Custom facts are written in Ruby, stored in the *lib/facter/* directory of Puppet modules, and register the fact name using `Facter.add()`.

Unless execution of a different language is required, you should write custom facts in Ruby. The interfaces for facts are stable, the syntax is simple, and native facts allow you to do anything an executable fact can, with the advantage of Ruby's excellent parsing functionality and access to Puppet configuration values and other facts.

External facts

Facter also supports external facts, which are files stored within the *facts.d* directory of Puppet module. If named with one of the following file extensions, they will be read as data facts:

.txt
> Read expecting text format

.yaml
> Read expecting YAML format

.json
> Read expecting JSON format

If the file does not have one of these file extensions, it will be executed as a program if one or the other of the following is true:

- It's on a Unix/Linux/POSIX system and the file has the execution bit set.
- It's on a Windows system and the file has one of the known Windows executible extensions, including *.exe, .com, .bat, .cmd,* or *.ps1.*

The expected output from each supported method is well documented at Custom Facts Walkthrough: External Facts (*http://bit.ly/2OUC275*).

Facts Puppet Can't Know

In the vast majority of situations, Puppet code can identify and source the appropriate data; for example, to perform the correct query to get the value. If Puppet has code that can determine the appropriate value for a node, it's always better to put the fact in a module and count on Puppet to synchronize the fact down before the initial catalog build.

For situations in which the node has data that Puppet cannot determine programatically, you can pre-create facts on the local filesystem to work around the shared-knowledge limitations; for example, data provided by a provisioning system which the node cannot query or retrieve. Create the unknowable data facts in the */etc/facter/facts.d* directory as part of the machine provisioning process. This ensures that the facts are available during the initial Puppet node classification.

Structured Facts

Puppet 4 and above utilizes structured facts by default, allowing facts to be presented as data structures in any valid Puppet data type. This makes it easy to supply hashes or arrays of values ready for use by modules without decoding.

When you're using structured facts, keep in mind the KISS and single responsibility principles. Avoid using a large, complex data structure where multiple facts would be cleaner and clearer.

Abusing Facts

Facters gather...well, FACTS about the node for use in the catalog build. That is the one and only thing fact code should do.

In our consulting experience, we've found a few abuses of facts that you should avoid. The most significant abuse of facts is to directly enforce policy on the client node. Even though facts do execute client side, you should design them to avoid having any effect on the system. You should use facts to discover details about the system, not to change the system.

As discussed in "Declarative Code" on page 1, facts provide necessary state information to Puppet, the Puppet data and code describe the desired state, and resource providers handle changing state on the node.

Trusted Certificate Attributes

As mentioned previously, because facts run on the node each time to supply data for the Puppet catalog, a compromised node could alter its facts. As discussed in "Use trusted facts when available" on page 155, data can be stored in a node's Puppet certificate, which cannot be changed by a compromised node (unless the compromised node is the Puppet certificate authority, which is a whole different level of problem).

For more information, refer to the documentation (*https://puppet.com/docs/puppet/latest/ssl_attributes_extensions.html*) for storing custom attributes in the node's certificate.

Custom Types and Providers

Although a core set of types and providers are built in with Puppet, you can add custom types and providers. The list of built-in resource types hasn't changed significantly since the Puppet 2.x days, and the trend is to move built-in providers out into modules to allow more selection and faster development of resource types.

You can add custom types and providers to any Puppet module and install them whenever the module exists in the Puppet environment's modulepath. All plugins available in the Puppet environment, including resource providers, are synchronized down to the node before the catalog is built. This ensures that custom providers are available to nodes during their first run of Puppet.

In most cases, modules that provide new resource types include both the type and its providers. For example, the puppetlabs/mysql (*https://forge.puppet.com/puppetlabs/mysql*) module contains custom types and providers for interacting with MySQL databases. However, there are cases for which a module might include a provider for an existing resource type, such as the *Chocolatey* or *Oneget* providers for the package resource on Windows platforms.

Users of Puppet will rarely if ever interact directly with resource providers. The most common interaction would be the explicit declaration of nondefault providers when needed, such as an alternative package manager on a platform. Only Puppet developers and contributors generally need to create or install providers.

Publicly available types and providers should be sufficient for the vast majority of sites. However, there are numerous good reasons to create your own types and providers:

- A resource type can be compared for compliance by using `puppet resource` and `--noop`.
- Resource attributes are stored and changes are logged.
- You can export resource attributes for use in other catalogs.
- No provider for an existing resource supports your platform or application framework.

An idempotent provider that can compare state and log changes is vastly superior to a fire-and-forget `exec` resource that knows only the command's return code.

If you are interested in developing resource types and providers, the foundation book is *Puppet Types and Providers* (*http://bit.ly/puppet-types-and-providers*) by Dan Bode and Nan Liu. Their book covers the basics of implementing types and providers. This chapter focuses on best practices and gotchas of resource type and provider development.

Avoiding Creation of Duplicate Types

Let's be honest: the best kind of code is code that you don't need to write. So before engaging in the creation of a new resource type or provider, make sure there's not already a well-written, idempotent provider that handles this need. Many of the following resource types can be utilized as building blocks of a defined type.

PowerShell DSC

Microsoft has put a fairly heroic effort into making Windows automation friendly in all supported versions. PowerShell Desired State Control (DSC) is your best bet for implementing Windows configuration changes.

In many cases, you probably won't need to write a custom type or provider for Windows; the dsc (*https://forge.puppet.com/puppetlabs/dsc*) resource type and provider should be able to handle most common tasks. If DSC does not offer a built-in resource that suits your needs, consider the Lite module.

PowerShell DSC-lite. The puppetlabs/dsc_lite (*https://forge.puppet.com/puppetlabs/ dsc_lite*) module is a lighter-weight version of the Puppet DSC module, providing more flexibility for advanced users. It allows you to manage target nodes using DSC resources using a generalized Puppet call, without the overhead of build or compilation steps used in the DSC module.

inifile

The puppetlabs/inifile (*https://forge.puppet.com/puppetlabs/inifile*) module has providers to parse files that use INI or Java properties syntax. This provider is useful for any file that uses a separator between key and value, such as `key = value`, `key: value` pairs to manage configuration settings. The `ini_setting` resource is fast, easy to use, and it handles all of the complexity in handling loosely or inconsistently formatted files.

 `ini_setting` allows you to overwrite the key/value pair delimiter, making it useful for parsing files that use INI-like syntax, not just files that follow strict INI formatting.

INI syntax files are surprisingly common in both the Windows and Linux/Unix worlds; this provider can easily be used to parse the following:

- EL interface configuration files and other files in */etc/sysconfig/*
- Java properties files
- Most application configuration files in */etc/* entries

XML

If you want to parse XML files, there are a few options available:

- Gary Larizza's xmlsimple (*https://forge.puppet.com/glarizza/xmlsimple*) module makes it easy to read XML into hashes for use in Puppet, and write them back out again.
- Ian Oberst's xml_fragment (*https://forge.puppet.com/ianoberst/xml_fragment*) makes it easy to ensure specific fragments of an XML file exist.
- You can use the built-in augeas (*https://puppet.com/docs/puppet/latest/ type.html#augeas*) resource type with the XML lens. This is a good approach to use if you're already familiar with Augeas and need to perform a fairly simple task.

The archive resource

The `archive` resource is a powerful type for deploying files from web sources. It implements methods to download files via the HTTP, FTP, and other protocols on multiple platforms. It can also extract the archives and run commands from the contents.

This resource can pull packages from sources not supported by the underlying package provider. For example, it can download an executable installer from a web server, which can then be run locally. It's useful in any situation for which you need to download a file from a source other than a Puppet mountpoint.

A huge benefit of `archive` is that it abstracts away the underlying tools. You can specify an FTP, HTTP, Puppet or local filesystem source, and `archive` will do the right thing, going so far as to use the correct platform-specific tools. This abstraction is invaluable for module development and testing; it avoids the need to set up a web server to perform simple experimentation. It allows for local fixtures to be used during testing rather than leaving you reliant on external infrastructure.

In a previous example, we used an `exec` resource to run `wget` for illustrative purposes. That's never the best way to do it. Use an `archive` resource, instead. In almost every single case, the best practice is to use an `archive` resource.

The `archive` resource depends on the availability of `wget`, `unzip`, and other tools that might or might not be installed on your hosts by default. It is a good idea to install these tools prior to invoking the `archive` resource. For more details, see Chapter 7.

The `archive` resource type is provided by the puppet/archive (*https:// forge.puppet.com/puppet/archive*) module.

Creating a New Resource Type

Custom types allow you to extend Puppet's ability to identify and manage resources present on a node.

Describing state with a type

Before writing a custom resource, decide whether your need would be satisfied by developing a provider for an existing resource type.

Puppet resource types describe the interface to your module; they model the resource declaratively. The provider has methods to acquire the existing state for comparison and to bring the resource to the desired state. If there is an existing resource type that provides a good interface, you can simply add a new provider for that resource type, as discussed in "Adding providers to a resource" on page 265.

Resource types attempt to be platform agnostic where possible. For instance, the user resource type creates users for Windows, Linux, and Solaris. It can also create users in Lightweight Directory Access Protocol (LDAP). Each platform has its own provider, but a single resource type provides a common interface for all of them. Platform-specific parameters are available where needed.

Defining the type's interface

Custom types are written in Ruby and created by the `newtype()` method of `Puppet::Type`. Puppet's type framework is relatively straightforward to implement: it is a simple interface between the Puppet DSL and underlying Ruby logic. The resource type (found in the *lib/puppet/type* directory of a module) is a declaration of the attributes accepted (and required) for the resource and invocations of the provider's method calls that get or set the current state.

Puppet Types and Providers (*https://bit.ly/puppet-types-and-providers*) by Dan Bode and Nan Liu provides an excellent reference for the types and providers interfaces. Although it predates Puppet 4, very little has changed in the creation of Puppet types and providers, so it remains relevant. See also Puppet's Custom Types (*https://puppet.com/docs/puppet/latest/custom_types.html*) documentation.

Resource types comprise the following components:

1. The type's name
2. Properties: measurable or comparable things to be evaluated (e.g., user uid and file mode)
3. Parameters: configuration options that inform the provider how to apply (path for exec command, options for package installation, etc.)
4. Input validation for parameters and properties
5. Method calls implemented by the underlying provider(s)
6. Documentation of the type and its parameters

It is possible to implement resource types that do not rely on a backend provider. This is practical only when a resource doesn't directly make changes. The following are circumstances in which a backend provider is not necessary:

The resource type can provide its own implementation
 The `notify` resource has no provider because it does nothing more than output a message within Puppet.

The resource type can declare other resources
 The `tidy` resource is a metatype. It declares one or more instances of the `file` resource, which has its own providers.

As shown in this description, the resource type provides a clean abstraction layer for declaration of the resource, without concerning itself with how to implement those changes on any given platform.

Custom Resource Providers

Providers are responsible for the functional aspects of implementation on a given platform or for a given need. A provider does all of the following:

- Evaluate the presence or absence of the resource
- Evaluate each of the properties of the resource
- Apply changes to bring the resource to the declared state

Adding providers to a resource

Puppet resource types are intended to be a generic interface to the resource, and providers are expected to implement the platform-specific calls to manage that resource. For example, the `package` resource has drastically different providers that implement the package management functionality for each operating system: *apt*, *yum*, and so on.

If you do choose to implement a new provider for an existing resource type, be aware that the resource type and resource provider interfaces are very tightly bound. Your provider will break if it does not handle all of the required attributes and parameters of the parent resource. This requires you to track changes to the resource type and implement the new features.

Note that feature-specific attributes do not need to be supported unless your provider explicitly states that it supports those features. This behavior allows a lot of leeway in implementing new resource parameters without breaking backward compatibility.

Inheriting an existing provider

It's fairly common to build a provider based on an existing provider. The most common reason to do this is for cases in which you need to change the behavior of an existing provider.

For example, the puppetserver_gem (*https://github.com/puppetlabs/puppetlabs-puppetserver_gem*) resource provider is based on the built-in `gem` provider. It overrides a few behaviors of the upstream gem provider so that it can manage gems installed into the Puppet server's library path rather than the system Ruby library paths:

```
Puppet::Type.type(:package).provide :puppetserver_gem, :parent => :gem do
```

To inherent a provider, you simply need to supply the :parent and, optionally, the :source arguments to your provider declaration. Internally, Puppet subclasses the parent class. You can override parent methods by using normal Ruby class inheritance design patterns, including the super() method call. This is well-documented behavior at Provider Development (*https://puppet.com/docs/puppet/latest/ provider_development.html*).

 The provider will be very sensitive to changes in parent provider. The provider will need to be tested before after each parent module upgrade to ensure that it hasn't been broken.

Creating a resource provider

Providers have the following components:

- A declaration of a new resource provider
- A list of constraints and requirements to determine when to use
- A list of conditions to help determine the correct provider for a platform
- An optional method call to find all instances of the resource
- A method call to retrieve a specific instance of a resource
- Method calls for getting and setting resource property states

Providers are tightly coupled to their types: resource types call provider methods directly. Each provider must implement the methods of the resource type. Because of the tight coupling of type to the provider, it's possible to find that an older provider is not compatible with an updated type, or vice versa.

Retrieving existing resource instances

Resource providers can *but are not required to* implement an instances method. The instances method discovers existing instances of a resource on the node. The instances can then be used by resource metatypes such as the resources resource to purge existing resources that are not declared in the catalog, or by the puppet resource command to output lists of existing resources.

Most package providers provide an instances method. In the case of the RPM provider, the method is implemented by using a simple rpm -qa exec and some regular expression magic.

Implementing the instances method is optional because discovering available instances might not be possible due to the nature of the resource, or might be impractical because of the impact of discovering the resource instances. For example, the file resource doesn't implement the instances method because discovering every file on a node would incur huge overhead and take far too much time.

The systemd instances method is very simple, and makes for a great example implementation:

```
def self.instances
  i = []
  out = systemctl(
    'list-unit-files','--type','service','--full','--all','--no-pager'
  )
  out.scan(/^(\S+)\s+(disabled|enabled|masked)\s*$/i).each do |m|
    i << new(:name => m[0])
  end
  return i
rescue Puppet::ExecutionFailure
  return []
end
```

The instances method is provider specific, and can be implemented for only some of the providers for a given resource.

Reuse Existing Frameworks

Providers rarely need to be implemented from scratch. In many cases, you can use an existing code library or framework. In this section, we list a few powerful frameworks that can greatly simplify provider development.

Text frameworks

Manipulation of text configuration files is fairly common with Puppet, and there are a number of frameworks to help you build custom providers for this task.

Puppet's IniFile (http://bit.ly/2nTi9Sm)
  This framework has documentation for using it as parent classes for providers that need to read and write a key/value pair configuration file. This is by far the easiest provider to use if it meets your needs.

Puppet::Provider::ParsedFile (http://bit.ly/2OVm50n)
  This framework is intended to be a parent class for any provider that parses or generates files. It is used in a large number of Puppet's built-in resource providers. ParsedFile is line oriented and quite fast.

herculesteam/augeasproviders_core (http://bit.ly/2nWtvVX)
  This framework is a parent class for any provider that uses Augeas to parse or generate files. It is used in a large number of Puppet *approved* Augeas provider modules. It's best if you already use and know Augeas lenses and actions.

Vox Pupuli's FileMapper (https://forge.puppet.com/puppet/filemapper)
> This framework provides a way to map resources to file providers. It is provided as a mixin (Ruby `require`) that you can include in a provider that has a different parent. It is well documented and thus easier to use than the ParsedFile or Augeas providers. It's possible to implement complex and recursive multiline parsers that would be very difficult to build with ParsedFile.

Each of these providers enable you to bundle the backend parsing and writing in your type and provide a clean and simple interface for others to consume.

JSON, YAML, XML, and other well-known formats

JSON, YAML, XML and other well-known formats already have excellent library support within Ruby. Don't attempt to reinvent the wheel and parse them yourselves. You can use these to provide the parsing implementations required by FileMapper. Use of FileMapper together with the appropriate parsing library can remove a lot, if not all, boilerplate tasks.

Windows Management Interface and object linking and embedding

Ruby's win32ole (*http://bit.ly/2nV48nh*) class (part of the Ruby stdlib) can interact with Windows applications and subsystems with object linking and embedding (OLE) support. Among other things, you can use OLE to issue you can use Windows Management Instrumentation Query Language (WQL) queries, allowing you to determine a lot of information about the system. Facter uses this approach internally to populate a few Windows facts.

Creating Custom Hiera Backends

If you need to introduce new data sources into Puppet, Hiera is a good place to do so. Hiera supports pluggable backends and allows you to easily query and combine data from multiple sources.

The good news is that custom Hiera backends are simply functions. Any code that provides a Puppet function can be a Hiera backend. The bad news is that Hiera is a highly stressed component of Puppet; you must carefully consider the performance and load impact of your new backend before deploying it.

Due to automatic parameter lookups, Hiera will be queried for every class declaration for which not every parameter is supplied in the declaration. At a typical site, this results in hundreds or thousands of Hiera calls per catalog build. A few strategies can be used to help reduce and control the load placed on your Hiera data source. We explore them in the next section.

Choose the Appropriate Backend Type

Hiera supports multiple different backend types based on the performance characteristics involved. Choose the appropriate one from the documentation at Writing new data backends (*https://puppet.com/docs/puppet/latest/hiera_custom_backends.html*). We'll call your attention to the three most commonly used. The provider must implement one or more of these functions:

data_hash
> For data sources for which it's inexpensive, performance-wise, to read the entire contents at once

lookup_key
> For data sources for which looking up a key is relatively expensive, performance-wise, like an HTTPS API

data_dig
> For data sources that can access arbitrary elements of hash or array values before passing anything back to Hiera, like a database

Creating a High-Performance Backend

The following are important issues to handle properly when building a Hiera backend:

Filtering out queries the backend can't answer
> If queries are costly to perform, create a mechanism to identify well-formed queries for that data source. Because any module's parameter query could reach this data source, filter out queries for which the data source is incapable of answering and return a null response immediately.
>
> If your backend is an API or database, this might mean querying and caching a list of tables or keys to which your backend can respond.

Enabling persistence
> Due to the high number of queries placed in a single catalog compilation, it's crucial to avoid creating and destroying a connection for each query. Establish a connection when your backend is initialized, and reuse the connection for the duration of its life.

Implementing caching
> Hiera backends persist after they're initialized. This behavior allows you to easily cache the results of queries. The JSON backend (*http://bit.ly/2BIt0Zt*) built into Hiera demonstrates a simple data-caching implementation and provides a good reference for a simple backend.

Puppet caches the entire result of `data_hash` providers after the first call. It's only necessary to implement caching for other providers.

Here are a couple of key things you should build into your cache:

- Create a negative cache as well as a positive cache. The vast majority of all Hiera lookups will return no data. A negative cache can short-circuit the vast majority of your queries.
- The caching strategy needs to account for likelihood of change in the source data. Either expire the cache in a timely manner or build into it an invalidation mechanism.

Using Puppet's Public Classes and Method Calls

All modern (2014+) releases of Puppet bundle Ruby and all Ruby dependencies in the All-in-One (AIO) installer. This makes the Puppet APIs inaccessible to the system Ruby interpreter.

If you want to write a utility that you should avoid Puppet's public method calls, there are a few practices that should be avoided:

- Avoid installing gems in Puppet agent's bundled Ruby that will not be used by Puppet.
- Avoid counting on Puppet agent's bundled Ruby for version-specific features or bundled libraries.
- Avoid installing Puppet as a system gem in order to satisfy the dependency.

All of these create long-term support problems. The next version of Puppet agent can upgrade the bundled Ruby interpreter or change the bundled gems. Installing Puppet into the system Ruby gem path creates potential compatibility problems and means that your script is running in a different environment than that of Puppet agent. Keep the worlds distinct. Run non-Puppet Ruby scripts in a system-installed Ruby environment. Run Puppet exclusively through the bundled AIO installation.

The recommended solution is to package your script as a gem, and deploy it into Puppet's gem path. How to accomplish this depends on how Puppet is run on the node.

- If the gem is used by a fact or resource provider, use the `puppet_gem` package provider.

- If the gem is used by a node using `puppet apply`, use the `puppet_gem` package provider.

- If the gem is used by Puppet Server to build the catalog for an agent, use the `puppetserver_gem` package provider.

Puppet Faces

The Puppet Faces API was intended to allow users to provide a method to add new subcommands to `puppet`. As of this writing, the API is deprecated and unsupported for external use. Puppet recommends to deploy a new subcommand as a standalone gem that provides an executable named `puppet-`*subcommand*. When you run the `puppet subcommand`, it automatically invokes the `puppet-`*subcommand* binary for any subcommands not built in.

Indirection

Indirectors provide an API to abstract data provider backends, also called *termini*. Puppet gathers the data through the indirector, making it possible to shim or replace many interfaces into and out of Puppet. Examples of indirectors include the following:

- The *facts terminus* used for fact aquisition
- The *node terminus* used for node classification
- The *file bucket terminus* used for file storage and retrieval

Indirectors can supply data in response to REST requests, or you can distribute them as Ruby classes within Puppet modules.

You can call indirectors explicitly in code. For example, `storeconfigs` resource collector explicitly references the resource indirector, and the catalog preview tool (*https://forge.puppet.com/puppetlabs/catalog_preview*) makes direct use of the catalog indirector.

If you have another data source that contains node data not available to Puppet, you might want to write a custom indirector for node classification. A custom indirector is considerably more flexible than writing an `exec` node classifier. You can find a list of all available indirectors and their internal data types in Puppet's Indirection Reference (*https://puppet.com/docs/puppet/latest/indirection.html*).

Deploying Extensions

It's relatively straightforward to deploy a simple extension (such as a custom fact) in a standard Puppet environment. The complexity of deployment increases significantly if Ruby dependencies are involved. The complexity of distributing extensions increase further in standalone Puppet environments.

pluginsync

The pluginsync mechanism copies libraries and extensions to the node for use. Libraries are copied from every module in the Puppet environment's modulepath to Puppet's library path. pluginsync happens early in the Puppet run, prior to the node evaluating facts. This allows custom facts and dependent libraries to be used in the first Puppet convergence.

Libraries copied using this mechanism are available offline. Custom facts will be available to the facter command, custom types and providers will be available to the puppet resource command, and so on. This behavior can, however, be somewhat confusing when developing libraries offline. If you are making changes to a library and those changes don't seem to be taking effect, be sure that there isn't a cached copy by running Puppet to synchronize the extension.

Deploying Gem Dependencies

When developing a Puppet extension, you might want to use Ruby gems that aren't bundled with Puppet. The Puppet Agent utilizes the reference Ruby interpreter supplied in the Ruby standard build. All standard Ruby gems work normally on the Puppet Agent if the gem dependencies are deployed to the Puppet AIO Ruby GEMPATH, not to the system Ruby GEMPATH.

Unfortunately, dependent gems are not copied down using pluginsync. Instead, they are installed during Puppet convergence. Using Puppet to deploy a gem it depends upon may appear to create a chicken-or-egg scenario, but there is a simple and elegant solution.

Add a Puppet feature to the Puppet module that contains the provider with this dependency. Features are just Ruby files placed in the *lib/puppet/feature/* directory of the module and declared with the constructor, as shown here:

```
Puppet.features.add(:speciallib, :libs => ["special"])
```

Then, instruct Puppet to confine the provider for use when the necessary feature is available. Just after the type declaration, confine the provider suitability based on the feature:

```
Puppet::Type.type(:foo).provide(:bar) do
    confine :feature => :speciallib
```

The final step is to add the dependent gem with a `puppet_gem` package provider and have the dependent resource type depend on that gem:

```
package { 'special':
  provider => 'puppet_gem',
}

# Apply the gem package before any instance of this type
Package['special'] -> Custom_Type <| |>
```

This solution works because resource provider selection is deferred until the resource is evaluated. By the time the custom type is evaluated, the dependent gem will already be installed. The solution can be found at *https://projects.puppetlabs.com/issues/17747* and *http://bit.ly/2LeuF8r*.

Deploying Ruby Gem Extensions on Puppet Server

To install a gem into Puppet Server for use when building catalogs, use the `puppet server_gem` provider:

```
package { 'special':
  provider => 'puppetserver_gem',
}
```

Puppet Server uses a JRuby interpreter rather than the standard Ruby interpreter. Even though this is highly compatible, it cannot utilize compiled C-language extensions. Many popular Ruby gems include Java language versions for this situation. In other cases, you must select appropriate replacement gems, such as the JDBC database connectors rather than the compiled C database connectors.

Debugging a running server will require the installation of the `pry` gem into the Puppet server. You can find more details at *https://puppet.com/docs/puppetserver/latest/dev_debugging.html*.

Summary

Puppet offers a tremendous number of extension points. Using the correct framework and interface can dramatically simplify the implementation of your extension. Applying best practices when developing extensions will make them simpler to understand, use, and maintain.

In this chapter, we looked at some of the tools available to Puppet developers. A robust development environment and continuous testing can help improve the quality of your code by allowing the development team to more easily catch defects before they make it to live systems. The ability to quickly build experimental environments can help improve development throughput.

Here are the key takeaways from this chapter:

- Attempt to use a public extension when possible. Don't reinvent the wheel.
- Use test cases to prevent regressions, ensure compatibility, and reduce upgrade stress.
- Deploy VMs or containers to run Puppet and evaluate results as acceptance tests.
- Carefully consider what kind of extension best suites your needs.
- Put custom facts in modules. Don't write facts using a file resource that's too late for use.
- Attempt to use an existing framework when creating new resource types.
- Types offer abstraction, but understanding the underlying platform is necessary to implement the resource provider.

Index

About the Authors

Chris Barbour is a practice leader at Taos Mountain, Inc. He specializes in IT automation and large-scale infrastructure and has been working with configuration management solutions in various forms since 2008. Chris has maintained and deployed a mix of Puppet and Puppet Enterprise in a number of large-scale multiplatform environments. In addition to his operational responsibilities, he provides training and professional guidance for consultants looking to learn Puppet or otherwise further their IT careers. Chris lives in the heart of Silicon Valley with his wife and son, and in his free time enjoys motorcycling, photography, and travel.

Jo Rhett is a network architect and DevOps engineer with 25 years of experience conceptualizing and delivering large-scale internet services. He focuses on creating automation and infrastructure to accelerate deployment and minimize outages. Jo has been using, promoting, and enhancing configuration management systems for more than 20 years. He builds improvements and plugins for Puppet, MCollective, Docker, Jenkins, AWS, and many other DevOps tools. He is the author of *Learning Puppet 4* and *Learning MCollective*.

Colophon

The animal on the cover of *Puppet Best Practices* is the Mongolian five-toed jerboa (*Allactaga sibirica*). This small, hopping rodent is found throughout the steppes, plains, and deserts of central Asia, preferring clay and stone environments to sand deserts. They subsist primarily on the bulbs of tulips and similar flowering plants, though they also eat leaves and insects when their preferred food is scarce.

In captivity, these jerboas have been observed to live three to five years, and they typically have one or two litters of around four pups each spring. Crepuscular in the spring and autumn, and nocturnal in the summer, these rodents create non-branching burrows approximately 5 meters in length and a half meter deep.

Many of the animals on O'Reilly covers are endangered; all of them are important to the world. To learn more about how you can help, go to *animals.oreilly.com*.

The cover image is from *Johnson's Natural History*, by S.G. Goodrich. The cover fonts are URW Typewriter and Guardian Sans. The text font is Adobe Minion Pro; the heading font is Adobe Myriad Condensed; and the code font is Dalton Maag's Ubuntu Mono.

Learn from experts.
Find the answers you need.

Sign up for a **10-day free trial** to get **unlimited access** to all of the content on Safari, including Learning Paths, interactive tutorials, and curated playlists that draw from thousands of ebooks and training videos on a wide range of topics, including data, design, DevOps, management, business—and much more.

Start your free trial at:
oreilly.com/safari

(No credit card required.)